Donnie Humphries

THE PRACTICAL WRITER

Paragraph to Theme

Edward P. Bailey, Jr.
Philip A. Powell
Jack M. Shuttleworth

THE PRACTICAL WRITER
Paragraph to Theme
FOURTH EDITION

HOLT, RINEHART AND WINSTON, INC.
Fort Worth; Chicago; San Francisco; Philadelphia;
Montreal; Toronto; London; Sydney; Tokyo

Publisher, Humanities: Charlyce Jones Owen
Associate Editor, English: Kate Morgan
Senior Project Manager: Sondra Greenfield
Senior Production Manager: Annette Mayeski
Design Supervisor: Lou Scardino
Text Design: Art Ritter
Cover Design: Fred Pusterla
Cover Photograph: Image Bank

Library of Congress Cataloging-in-Publication Data

Bailey, Edward P.
  The practical writer / Edward P. Bailey, Philip A. Powell, Jack M.
Shuttleworth.—4th ed.
  p. cm.

  Includes index.
  ISBN 0-03-023747-5
  1. English language—Rhetoric.   I. Powell, Philip A.
II. Shuttleworth, Jack M.   III. Title.
PE1408.B226   1988   88-19757
808'.042—dc19   CIP

ISBN 0-03-023747-5

Printed in the United States of America

9 0 1 2   039   9 8 7 6 5 4 3 2

Holt, Rinehart and Winston, Inc.
The Dryden Press
Saunders College Publishing

Copyright Acknowledgments

    p. 164 *Readers' Guide to Periodical Literature*, May 1987 issue,
page 193. Copyright © 1987 by the H. W. Wilson Company. Material
reproduced by permission of the publisher.
    p. 165 Reprinted from PAIS BULLETIN. 73(3):130–31; Oct.–Dec.
1986. Copyright 1987 Public Affairs Information Service, Inc.
    p. 166 Copyright (1987) by the American Psychological Association.
Reprinted by permission of the publisher.

Preface to the Fourth Edition

This edition remains true to our original conception of *The Practical Writer* when we first began work on it in 1977: a step-by-step introduction to the fundamentals of composition presented in a clear, straightforward style.

In this edition we've made many changes. First, we've added three chapters:

- Chapter 22, "Works Cited," which helps students understand this key part of a research paper.

- Chapter 28, "Colon," which presents one good (and simple) rule to help students use this important mark of punctuation.

- Chapter 29, "Dash," which presents two (easy) rules and encourages students to use this mark of punctuation.

We've also thoroughly revised the exercises in the book, keeping some workhorses but replacing many and adding a substantial number to Part Six, "Punctuation," and Part Seven, "Expression."

And we've added extra sample essays to the chapters in Part Four, "More Patterns of Development."

In each edition, we've acknowledged our indebtedness to Professor Paul Knoke, who worked closely with us on every word in the first edition of this book. Paul has our continuing thanks.

Our editors at Holt, Rinehart and Winston are true professionals who share our enthusiasm for this book and always "go the extra mile": Our special thanks to Charlyce Jones Owen, who helped us develop our ideas for this edition (and who has no doubt memorized our phone numbers—as we have memorized hers); to Kate Morgan, who worked closely with us to develop our ideas into words; and to Sondra Greenfield, who turns all of our words and ideas into the real thing—a typeset book that looks (and is) professional. Our thanks to all of you.

The reviewers for this edition were especially insightful, confirming our concerns and offering us new approaches. Our particular thanks to all of them: Paul Devlin, Ferris State College; Beverly Elliott, Peirce Junior College; Beverly Farris, Hinds Junior College; James Helvey, Davidson County Community College; Robert Jenkins, Florence Darlington Technical College; Linnie Jones, New Mexico State University; Patricia Kuett-Wellington, University of Miami; Ann Morton, Portland Community College; Mary Catherine Park, Brevard Community College; Kathleen Tickner, Brevard Community College.

And our students, of course, deserve special recognition. We admire their talent and creativity. We especially thank those students who contributed sample papers: Andrea M. Bopp, Louise A. Burket, Anthony J. Comtois, Robert T. Cunningham, Erik A. Emaus, George M. Fox, James C. Gall, James E. Kinzer, Janet C. Libbey, Rodney L. Marshall, Jay D. McFadden, Susan J. Timmons, Rodney R. Williams, and Lawrence A. Wolf.

September 1988

Edward P. Bailey, Jr. *Marymount University*
Philip A. Powell *Burke, VA*
Jack M. Shuttleworth *US Air Force Academy*

Contents

Contents

How This Book Works

The *Practical Writer* is intended for typical first-year college students, who perhaps lack knowledge but don't lack intelligence. We assume that these students can learn quickly and well from a step-by-step approach to the fundamentals, good examples to follow, and carefully designed exercises.

We begin by presenting the fundamentals (organization, support, unity, coherence)—one at a time—in a tightly structured one-paragraph essay. The paragraph, we've found, is a unit large enough for students to demonstrate their understanding of the fundamentals and small enough for them to work toward mastery. At this point, we don't overwhelm them while they're learning the fundamentals by making them struggle to find support; instead, we ask them to write about personal experiences and the people and things they know well. We encourage them to be colorul, interesting, and—above all—specific.

We then move through several longer stages of writing to a 1000-to-2000-word research paper. By the time students complete the research block, they can write a serious paper—the kind they will have to write in other college courses and beyond them—with a less mechanical structure than we required earlier. We still offer a model, of course, but it becomes a guide rather than a goal.

The last two topics of our book, punctuation and expression, are not part of the step-by-step approach. These chapters can be studied anytime, whenever your students are ready for them. They are not typical handbook material, though, because we've been careful to select only what first-year students need to learn, leaving out the skills they probably know and those they're not yet ready to apply.

Finally, we try to avoid the "scholarly" style of writing and speak personally to the students, as though we're talking to them in class.

SECTION ONE

A MODEL FOR WRITING

PART ONE
The One-Paragraph Essay (Stage I)

This section teaches you how to write a good one-paragraph essay. Though you rarely see one-paragraph essays in publications, you'll find them remarkably handy for improving your writing. One obvious advantage is that they are short enough to allow you to spend your study time writing a really good one. Yet they are long enough for you to practice and demonstrate the fundamentals of writing. A final advantage is that what you learn about one-paragraph essays transfers nicely to larger themes and research papers.

In Part One you'll learn about the simplest one-paragraph essay, which we call Stage I. Later, in Part Two, you'll study the organization for a slightly more sophisticated one-paragraph essay, which we'll call Stage II.

Part One presents a very tightly structured model for a paragraph. You may wonder if all good writers follow such a structure for persuasive writing. No, of course not. This structure is not *the* good way to write a paragraph, but it is *one* good way. And this way has a very real advantage: it automatically gives your paper organization so that you have one less thing to worry about. You can then concentrate on learning the other fundamentals that experienced writers already know. And by working constantly with this model paragraph, you will learn organization too, the easy way.

Support for the paragraph's main idea is also easy. Right now we don't care if you know how to find facts in the library. We're much more concerned that you can recognize and use good support once you find it. So we make finding it simple. You don't need to go any further than your own mind: you can use either your experiences or your imagination for support. As a result, you can have fun with your one-paragraph essays. They can be intriguing and perhaps humorous. Writing doesn't have to be dull!

1
Overview of the One-Paragraph Essay (Stage I)

You may already be familiar with a common organization for good writing:

• Tell the readers what you're going to tell them.

• Tell it to them.

• Then tell them what you just told them.

This chapter shows you how to apply that organization to the one-paragraph essay: the first sentence states the idea you want your readers to accept (we call this a *topic sentence*), all middle sentences present specific support for that idea, and the last sentence rewords the topic sentence—to remind your readers of the point you've just made.

THE MODEL FOR THE ONE-PARAGRAPH ESSAY (STAGE I)

The model for a Stage I one-paragraph essay looks like this:

Topic Sentence
  Specific Support
  Specific Support
  Specific Support
Reworded Topic Sentence

Now let's look at a "real" paragraph—one that follows the model we've just shown you:

Topic Sentence   { The Boundary Waters Canoe Area, a wilderness park in northern Minnesota, is a refreshing change from the city. Away from the din of civilization, I

Specific
Support { have canoed silently across its waters for an entire afternoon and not heard a single noise except an occasional birdcall and the sound of waves beating against the shore. Also, my partner and I were able

Specific
Support { to navigate our way through a string of five lakes by following a campfire's scent drifting through the pure air. Most refreshing, the park is so magnifi-

Specific
Support { cently beautiful that even the voyageurs of old were willing to endure its hardships in order to settle

Reworded
Topic Sentence { there. The Boundary Waters Canoe Area is thus an ideal place to clear your head of the congestion of urban life.

Now look at an outline of this paragraph:

Topic Sentence The Boundary Waters Canoe Area is a refreshing change.
  Specific Support quietness
  Specific Support purity of the air
  Specific Support beauty
Reworded Topic Sentence It's an ideal place to clear head of congestion of urban life.

ANOTHER EXAMPLE

Here's another sample one-paragraph essay. Notice that it, too, follows the model perfectly.

Topic
Sentence { Even though I have never really lived there, going to my grandmother's farm always seems like

Specific
Support { coming home. The feeling begins as soon as I cross the threshold of that quaint little house and tumble into the arms of waiting aunts and cousins. The

Specific
Support { sense of welcome overwhelms me. Then there are the cozy rooms—the ceilings don't seem higher than six feet—with their crackling fireplaces that make me want to snuggle down into the feather-

Specific
Support
Reworded
Topic
Sentence { stuffed chairs. But the memory that always lasts the longest is the smell of Grandma's biscuits and pastries cooking in her coke-fed stove. Yes, only in Grandma's house do I feel the warmth and welcome that always seems like coming home.

Again, let's outline it:

Topic Sentence Going to my grandmother's farm seems like coming home.
   Specific Support greeting by relatives
   Specific Support coziness of house
   Specific Support smell of home-cooked food
Reworded Topic Sentence Visiting Grandma's seems like coming home.

Notice that each of these sample paragraphs has three items of specific support. Sometimes five or six items are necessary to be persuasive; other times, one long example will do. As a general rule, though, three seems to work well.

Although the sample paragraphs in the first two or three chapters of this book are good, they are intentionally fairly simple so you can easily see the basic organization. But if you don't fully understand the one-paragraph essay yet, don't worry. The rest of Part One explains the fundamentals.

You can find a checklist for these fundamentals on page 54.

EXERCISES

A. Outline the following paragraph the same way we outlined the two paragraphs in the chapter:

> Three common electrical distractions on my desk waste my precious study time at night. The worst distraction is my clock, constantly humming to remind me how little time I actually have. Another interruption is the "high-quality" fluorescent desk lamp that sometimes buzzes, flickers—and then goes out. And, finally, consider that fascinating little invention, the computer, which not only does all kinds of complicated math problems, but also challenges me to games and helps me write letters home. After stopping to worry about the time, fix my lamp, and play with the computer, I am too tired to study, so I just go to bed.

Topic Sentence _____

_____

   Specific Support _____

   Specific Support _____

   Specific Support _____

Reworded Topic Sentence _____

_____

B. Outline this paragraph:

Old, stiff, and weathered, my grandfather's hands show the strenuous way of life he has known as a working man. Many hot summer days tilling the stubborn soil of West Texas have left their lasting mark in the form of a deep and permanent tan. Grandpa's hands are also covered with calluses—begun, perhaps, when he split cordwood for two dollars a day in an effort to pull his family through the Great Depression. Most striking, though, are the carpenter's scars he has collected from the days of building his house, barn, and fence, and from the unending repair jobs that still occupy his every day. Although small and battered, Grandpa's hands bring back images of a time when men and women worked from dawn to dusk just to survive, a difficult but respected way of life.

Topic Sentence _____

_____

Specific Support _____

Specific Support _____

Specific Support _____

Reworded Topic Sentence _____

_____

C. Outline this paragraph:

The East Wing of the National Gallery of Art in Washington, D.C., is a showplace of modern art. Inside, it houses collections of such artists as Picasso and Matisse, artists well known for their nonrepresentational works. Hanging from the ceiling is a mobile, normally thought of as a dangling toy parents hang above their infant's crib. This one, however, is several stories high and much more impressive to the parents (and children, too). Even the building is in keeping with its contents—it has lots of glass, open spaces, and strange angles and corners. For modern art, then, this wing of the gallery is an excellent place to visit.

Topic Sentence _____

_____

Specific Support _____

Specific Support _____

Specific Support _____

Reworded Topic Sentence _____

_____

2
Support: Examples, Statistics, Statements by Authorities

The first sentence in our model paragraph is the topic sentence, but let's save that for the next chapter. Instead, we'll start with support. Once you understand support—and how specific it must be—you'll understand much more easily how to write a good topic sentence.

This chapter examines three different kinds of support: examples, statistics, and statements by authorities.

EXAMPLES

"The secret of good writing—the real secret," many professional writers would tell you, "is using examples."

"The biggest problem with undergraduate writing—the one that almost all students have," many teachers would tell you, "is that they don't know how to use examples."

So here you go: a chance to solve a problem by learning a secret. Let's begin with two different kinds of examples: *quick examples* and *narrative examples.*

Quick Examples

You already know from your everyday experience what a quick example is: *a quick example is one instance, one occurrence of whatever you're talking about.* If you're discussing the meals available at fast-food restaurants, a hamburger is one example—one of several possibilities. You could have named fried chicken, tacos, roast beef sandwiches, or (at the waterfront of San Francisco) even sourdough bread and crabs.

For a quick example to be effective, it must be very specific. If you want to show that Constance Dilettante can't stick with anything, don't say, "She changes her mind a lot." Don't even just say, "She changed her major fre-

7. _____

8. _____

9. _____

10. _____

11. _____

12. _____

13. _____

I encountered a careless driver on the way back from the beach a couple of weeks ago. (7) I was going about sixty in the right lane on a four-lane road. (8) Suddenly, a man decided that he want to use the same lane that I was in. (9) I found myself in the ditch scared half to death.

(10) Another kind of driver that upset me is the paranoid driver. (11) A paranoid driver slows down at a green light, comes to a complete stop when making a right turn, or waits until every car within a mile has passed by before entering the highway. (12) For example, I almost hit the rear end of a woman's car because she came to a complete stop and looked both ways at a green light.

(13) Finally, the kind of driver that I hate the most is

ENGLISH 099

DEVELOPMENTAL ENGLISH II

EDITING EXERCISE #2B1 (edex2b1)

S-V AGR, VERB FORM ERRORS

DIRECTIONS:

The following essay contains several errors in subject-verb
agreement and verb form. Going backwards through the essay,
find and correct these errors by following these steps:

1. Using a pencil, label all the subjects and main verbs
   (S=Subject, V=Verb) in all the clauses, independent and
   dependent.

2. Check each sentence, following the guidelines in your
   grammar handbook. Using a blue pen (not the erasable
   kind), label each sentence as correct (C) or incorrect
   (I).

3. Using a blue pen (not the erasable kind), correct all
   errors by making changes within and above the lines using
   standard editing symbols. Correct only major errors; do
   not concern yourself with minor errors. NOTE: Some
   sentences may contain more than on

HINT: There are 10 major errors and 8 incorrect sentences.

A Driver's Worst Nightmare

(1) What are one of the worst things that could possibly

happen when you be late for work? (2) For me, it is usually
are

a little old lady pulling out in front of me and going

fifteen miles an hour in a forty-five miles an hour zone.

(3) Although careless drivers makes me angry, it is the

ignorant ones that drives me up the wall.

(4) The first kind of driver that upsets me is the

careless driver. (5) Careless drivers are the ones who

change lanes without a signal, fail to look both ways at a

stop sign, or turn left in the far right lane. (6) In fact,

1. ___T___

2. _____

3. ___C___

4. ___C___

5. ___C___

6. ___T___

15. _____ this type of driver passed the driver's exam. (15) Ignorant

16. _____ drivers have many things in common. (16) Most of them do not
know which car goes first at a four-way stop, that the left
lane is for faster traffic, or that they cannot turn left at

17. _____ a red light. (17) For instance, many times I have been tempt
to get out of my car and direct traffic at a four-way stop
because the other cars cannot decide which one goes first.

18. _____ (18) The way that people drive seems to amaze me every

19. _____ time that I enter the road. (19) Although careless,
paranoid, and ignorant drivers stand out in my mind, these
are only a few of the lunatics that enters the highways
daily.

quently in college." Be still more specific: "She changed her major from philosophy to computer science to animal husbandry—all in one semester."

Do quick examples really make any difference? We think so. Consider the following:

Without Quick Examples

There were many expensive cars in the school's parking lot during the football game.

You could tell spring was here because of all the flowers in bloom.

Why do lawyers use words that mean one thing to them and something else entirely in ordinary English?

With Quick Examples

There were many expensive cars in the school's parking lot during the football game—Mercedes convertibles, low-slung Porsches, red Ferraris.

You could tell spring was here because of all the flowers in bloom: tulips of all colors, yellow daffodils, and (if you want to call them flowers) even a few early dandelions.

Why do lawyers use words that mean one thing to them and something else entirely in ordinary English (words like "party" and "action" and "motion")?

See the difference that quick examples make? They take something rather abstract—cars, flowers, legal words—and make them much more concrete. It's almost as if the abstract words don't really communicate, don't really find a place to lodge in the brain cells. But the more concrete words—Mercedes, tulip, party—do.

When should you use quick examples? Well . . . how often do you like to have such examples when you're a *reader*? Pretty often, right? And that's how often you should use them when you're a writer.

Quick examples, of course, don't have to come at the ends of sentences. You could have a paragraph—probably a very short one—that depended entirely on quick examples:

Chairs come in many different designs. Easy chairs—designed for people who like to lounge back—usually have lots of padding, perhaps a curved back, and comfortable armrests. Straight chairs usually have minimal padding, a vertical back, and sometimes no armrests. Some contemporary chairs—kneelers—have padding for the knees and seat, but no back at all and no armrests. So, depending on their purposes, chairs differ quite a bit.

The topic of that paragraph may not be exciting, but the quick examples—easy chair, straight chair, kneeler—certainly communicate much more than the abstract beginning: "Chairs come in many different designs."

A quick example is just one instance, one occurrence. *But a narrative example is a brief story.* A narrative example can be terrific support, so we really emphasize it in this book.

Sometimes you want to emphasize an idea, to really help your readers understand what you mean. So you decide to run a little "motion picture"; that is, you decide to tell a story that will help your readers almost see what you are saying—as though they are watching a short motion picture rather than simply reading words.

For example, if you want to show that shark hunting is dangerous, you could give a quick example by saying "a friend of mine was once maimed while hunting sharks." Or you could really make your point by telling the story:

> I still have nightmares about the time last June when Rocky and I were scuba diving off the coast of Baja California. Rocky spotted a great white shark and tried to shoot it with his spear gun. As he fired, the shark spun suddenly toward him. Before I knew what happened. . . . [Then—poor Rocky—finish the story.]

Can you see how a narrative example really drives the point home?

A narrative example, then, is a specific incident (usually with names, dates, other details). It is not the *kind* of thing that happens (not "sometimes people get hurt when they try to shoot sharks with spear guns"). It is the story of something that *did* happen (June, Rocky, Baja California, great white shark).

Let's take another narrative example. You might find a paragraph like this in *Time* or *Newsweek:*

> Alison Marks, a twenty-three-year-old graduate student in architecture at the University of Colorado, had a blood pressure of 180/120 in February 1988. Her doctor prescribed Elavil, which Alison took for three months until she became so busy with exams that she found taking medicine too much trouble. After exams, she still neglected her medicine. As a result, her blood pressure rose so sharply that in September she was rushed to the hospital with a stroke.

Do we care that this patient was an architecture student, or that she was twenty-three, or that she was named Alison Marks? Yes, somehow we do. Alison becomes more real to us, someone we can sympathize with, and because Alison's case becomes believable and typical, we begin to be convinced that people with high blood pressure should take their medicine. The narrative example has helped convince us.

Now let's apply what we've learned about narrative examples to the one-paragraph essay. Suppose you are sitting in your room trying to write your first college English paper—the one for this course. You remember your instructor's words: "I want to see examples—specific examples—whatever else you do on this paper!" She's told you to write about something that distracts you. You look aimlessly around the room, your eyes suddenly brighten, and you slap down this sentence:

My roommate distracts me when I try to study.

Now you need some examples. Let's see: she has that record player going again, she's smacking her gum again, and you remember all those dumb questions she asks every few minutes. Here goes:

> Although my roommate is a helpful companion at times, she is a distracting nuisance whenever I try to study. Throughout the evening, her stereo blares in my ears. Even worse, she insists on smacking her gum. She also interrupts me with questions that have nothing to do with homework. At any other time my roommate is a friend, but while I'm studying, she's my greatest enemy.

"Pretty good," you say. "I think I'll show it to my roommate to see what she—on second thought. . . ."

Now suppose you're sitting in your room a couple of days later, ego deflated by a bad grade, trying to *rewrite* that paper. Your examples seemed specific enough to you—stereo, gum, questions—but they obviously weren't. You used quick examples when a narrative example might have been more effective.

Instead of presenting the *kinds* of things your roommate does to distract you, you could have used a narrative example—a story of something that actually did happen, at a particular time and a particular place. In other words, you could have talked about one specific study period. Then you could have told us not just that her stereo was going; you could have told us what record she was playing. You could have told us what kind of gum she was chewing. You could even have told us what specific "dumb" questions she asked you. In other words, you could have written this paragraph:

> Although my roommate is a helpful companion at times, she is a distracting nuisance whenever I try to study. Just last Wednesday night, Anna decided to spend the evening playing her "classic" Bob Dylan records. While I was trying desperately to integrate a math function, all I could hear was that the answer was somewhere "blowin' in the wind." Even worse, the entire time Dylan was rasping away, Anna accompanied him by smacking and popping her Bazooka bubble gum. I'd finally given up on math and started my struggle with chemistry when she abruptly asked (loudly, of course, so I could hear her over the music), "Do you think any Cokes are left in the Coke machine?" My stomach started rumbling and my throat suddenly felt dry—even drier than the chemistry text I

was trying to read. As I dropped the change into the Coke machine, I realized that although Anna is usually a friend, while I'm studying she is my greatest enemy.

We can now picture you, Anna, and all those distractions. You've told us the "story" (a narrative example) of your evening trying to study, helping us to see you and feel your frustration. That's communication.

So remember the "secret" that all professional writers know: *examples!*

STATISTICS

Examples are an important form of support. They help convince your readers and make the essay more interesting. Examples alone, though, may not be enough. We need something else; we need some *numbers.* Who doesn't love numbers, trust them, believe in them? Give us a statistic we don't suspect is phony, and we are probably convinced right there. Alison Marks and her trouble with high blood pressure may move us emotionally, but we will more likely be persuaded by a medical report like this:

> Recent statistics show convincingly that jogging is saving the lives of many Americans. Of the 12.5 million who jog at least 10 miles a week, 78 percent have a pulse rate and blood pressure lower than nonjoggers the same age have. Estimates indicate that these joggers can expect to live to an average age of 77— more than three years longer than the average age of their contemporaries. The lesson seems clear, doesn't it?

To be convincing, statistics must be unambiguous. We are not necessarily alarmed, for example, to hear that 47 of 54 football players were injured in a practice session because we have no way of knowing how serious the injuries were. Perhaps 46 of the players were treated with Band-Aids. We would become alarmed, however, to hear that 47 of 54 football players were hospitalized for at least one night following a practice session. The second statistic defines *injury* more clearly, so it is more convincing than the first.

STATEMENTS BY AUTHORITIES

The last kind of support we will consider in this chapter is the statement by an authority, a person who is in a position to know about something. If someone we trust tells us something, we just might believe him. But we do so because we trust *him:* his character, his judgment, and his knowledge of the subject. We would never believe Alison Marks, the architecture student who forgot to take her pills, if she tells us that shark hunting is one of the safest sports, but we might listen to her if she tells us that patients with high blood pressure should take their medicine. We might also believe the president of the American Medical Association or a research specialist in high blood pressure or our family doctor—people who know what they're talking about.

Who are some people whose unsupported opinions about high blood pressure would not be convincing? We would not trust someone whose character, judgment, or knowledge of the subject is questionable. We would not trust the unsupported opinion of the druggist convicted of selling overpriced drugs to people who did not need them anyway; we would not trust the doctor being investigated for gross incompetence by the American Medical Association; and we would not trust our roommate, who thinks blood pressure is measured by a thermometer. The first has doubtful character; the second, doubtful judgment; and the third, doubtful knowledge.

By the way, the use of authority is particularly important when you are presenting statistics. Remember all those impressive figures about people who jog? Guess where the numbers came from. For all you know (and, in fact, for all those statistics are worth), they came from Miss Fisher's sixth-grade creative writing class. The point, of course, is that unless the writer tells you the source of the statistics, you don't know whether or not you should trust them.

Here's a revision of that paragraph showing the use of authorities, both with and without statistics:

> Recent statistics show convincingly that jogging is saving the lives of many Americans. According to the Congressional Subcommittee on Physical Fitness, 78 percent of the 12.5 million people who jog at least 10 miles per week have a pulse rate and blood pressure lower than nonjoggers the same age have. This committee estimates that these joggers can expect to live to an average age of 77—more than three years longer than the average age of their contemporaries. Dr. Hans Corpuscle, chief adviser to the committee, says that "joggers are the healthiest single group of people in America today." The lesson seems clear, doesn't it?

COMBINED TYPES OF SUPPORT

A paragraph that uses one type of support—examples, maybe—is often convincing, but many good paragraphs contain several types: a couple of examples and some statistics, or a statement by an authority and an example, and so on.

The following paragraph attempts to show that people attend yard sales for entertainment. Can you identify the types of support?

> Although you might think that most people attend yard sales for the bargains, the main reason they attend is for the entertainment they find there. For example, consider what happened to my family last summer when we held a yard sale to get rid of some old things before moving to a new place. Many people came, but few bought. Each new carload of people disgorged a new group that would while away an hour or so on a Saturday by caressing the sun-faded curtains,

thumbing through ancient *National Geographic* magazines, and carefully considering sweaters eight sizes too small for them or anyone else in their group. Then the group would gather around a folded section of the classified ads and pick the next sale they'd visit. My suspicions about why those people came to our sale were confirmed a few months later by a survey I read in *Psychology Monthly.* The survey showed that seven of ten people who attended yard sales admitted they did so "just for the fun of it." The psychologist who conducted the survey then reached a conclusion I could have told him last summer: "The real bargain that people seek at yard sales, if only subconsciously, is not another frying pan or partially burned plastic spatula, but just a little weekend entertainment."

Notice that the statement by the authority is an effective rewording of the topic sentence, so no separate concluding sentence is necessary for this paragraph.

The above paragraph uses all three kinds of support—all of it invented by the writer. When you are inventing support for exercises or when you find it in books or magazines, statistics and statements by authorities are no problem. If, however, you are writing paragraphs based on personal experiences (much like many samples in Section One), you will naturally rely heavily on examples. Fortunately, the example is one of the most colorful and convincing kinds of support.

INVENTED SUPPORT

Before you begin the exercises, let's have a word about invented support. It greatly simplifies the learning process. You don't have to struggle to find real support at the same time you're trying to figure out just what good support is. You don't have to search any further than your own mind, and you can be as specific as you like.

But please remember, inventing evidence is just an exercise, a convenience for you and your instructor. So you must follow these rules:

- Never write invented support unless your readers know that is what they are reading.
- And never write invented support unless your instructor approves.

Within these two guidelines, you can have fun with your writing. All the examples we've used in this chapter were "invented"—you could easily tell that. So try to be imaginative.

At the same time, though, try to be realistic. Don't, for instance, try to convince us that the Grand Junction School of Cosmetology is noted for its scholarly excellence because it had thirteen Rhodes scholars last year. The school may be good, but such an exaggerated figure is bound to raise eyebrows.

EXERCISES

A. We'll examine the topic sentence in detail in the next chapter. For now, keep in mind that a topic sentence for a paragraph states the idea you want your readers to accept, and the rest of the paragraph supports and reinforces that idea. Our attention for the moment is on that supporting material. Therefore, for each of the topic sentences below, invent (in other words, simply make up) a quick example (1 sentence), a narrative example (3–5 sentences), a statistic (1–2 sentences), and a statement by an authority (1–2 sentences), as required. Use the sample paragraph on yard sales, which has invented support, as a model.

1. Sometimes women are discriminated against in the workplace.

    a. Narrative Example _____

    _____

    _____

    _____

    _____

    b. Statistic _____

    _____

    _____

    c. Statement by an Authority _____

    _____

    _____

2. Computers save people time.

    a. Statistic _____

    _____

    _____

    b. Narrative Example _____

    _____

    _____

    _____

    _____

    _____

c. Statement by an Authority _____

_____

_____

3. Twentieth-century medicine really works.

   a. Quick Example _____

   _____

   _____

   b. Quick Example _____

   _____

   _____

   c. Narrative Example _____

   _____

   _____

   _____

   _____

B. Follow the same instructions for these topic sentences:

1. Women are rarely discriminated against in the workplace.

   a. Statement by an Authority _____

   _____

   _____

   b. Statistic _____

   _____

   _____

   c. Narrative Example _____

   _____

   _____

   _____

   _____

2. Too often, computers waste people's time.

   a. Narrative Example _____

_____

_____

_____

_____

b. Statistic _____

_____

_____

c. Statement by an Authority _____

_____

_____

3. Twentieth-century medicine sometimes causes problems.

   a. Quick Example _____

   _____

   _____

   b. Quick Example _____

   _____

   _____

   c. Narrative Example _____

   _____

   _____

   _____

   _____

C. Invent support for the same topic sentence four different ways:

   1. Putting animals in zoos is inhumane.

   a. Statistic _____

   _____

   _____

   b. Statistic _____

   _____

   _____

c. Statistic _____
_____
_____

2. Putting animals in zoos is inhumane.

a. Statement by an Authority _____
_____
_____

b. Statement by an Authority _____
_____
_____

c. Statement by an Authority _____
_____
_____

3. Putting animals in zoos is inhumane.

a. Quick Example _____
_____
_____

b. Quick Example _____
_____
_____

c. Quick Example _____
_____
_____

4. Putting animals in zoos is inhumane.

a. Narrative Example _____
_____
_____
_____

b. Narrative Example _____
_____

D. Answer these questions about Exercise C:

1. Which form of support was most effective? Why?

2. Which form of support was least effective? Why?

3. For that topic sentence, what combination of support (examples, statistics, quick examples, narrative examples) would you recommend? Why?

E. Look again at the paragraph on yard sales at the end of the chapter. Now intentionally destroy the effectiveness of the paragraph: rewrite the narrative example (the second through the fifth sentences) by making it much shorter—and therefore too general.

F. Now let's reverse Exercise E. Each of these topic sentences is followed by an example that's too general. Improve the italicized example by converting the dull generality into a narrative example. You'll need several sentences for each one.

1. Vacations to foreign countries can be exciting. *Last summer, for example, I had quite an experience.*

2. Floods can cause tremendous damage. *Once the Mississippi River over-flowed and many people lost everything.*

_____

_____

_____

_____

3. Actresses can become quite popular. *There's one on television most people really like.*

_____

_____

_____

_____

G. In Exercises A, B, and C you outlined several paragraphs. Choose the one that interests you the most and use the support you invented to write the paragraph. The Appendix (pages 323–326) gives you a suggested format.

3
Topic Sentence

Now we move to the first sentence of the one-paragraph essay, to its intellect—the thought at the head of the body. That thought, called the *topic sentence,* is the primary idea of the paragraph, the central idea you wish to persuade your readers to accept. (In addition, in a larger essay the topic sentence also introduces the paragraph, relates to the thesis statement, and helps make a transition from the previous paragraph. You'll learn more about these functions in later chapters.)

Writing texts try to define the topic-sentence idea with a number of terms: it is the writer's "viewpoint" of the topic, the writer's "judgment" about the topic, the writer's "conviction," the writer's "assertion" of truth. Those texts are right; the topic-sentence idea is all these things. However, we prefer the term *opinion:* the topic sentence is a precise statement of opinion you wish to persuade your readers to accept.

Why do we associate a topic sentence with the word *opinion*? An opinion is a judgment that seems true only for the person who believes it. Imagine for a moment that you're telling a friend something you believe—a viewpoint, a judgment, a conviction, an assertion you hold to be true. Your friend replies, "That's just your opinion." He's not denying that you believe what you say, but he is letting you know that you'll have to persuade him to agree with you. He's placing the burden on you to support your belief so that he can accept the idea as fully as you do. A similar relationship exists between you (the writer) and your readers. Your topic sentence stands as a statement of your opinion *until* you persuade your audience to accept it fully. Thus, recognizing that the topic sentence is a statement of opinion will help you remember your obligation to support your idea.

Why should the topic sentence be an opinion instead of a fact? If you state your idea and your readers respond with "Oh, yes, that's true" or "That's a fact," what more can you say? Suppose you write this topic sentence:

William Shakespeare wrote *Hamlet.*

In your paragraph you could discuss Shakespeare or his play, but you wouldn't be trying to convince a reader to accept the topic sentence itself. That Shakespeare wrote *Hamlet* is accepted as fact. And statements of fact (or at least what everyone accepts as fact) don't make good topic sentences because they leave the writer nothing important to say. On the other hand, suppose you try this topic sentence:

Francis Bacon wrote *Hamlet.*

Now you've stated an opinion. Unfortunately, hardly anyone believes it. You've crossed into such extreme controversy that you'll have to really work to convince readers to accept your topic-sentence idea.

Your topic-sentence opinion doesn't need to arouse instant doubt. You don't need to take outrageous stands like these:

Dogs are really man's greatest enemy.

A toupee is better than real hair.

In fact, most good topic sentences bring neither instant acceptance nor instant doubt. Usually readers have not formed their own judgments, and they're willing to accept yours if you persuade them. For example, consider this topic sentence:

Today's toupees are so well made that they look like a person's own hair.

The writer is stating what she believes to be fact. Although readers have no reason to doubt her, they are not obliged to believe her either. They will probably agree with what she says once she provides specific support for her opinion. And it *is* her opinion—until she persuades the audience to accept it as fully as she does.

When you write a one-paragraph essay, you'll begin with a topic sentence and follow it with specific support (examples, statistics, or authoritative statements). If you structure the topic sentence well and support it well with specifics, you'll persuade your readers to accept your idea fully. The rest of this chapter shows you how to write a good topic sentence.

A good topic sentence contains two parts: a *limited subject* and a *precise opinion* about that subject.

LIMITING THE SUBJECT

The first step in writing a good topic sentence is to choose a subject limited enough to support in a single paragraph. If you try to support a large subject in a one-paragraph essay, your argument is not likely to be convincing because the subject (which is too general) will demand more support than you can develop in one paragraph. Thus, limiting the subject is the first step toward writing a good topic sentence.

Let's examine a sample case. You begin with a general subject: say, *advertising*. Since the topic is obviously too large for a one-paragraph essay, you must limit it. Of the many types of advertisement (television, radio, newpaper, billboard, and the like), you choose one—for instance, magazine advertising. As you glance at the advertisements in your favorite magazine, three attract your attention. In one advertisement you see a scantily clad woman holding a tape recorder she wants you to buy. In another a shapely blond is stroking a luxury automobile. And in a third ad a couple embrace in delight as they hold cigarettes in their free hands. You see a common element in each sales pitch: the advertisers use sex appeal to make you want the things you see before you. In this way you limit the subject from *advertising* to *magazine advertising* to *sex appeal in magazine advertising*.

Consider the process you just went through. You might have noticed the lack of color in the tape-recorder advertisement, the large amount of space wasted in the automobile ad, or the small print that obscures the Surgeon General's warning in the cigarette advertisement. Instead you focused your attention on sex appeal in the ads, thereby limiting the subject.

STATING THE PRECISE OPINION

The second part of the topic sentence tells your opinion about the limited subject. Although limiting the subject is a step toward precision, an opinion about even a limited subject will remain vague unless you tell the readers what your idea is exactly.

The precise-opinion part of the topic sentence is a word or phrase that makes a judgment, such as *dangerous* or *exciting*. But a warning is necessary here, for not all judgment words will express precise opinions. Words like *interesting, nice, good,* or *bad* start to take a stand but remain vague. What do you really mean when you say something is "interesting"? What have you said about a person you call "nice"? Such vague judgments make imprecise opinions. On the other hand, precise judgments combine with a subject to define your opinion about the subject.

Again, let's apply this theory to our sample case, sex appeal in magazine advertising. So what if advertisers support sales with sex appeal? You look again at the ads that will support your argument only to find another common element: sex appeal isn't really related to the items for sale. The ads hold your attention because sex appeal was connected to nonsexual items. You are irritated because the advertisers are trying to manipulate your senses so that you will buy whatever they put in the advertisements. Thus, you are ready to state precisely your opinion about sex appeal in these three advertisements: it *irritates* you.

Again consider the process you used. You had to make a judgment about sex appeal in the advertising; you had to establish your precise opinion about the subject. Because you didn't like the sex appeal in the ads, you might have said that the sex appeal was bad. But what would *bad* mean? Did the sex appeal disgust you? Did it appeal to your prurient interests in a manner not consistent with community standards (whatever that means)? Did the sex appeal in the ads merely irritate you? Just what was the *badness*? When you made the precise judgment that sex appeal in some magazine advertisements is irritating, you established your exact stand on the subject.

WRITING THE TOPIC SENTENCE

Once you have limited the subject and have decided precisely your opinion about it, you have formed the two basic parts of the topic sentence—a *limited subject* and a *precise opinion* about that subject. You can easily structure a topic sentence by stating the precise opinion in some form after the sentence's subject, as in the following:

For me, dieting is futile.

Dieting, the subject of the sentence, is the limited subject, and *futile,* which follows, is the precise opinion about it.

Now we can write the topic sentence for the paragraph on sex appeal in magazine advertisements.

Magazine advertisments that try to use sex appeal to sell any product are irritating.

We can see, then, that the basic pattern for the topic sentence is *"limited subject* is *precise opinion."* Consider these examples:

Arcade video games are challenging.

Restoring old houses is rewarding.

In the first sentence, *arcade video games* is the limited subject and *challenging* is the precise opinion. In the second, you intend to persuade the readers that *restoring old houses* (the limited subject) is *rewarding* (the precise opinion).

REFINING THE TOPIC SENTENCE

Even though this pattern is basic for a topic sentence, you need not feel restricted to it. Perhaps the model seems too mechanical. You can easily convert the topic-sentence model to a more sophisticated form. Look at the following topic sentence in the basic pattern:

Overpackaging of supermarket items is seriously wasteful of natural resources.

Here is the same idea in another form:

The overpackaging of supermarket items seriously wastes natural resources.

Notice that the verb *is* and the precise opinion *wasteful* (the basic pattern) became the verb *wastes* in the second sentence form. Now look at a topic sentence from an earlier chapter:

Even though I have never really lived there, going to my grandmother's farm always seems like coming home.

Converted to the basic pattern, the idea of the sentence is as follows:

Going to my grandmother's farm is like coming home.

In another topic sentence we may say this:

Hitchhiking is dangerous.

But we may also state the sentence more imaginatively:

Hitchhiking has proved to be the last ride for many people.

The important point is that refined topic sentences, such as those above, can always be converted to the model: *"limited subject* is *precise opinion."* When you write a topic-sentence form beyond the model, take a moment to ensure that you can still convert it to the two basic parts.

Whatever the pattern of the topic sentences, the result is the same. When you have limited your subject and precisely defined your opinion about it, you have formed the necessary parts of the topic sentence. You have created an assertion that will guide both you and your readers through the supporting material of the paragraph. In one sentence you've taken a stand that you will then persuade your readers to believe. You've given form to the idea that rests at the head of the body.

EXERCISES

A. Place a check mark by the sentences that would *not* make good topic sentences because they do not state precise opinions.

1. _____ Baked potatoes are nutritious.

2. _____ Kerosene heaters are dangerous.

3. _____ Submarines are terrific!

4. _____ Submarines are technological marvels.

5. _____ According to the U.S. Weather Service, eight inches of snow fell overnight.

6. _____ The snowfall turned the city's streets into a nightmare for commuters.

7. _____ The wind in Maine can be quite damaging.

8. _____ Let me describe the new stadium.

9. _____ Babies tend to cry when upset.

10. _____ Wolves are loyal to each other.

B. For these topic sentences, underline the subject once and the opinion twice. Also, circle any subjects that aren't limited enough and any opinions that aren't precise enough.

1. Tigers are crafty hunters.
2. The time machine was unreliable.
3. Pool halls are lousy.
4. Associating with students from different backgrounds has made me more tolerant of other people's behavior.
5. Transportation is important.
6. Today's golfers are extraordinary athletes.
7. Summer vacations are wonderful.
8. Insecticides can be harmful to human beings.
9. The early explorers were daring.
10. Soccer is great.

C. Limit the general subjects below and then state a precise opinion about each limited subject:

Example: **General Subject** Traveling

_____Hitchhiking_____ is/are _____dangerous_____ .
             (Limited Subject)   (Precise Opinion)

1. **General Subject** Science Fiction

_____ is/are _____ .
             (Limited Subject)   (Precise Opinion)

2. **General Subject** Diseases

_____ is/are _____ .
             (Limited Subject)   (Precise Opinion)

3. **General Subject** Dangerous Animals

_____ is/are _____ .
             (Limited Subject)   (Precise Opinion)

4. **General Subject** City Transportation

_____ is/are _____.
(Limited Subject)   (Precise Opinion)

5. **General Subject** Agriculture

_____ is/are _____.
(Limited Subject)   (Precise Opinion)

6. **General Subject** Criminals

_____ is/are _____.
(Limited Subject)   (Precise Opinion)

4
Unity

You know a topic presents a precise opinion about a limited subject. Now we can go to the next step in good writing: unity.

Think about the word *unity* for a moment. It means "oneness," doesn't it? So for a paragraph to have unity, it must have "oneness." More specifically, each idea in the paragraph should be clearly supporting the "one main point," the topic sentence; normally there shouldn't be any ideas that are irrelevant, that aren't supporting the point of the paragraph.

If, for example, you're writing about the dullest class you ever took, you'd destroy the unity by talking about the fascinating lectures and exciting field trips. Or if you want to show that your mynah bird is an ideal pet, the friendliness of the boa constrictor is off the subject and, therefore, irrelevant. In other words, everything you say in a paragraph must support your paragraph.

Can you find the two places in this next paragraph where the writer loses her sense of unity?

> My most frustrating job was cooking for the dorm cafeteria during my freshman year. No matter how hard I tried, I never could cook what the menu said because the food company always delivered the wrong food or brought it late. I was also frustrated because I had trouble estimating how much food to cook—many times we ran short of hamburgers or had to throw away pounds and pounds of french fries. Sometimes we ate the extra french fries, though, and we'd sit around, joking and having a good time. The worst thing, however, was the condition of my clothes after the meal was over. Even if I hadn't spilled anything (and I usually had spilled spaghetti or something worse), my clothes smelled awful. I'd want to go home to change before going anyplace else. Some of the other students who didn't work in the cafeteria also spilled food and had to change, too. No wonder, then, I thought cooking for the dorm cafeteria was frustrating.

Did you find the two sentences? The first one is when the writer talks about eating the french fries and having a good time; the second is the sentence about the students not working in the cafeteria spilling food on themselves. Neither of those sentences has anything to do with the main topic of the paragraph: working in the cafeteria being *frustrating*.

Here's a diagram showing what we mean:

Topic Sentence
My job as cook was frustrating.

Support
Wrong food was delivered.

Support
I had trouble estimating amounts.

Support
I had fun eating extra food.

Support
My clothes were messy.

Support
Other students were messy.

Reworded Topic Sentence
My job as cook was frustrating.

Now let's fix the unity of that paragraph:

My most frustrating job was cooking for the dorm cafeteria during my freshman year. No matter how hard I tried, I never could cook what the menu said because the food company always delivered the wrong food or brought it late. I was also frustrated because I had trouble estimating how much food to cook—many times we ran short of hamburgers or had to throw away pounds and pounds of french fries. The worst thing, however, was the condition of my clothes after the meal was over. Even if I hadn't spilled anything (and I usually had spilled spaghetti or something worse), my clothes smelled awful. I'd want to go home to change before going anyplace else. No wonder, then, I thought cooking for the dorm cafeteria was frustrating.

Note the difference: the writer sticks to the subject. All the examples help show that being a cook for the dorm cafeteria was frustrating. A diagram of this paragraph looks unified, showing that all the blocks fit:

Topic Sentence My job as cook was frustrating.
Support Wrong food was delivered.
Support I had trouble estimating amounts.
Support My clothes were messy.
Reworded Topic Sentence My job as cook was frustrating.

As you can see, the idea of unity is really simple: stick to the point. Don't be led astray by a word or idea in one of your sentences the way the writer was in the first paragraph. Make sure everything in your paragraph belongs there. That way, your readers won't be distracted—or worse, confused.

EXERCISES

A. Read these paragraphs and underline the precise opinion in the topic sentence. Then identify those sentences that don't help support the precise opinion.

1. ¹Television comedy shows are undermining America's social values. ²The most obvious way is that these shows usually show the father or other male power figure as foolish, incompetent, or corrupt. ³The shows also make women only sex objects, bouncy but brainless. ⁴Likewise, people who are honest or hardworking often appear stupid. ⁵Some of the "one-liners" in these shows are pretty good, though. ⁶It's clear that sit-coms are harming America's values.

The irrelevant sentence is _____.

2. ¹Compared with the Earth, the moon is an unusual geological specimen. ²Its surface, once turbulent, is now so tranquil that the astronauts' footprints probably still remain virtually unchanged. ³Also, the surface of the moon is, of course, entirely barren and, except for its shape, almost dully consistent. ⁴The view from there is spectacular, which makes me really want to visit it. ⁵In summary, the moon has some important geological differences from Earth.

   The irrelevant sentence is _____.

3. ¹Railroad trains can haul freight much more efficiently than trucks can. ²For one thing, trains can have many cars—sometimes well over a hundred—and each railroad car can hold many times what a truck (or tractor-trailer) holds. ³Therefore, a relatively short train carrying only a small crew can carry thousands of tons more than a truck can for each trip. ⁴For another thing, trains use much, much less fuel per ton of freight than the trucks do. ⁵Finally, trains are breathtaking to watch, moving powerfully and smoothly across the country as they have for well over a century. ⁶Let's not forget, the trains helped open the West. ⁷So let's give trains their due: they are much more efficient than trucks at hauling freight.

   The irrelevant sentences are _____ and _____.

B. In the following examples, provide unified support for the topic sentence. If you need to, invent specific details for your support.

1.

Topic Sentence **Aerobic exercise has many benefits.**
Support
Support
Support
Reworded Topic Sentence **Therefore, aerobic exercise has many benefits.**

2.

Topic Sentence Fireplaces can be dangerous.
Support
Support
Support
Reworded Topic Sentence So fireplaces can be dangerous.

3.

Topic Sentence Many farmers have hard days.
Support
Support
Support
Reworded Topic Sentence Therefore, many farmers have hard days.

C. 1. Write a paragraph on one of the topic sentences in Exercise B; use your
invented support. Add two irrelevant sentences to destroy the paragraph's
unity.

2. Now write the same paragraph but eliminate the irrelevant sentences so
that your paragraph is unified.

5
Coherence

A one-paragraph essay must have not only unity but also coherence, a word few students can define, though nearly everyone can recognize the opposite, incoherence. If a man runs into the room screaming, "Fire! Dog! House!" we call him incoherent. Does he mean that a dog is on fire in the house? Or that the house is on fire with the dog inside? Or that a doghouse is on fire? We don't know. Although the man apparently has some very important ideas he wishes desperately to communicate, he has left out the essential links of thought. Coherence, then, requires including those links.

This chapter discusses three important ways to achieve coherence in the one-paragraph essay: *explanation of the support, reminders of the opinion in the topic sentence,* and *transitions.* These important links will help your readers move smoothly from idea to idea within your paragraph. Then when your doghouse catches on fire, you will know exactly how to ask for help.

EXPLANATION OF THE SUPPORT

Don't assume that your readers are specially gifted people able to read minds. You must not only present the support to the readers but also explain how it is related to the topic sentence. In other words, you must link your support—clearly and unambiguously—to the topic sentence. The author of the following paragraph does not explain his support at all, apparently hoping that his readers are clairvoyant:

> In the early morning, I am easily annoyed by my roommate. I have to shut the ice-covered windows. A white tornado of dandruff swirls around the room. A mass of smoke from cigarettes hovers near the door. No wonder I find my roommate annoying!

No wonder, indeed! The paragraph is incoherent because the author has failed to explain how his support relates to the topic sentence. Does he mean that his roommate is annoying because he does not close the window in the morning? Or is he annoying because he opens the window every night, even in winter, thus causing the writer to be cold in the morning? Or what? And who has dandruff, and who smokes? Is it the roommate or is it the author, who is upset because the roommate does not understand? After all, the author may be doing the best he can to get rid of the dandruff, and he is smoking heavily only because he is trying to distract himself after waking up every morning in a cold room.

By being incomplete, by not explaining the support fully, the paragraph demands too much of readers. Let's guess what the writer really meant and then revise the paragraph to add coherence:

> In the early morning, I am easily annoyed by my roommate. I have to shut the ice-covered windows *that John, my roommate, insists on opening every night, even during the winter.* A white tornado swirling around the room *shows me that his dandruff problem is still in full force.* A mass of smoke *from John's pack-a-day habit* hovers near the door. No wonder I find my roommate annoying.

We have now explained that John, the roommate, is guilty of the indiscretions. The coherence is improved greatly, but the paragraph still needs work.

REMINDERS OF THE OPINION IN THE TOPIC SENTENCE

In the preceding section we learned not to assume that readers can read minds. In this section, however, we will make an assumption about readers: readers, like all of us, prefer being mentally lazy. They don't like remembering too much at once. While they are reading the support, they like occasional reminders of the opinion stated in the topic sentence so that they will remember why they are reading that support. We can remind them of the opinion in the topic sentence with either of two techniques at the beginning of each item of support: we can repeat the exact words of the opinion or use other words that suggest the opinion. In the sample paragraph about the roommate, we can use the word *annoy* in presenting each example, or we can use words such as *disgusted* or *choking on stale smoke*, which *suggest* annoyance. Notice the reminders in the revised paragraph:

> In the early morning, I am easily annoyed by my roommate. *I am annoyed* each time I have to shut the ice-covered windows that John, my roommate, insists on opening every night, even during the winter. *A disgusting* white tornado swirling around the room shows me that his dandruff problem is still in full force. *A choking mass of stale smoke* from John's pack-a-day habit hovers near the door. No wonder I find my roommate annoying.

By reminding the readers that each example presents something annoying, the paragraph becomes more coherent.

TRANSITIONS

Each example in the sample paragraph now has a clear explanation of the support and a reminder of the opinion in the topic sentence, but the paragraph is still rough. It moves like a train with square wheels, chunking along abruptly from idea to idea. To help the paragraph move more smoothly, we must add transitions.

Transitions are like road signs that tell readers where they are going. If you live in Louisville and wish to drive north to Indianapolis, you don't want to stop to consult a map to find out you are on the right road. You would rather have road signs. Similarly, readers don't want to run into an example that slows them because they don't understand how it relates to the previous example or, worse yet, how it relates to the topic sentence. In a paragraph, the road sign could be *however* to tell readers that the next idea is going to contrast with the one just presented; or it could be *also* to tell readers that another idea like the preceding one is about to be presented; or it could be *therefore* to tell readers to prepare for a conclusion. These and other transitions will keep your Indianapolis-bound driver from losing valuable time because he has to stop, or, if he takes a chance and presses on, from arriving nowhere, which is where he may end his trip in a paragraph without transitions.

Here are some common transitions:

To add an idea: also, and, another, equally important, finally, furthermore, in addition, last, likewise, moreover, most important, next, second, third

To give an example: as a case in point, consider . . . , for example, for instance, as an illustration

To make a contrast: and yet, but, however, instead, nevertheless, on the contrary, on the other hand, still

To begin a conclusion: as a result, clearly, hence, in conclusion, no wonder, obviously, then, therefore, thus

A paragraph must have transitions, but where should these transitions be placed? This diagram shows the critical locations:

	Topic Sentence
Transition ⟶	
	Specific Support
Transition ⟶	
	Specific Support
Transition ⟶	
	Specific Support
Transition ⟶	
	Reworded Topic Sentence

Sometimes you will find that no transition is necessary between the topic sentence and the first item of specific support because the second sentence of the paragraph is so obviously an example that a transitional expression seems too mechanical. For instance, you might be able to omit the first transition in this final revision of the sample paragraph about the roommate. The remaining transitions, however, are all desirable.

> In the early morning, I am easily annoyed by my roommate. *For example,* I am annoyed each time I have to shut the ice-covered windows that John, my roommate, insists on opening every night, even during the winter. I am *also* disgusted by a white tornado swirling around the room, which shows me that his dandruff problem is still in full force. *Most bothersome, though,* is the choking mass of stale smoke—from John's pack-a-day habit—that hovers near the door. *No wonder* I find my roommate annoying.

Our sample paragraph is finally coherent. We have explained the support, reminded the reader frequently of the opinion in the topic sentence, and added transitions at the critical locations.

You're so familiar with the above paragraph by now, and it's so simple, you may believe the transitions aren't really necessary. Perhaps you're right. But what if you read a paragraph that began like this?

> If you've ever bought a pomegranate, you probably know that it's one of the most difficult foods to eat. The juice is delicious and a beautiful ruby color. It drips everywhere, staining whatever it hits. The bitter, inedible pulp seems impossible to avoid. . . .

By now, you're probably lost. If the writer has trouble eating a pomegranate, then why start by telling us how delicious and beautiful it is? The writer knows why, but the readers don't because there aren't any transitions. Let's put them in:

> If you've ever bought a pomegranate, you probably know that it's one of the most difficult foods to eat. *Although* the juice is delicious and a beautiful ruby color, it *unfortunately* drips everywhere, staining whatever it hits. *Also frustrating,* the bitter, inedible pulp seems impossible to avoid. . . .

The transitions (and the reminder *frustrating*) make the paragraph easy to understand the first time through. Good writing shouldn't be an IQ test or a guessing game for the readers, so let them know what you're thinking as your ideas shift directions. For now, use the three techniques demonstrated in this chapter, even if they seem mechanical. As you gain experience as a writer, you will learn more subtle ways to link your ideas to each other and to the topic sentence. Your immediate goal now, though, is to communicate coherently with your readers.

EXERCISES

Outline this paragraph and indicate the *transitions* by filling in the blanks below. Merely summarize the topic sentence, the support, and the reworded topic sentence rather than writing them in full.

> A significant change I have noticed in myself since entering college is a fear of mathematics. The mere sight of a three-hundred-fifty-page math text, for instance, causes a cold shiver to run the length of my spine. As I cautiously open the front cover of the text, a myriad of complex formulas springs at me, quickly eliminating any trace of confidence I may have had. My dread of math is also strengthened each time I enter the small, dismal classroom. I can find no consolation in watching my classmates cringe behind open briefcases as they prepare to do battle with a common enemy capable of engulfing us all in a blanket of confusion. Finally, my greatest fears are realized as my instructor self-consciously adjusts his glasses and admits that he majored in English and never truly mastered, or even understood, calculus. Then I suddenly realize that the Cartesian plane has snared me in its nightmarish world for another semester.

Topic Sentence _____

Transition _____

Specific Support _____

Transition _____

Specific Support _____

Transition _____

Specific Support _____

Transition _____

Reworded Topic Sentence _____

The opinion the above paragraph demonstrates is *fear*. Circle all *reminders* of that opinion in the paragraph; that is, circle all words that either repeat the word or suggest the meaning *fear*.

B. Outline this paragraph and show the *transitions* by filling in the blanks. Again, simply summarize the topic sentence, the support, and the reworded topic sentence rather than writing them in full.

> Since becoming a college student, I have learned many ways to study faster than I did in high school. As an example, I discovered that spending three-fourths of my study time sprawled across a desk in deep slumber has helped me find a sudden aptitude for instantly memorizing five chapters of chemistry the period before a test. Another way I have developed my study skills is reading magazines at the bookstore on free afternoons. When my classmates (and occasionally the professors) ask me to justify this practice, I calmly tell them that the rate at which I study is sure to increase if I study only in the evenings. But by far my most useful device for sharpening my study habits is my custom of writing my girlfriend during finals. What else could teach me to study an entire semester's material in only an hour and a half? So, since becoming a college student, I have developed many ways to study far faster than I ever had before.

Topic Sentence _____

Transition _____

Specific Support _____

Transition _____

Specific Support _____

Transition _____

Specific Support _____

Transition _____

Reworded Topic Sentence _____

The opinion in the above paragraph is *study faster*. Circle all *reminder* words that either repeat the phrase or suggest the meaning *study faster*.

C. Using another paragraph in this book assigned by your instructor, underline all the transitions and circle all the reminders.

D. Rewrite this paragraph, adding transitions and reminders of the opinion in the topic sentence. You may also need to add some support to fully explain the relationship of the support to the topic sentence.

> The city of Stockholm is among the loveliest in the world. Slum districts, prevalent in almost all large cities, are nearly nonexistent in Stockholm, having been replaced by government housing. The citizens are careful to dispose of their litter properly and to pick up litter other people may have dropped. Stockholm has a unique layout: it is built on twenty-three islands. Water winds throughout the city. The beauty of Stockholm makes it one of the most alluring cities in the world.

E. Follow the same instructions as for Exercise D.

> Overnight camping can be disenchanting if you are a novice. Whether you hike in (carrying pounds and pounds of food and equipment on your back) or whether you drive (with all the monotony car trips are infamous for), you will probably be tired once you are ready to set up your camp. When you settle back to admire the stars at the end of the day, you will probably be besieged by bugs—mosquitoes and sand flies seem to prefer making their homes in scenic places. When you go to bed, you may find that your sleeping bag, especially if you have a cheap one, may be quite uncomfortable. Camping for newcomers can be quite different from a purely romantic adventure.

F. Write a paragraph that convinces readers that some*thing* (not some*one*) has a particular characteristic. On the final copy, underline all the transitions and circle all the reminders. Ensure you have met the other requirement for coherence by explaining your support fully. (Notice the paragraph in Chapter 1 on the Boundary Waters Canoe Area could have been a response to this exercise.)

G. Write a paragraph that convinces readers of one significant way in which you have changed since entering college. Use examples from your own experience as support. On the final copy, underline all the transitions and circle all the reminders. Ensure you have met the other requirement for coherence by explaining your support fully. (Exercises A and B are on the same subject.)

H. Write a paragraph that convinces readers of one important characteristic you like your friends to have. Use examples from your experience as support. On the final copy, underline all the transitions and circle all the reminders. Ensure you have met the other requirement for coherence by explaining your support fully.

PART TWO

The One-Paragraph Essay (Stage II)

In this section you'll learn a slightly more sophisticated way to organize a one-paragraph essay. You'll find out when you reach Part Three that this new type of paragraph is actually a stepping-stone to larger themes and research papers. Once you learn how to write a Stage II paragraph, the full-length essay will be simple for you to learn.

6
Overview of the One-Paragraph Essay (Stage II)

Good Stage I and Stage II paragraphs have a lot in common:

- a topic sentence
- specific support
- unity
- coherence
- a reworded topic sentence

So how are Stage I and Stage II paragraphs different? The answer: while a Stage I paragraph has just one opinion, *a Stage II paragraph has more than one opinion*—the opinion in the topic sentence (which is the main opinion) *and* the opinions in the subtopic sentences (which are supporting opinions). Each subtopic sentence is a separate idea in the paragraph that helps support the main idea, the topic sentence.

Let's look at a sample Stage II paragraph. The sentences in italics are the subtopic sentences.

Computer manuals can be really frustrating to use. *For one thing, the indexes are usually frustrating because they are hard to decipher.* I remember when I was trying to find out how to print my paper: I tried to find the word "print" in the index. Believe it or not, the word wasn't even there. I finally asked the person next to me, who said the term for printing in that manual isn't "print"; instead, it's "concatenate." No wonder I had trouble! *Aside from the indexes, the general quality of writing in the manuals themselves is frustrating.* The manual for my spreadsheet program doesn't have any diagrams at all, asking me to visualize what a spreadsheet looks like. And my word processing manual assumes I know as much as the software developers do. As you can tell, I think computer manuals need a lot of work.

Here's an outline of this paragraph:

Topic Sentence Computer manuals are frustrating.
  Subtopic Sentence Indexes are hard to use.
    Specific Support One index didn't use the word "print."
  Subtopic Sentence General quality of writing is poor.
    Specific Support Spreadsheet program has no diagrams.
    Specific Support Word processing program assumes too much.
Reworded Topic Sentence Computer manuals need work.

Notice that each subtopic sentence has the kind of specific support we discussed in Chapter 2. We use examples here (a narrative example for the first subtopic sentence and two quick examples for the second one), but statistics and statements by authorities would do as well.

Notice also that if you remove the subtopic sentences above, you would have a Stage I paragraph. Sometimes the relationship between Stage I and Stage II paragraphs is not so simple. You could add subtopic sentences to the Boundary Waters Canoe Area paragraph in Chapter 1, but you would end up with a worse paragraph because the support is so meager—the paragraph would have more topic and subtopic sentences than support sentences. Also, some Stage I paragraphs cannot become Stage II paragraphs because they were never divided into subtopic ideas. The sample paragraphs about fearing mathematics and learning to study faster in the exercises for Chapter 5, for example, do not have subtopic ideas, so you could not easily convert them into Stage II paragraphs.

Let's look now at a general model of the Stage II paragraph:

Topic Sentence
  Subtopic Sentence
    Specific Support
    Specific Support
  Subtopic Sentence
    Specific Support
    Specific Support
Reworded Topic Sentence

This outline is not rigid, of course. Your Stage II paragraph may have two, three, or four subtopic sentences, and each subtopic sentence may have one to four items of support, depending on the subject and your approach to it. The paragraph above, for instance, had just two subtopic sentences, and one of those subtopic sentences has just one item of support—a narrative example.

Our sample paragraph about computer manuals might have worked as a Stage I paragraph without subtopic sentences, but some paragraphs are so complex that they need subtopic sentences just to keep the readers (and maybe the writer) from getting lost. Look at this one:

> Although apparently just an assortment of oddities from the National Museum of American History, a 1980 special exhibit called "The Nation's Attic" struck me as a tribute to American ingenuity. *One part of the exhibit demonstrated the ingenious ways Americans have found to shape everyday items.* For instance, a large collection of hand sewing accessories—hundreds of thimbles, needle cases, sewing cases, and pincushions—showed how simple things could be made more useful, more beautiful, or more entertaining. *More imaginative, though, were the things made apparently just because Americans wanted to accept the challenge of making them.* There was an intricate model of the U.S. Capitol constructed entirely of glass rods. Someone else had engraved the Lord's Prayer on a single grain of rice. And a group of chemical engineers had even managed to do the proverbial "undoable": they had actually created a silk purse from a sow's ear—just to prove it could be done. *The most interesting part of the exhibit to me, however, was some of the bizarre but ingenious failures among the models submitted for approval to the U.S. Patent Office.* I haven't been able to forget an early attempt at creating an electric razor. The inventor had mounted some razor blades on a rotating wheel so it looked something like the paddle wheel of a riverboat, and this wheel was attached to a small hand-held electric motor. There were no guards to control the depth at which the blades cut, so anyone foolish enough to use the razor would no doubt have lost much more than a few whiskers from his face. Still, although I would never have sampled this inventor's work, I had to respect his resourcefulness. This invention, like the other unusual items in "The Nation's Attic," showed the mark of American ingenuity.

Here is an outline of the paragraph:

Topic Sentence "The Nation's Attic" was a tribute to American ingenuity.
   Subtopic Sentence Some everyday items were ingenious.
      Specific Support Sewing items.
   Subtopic Sentence Some items made just for the challenge were imaginative.
      Specific Support Capitol from glass rods.
      Specific Support Lord's Prayer on grain of rice.
      Specific Support Silk purse from sow's ear.
   Subtopic Sentence Some bizarre failures were ingenious.
      Specific Support Attempt to create electric razor.
Reworded Topic Sentence The unusual items showed American ingenuity.

You might notice that the last sentence of the sample paragraph ties together the last item of support with all those that preceded it. That's not a necessary attribute of a reworded topic sentence, but it works nicely here.

Notice that even though a paragraph follows a model, as does the paragraph above, it can still be very good writing. The model is like a skeleton, and the content is like the body on that skeleton. We know that most people have skeletons that look about alike, but to a man looking at a woman—or to a woman looking at a man—the bodies can appear considerably different. Similarly, the content of an essay—what *you* have to say—can make an essay rather dowdy or very appealing.

EXERCISES

A. Outline this paragraph.

> To play water polo well, you have to learn to cheat. The only way you can keep the ball is by making a few slightly illegal moves. Pushing off your opponent's stomach can give you the elbowroom necessary to make a good pass or score a goal. Likewise, kneeing your attacker in the ribs can keep him from stealing the ball while you are setting up a play. When the opposing team does get possession, the unapproved solution for retrieving the ball is again through cheating. Pulling back on your adversary's leg is an effective means of slowing him down to give you a fairer chance at guarding him. But the most effective method of getting the ball is simply to pull his suit down, which immediately stops all his competitive activity. Fortunately, water polo is played in the water, since it hides the cheating all players must do in order to be successful.

Topic Sentence _____

  Subtopic Sentence _____

    Specific Support _____

    Specific Support _____

  Subtopic Sentence _____

    Specific Support _____

    Specific Support _____

Reworded Topic Sentence _____

B. Outline this paragraph:

> Giving a good speech takes a lot of work. For instance, it takes hard work just to prepare the content—to write it. Last year I had to give a speech to our entire graduating class in high school. I wanted to impress my friends and their families, of course, but the words I wrote always sounded phony—too "elevated" in tone. I wrote and wrote and rewrote until I finally decided not to be impressive but just to say the good things I felt about the school. I had spent more than hours; I had spent days getting the words right. Once I had the words, the hard part really started: practicing my delivery. I gave my speech to my empty room. I gave my speech to my mirror. I gave my speech to my twin sister. I even gave my speech to my parents! So don't let anybody tell you that giving a good speech is easy.

Topic Sentence _____

  Subtopic Sentence _____

    Specific Support _____

Subtopic Sentence _____

    Specific Support _____

    Specific Support _____

    Specific Support _____

    Specific Support _____

Reworded Topic Sentence _____

7
Support: Subtopic Sentences

A *sub*topic sentence is very much like a topic sentence:

- A topic sentence and a subtopic sentence both state opinions that need specific support.
- And both are divisible into two parts: the subject (which must be limited) and the opinion (which must be precise).

The difference is that a subtopic sentence serves as a *support idea* to help show your readers that they should accept your main idea, the topic sentence. Theoretically, if you can persuade your readers to accept each subtopic sentence, then they should accept your topic sentence as well.

The precise opinion in each subtopic sentence is usually identical to the precise opinion in the topic sentence. For example, we showed you a sample Stage II paragraph in the last chapter. These were the two subtopic sentences—notice that the opinions in them are identical:

> For one thing, the indexes are usually *frustrating* because they are hard to decipher.

> Aside from the indexes, the general quality of writing in the manuals themselves is *frustrating*.

The rest of this chapter shows you three different kinds of subtopic sentences: subtopic sentences that answer the questions "Why?" "How?" or "When?" There are other kinds of subtopic sentences than these, of course, but these three ways can get you started quickly.

SUBTOPIC SENTENCE: "WHY?"

One of the easiest ways to find a subtopic sentence is to state the topic sentence and then ask, "Why?"

Suppose this is your topic sentence: "Vegetable gardens take a lot of planning." If you ask yourself, "Why do vegetable gardens take a lot of planning?" you might come up with these two subtopic sentences:

Vegetable gardens take a lot of planning because the soil needs to be prepared.

Vegetable gardens take a lot of planning because the vegetables need to be planted at specific times.

Here is a possible outline, including the specific support you might want to use:

Topic Sentence Vegetable gardens take a lot of planning.
   Subtopic Sentence They take planning because the soil needs to be prepared.
      Specific Support Soil should be tilled in the fall, after the last harvest.
      Specific Support Soil should be tested in the spring, especially for acidity and nitrogen.
   Subtopic Sentence They need to be planted at specific times.
      Specific Support Last year, I planted the lettuce too late, so that by the time it should have been ready for harvest, it had died. (Narrative example)
Reworded Topic Sentence Therefore, you should plan your garden in advance.

In this outline, the subtopic sentences give some reasons why the topic sentence is true; the specific support then gives the concrete support for the subtopic sentences.

By the way, subtopic sentences that answer the question "Why?" can always be joined to the topic sentence with the word *because:*

Vegetable gardens take a lot of planning *because* the soil needs to be prepared.

Vegetable gardens take a lot of planning *because* the vegetables need to be planted at specific times.

You don't have to use the word *because* to join the "Why?" subtopic sentence to the topic sentence, but you can. Whenever you write "Why?" subtopic sentences, then, you might want to test them by joining them to the topic sentence with the word *because.*

Notice that you can support your subtopic sentences with the same kind of specific support you learned in Chapter 2: examples (quick or narrative), statistics, and statements by authorities.

SUBTOPIC SENTENCE: "HOW?"

Another common type of subtopic sentence answers the question "How?" Look at this paragraph that has subtopic sentences answering the question "How?"

Topic Sentence Heavy rush hour traffic brings out the worst in many drivers.
  Subtopic Sentence Traffic conditions make some drivers overly nervous.
    Specific Support Uncle Billy, usually a calm and careful driver, becomes so flustered in rush hour traffic that he can't carry on a conversation and forgets to check the rearview mirror when he changes lanes.
    Specific Support A 1987 study of traffic flow in the Los Angeles area showed that the average waiting time at freeway entrance ramps increased to 1.5 minutes during rush hour because of the number of drivers who were afraid to merge into the heavy stream of cars.
  Subtopic Sentence Heavy rush hour traffic reinforces the aggressiveness of some drivers.
    Specific Support Often drivers follow too closely during rush hour because they're afraid other drivers might slip in ahead of them.
    Specific Support Drivers continue into intersections on yellow lights even though they will get caught there and block cross traffic.
    Specific Support A psychologist who has studied driver reactions concluded that "stress conditions of rush hour traffic cause physical and emotional reactions like those of a soldier in combat."
Reworded Topic Sentence Rush hour traffic conditions show many drivers at their worst.

Notice that these subtopic sentences clearly answer the question "How?" and not the question "Why?" "Why?" subtopic sentences probably would state something about the cause-effect relationship between rush hour traffic and the way drivers present themselves in it; "How?" subtopic sentences, on the other hand, show the results of the traffic on driver behavior.

We need to add a word of caution here. Sometimes subtopic sentences clearly answer "Why?" and sometimes they clearly answer "How?" At other times the questions appear to overlap. In other words, sometimes we can't be sure which of these two questions the subtopic sentences answer. Don't worry. The fine distinctions you would have to make are more fitting for a class in philosophy or semantics than for one in composition. Treat these questions for what they are—a quick and effective way to find subtopic sentences.

SUBTOPIC SENTENCE: "WHEN?"

Another type of subtopic sentence answers the question "When?" For example, to show that your roommate is constantly sleepy, you could ask yourself "When?" The resulting paragraph might look like this one:

Topic Sentence My roommate is constantly sleepy.
  Subtopic Sentence He is sleepy in the morning when he gets up.
    Specific Support He fumbles with the alarm clock.
    Specific Support He once put his trousers on backward.
  Subtopic Sentence He is sleepy when he is in class.
    Specific Support He once fell asleep in Math III and crunched his jaw on the desk.
    Specific Support He does not even remember the subject of the lecture he attended yesterday in chemistry.
  Subtopic Sentence He is sleepy in the evening.
    Specific Support His typical study position is a comatose sprawl with his head on his desk.
    Specific Support He is always in bed by 8:30 P.M.
Reworded Topic Sentence My roommate is sleepy all the time.

PARALLEL SUBTOPIC SENTENCES

In the examples in this chapter, all the subtopic sentences within a one-paragraph essay answer the same question: "Why?" "How?" or "When?" Your Stage II paragraphs should do the same. In other words, if you are supporting the idea "Hitchhiking is dangerous" in a Stage II paragraph, do not answer the question "Why?" for one subtopic sentence ("Hitchhiking is dangerous because too many drivers are deranged") and the question "When?" for another subtopic sentence ("Hitchhiking is dangerous at night, when the streets are poorly lighted").

These ideas may both work to support your topic sentence, but they do not work well together. They are not parallel and seem like a mixture of apples and oranges when you are selling only apples.

Once you have outlined your Stage II paragraph, be sure your subtopic sentences answer the same question: "Why?" "How?" or "When?"

EXERCISES

A. For each of these topic sentences, invent subtopic sentences and specific support. Be sure all your subtopic sentences answer the same question: "Why?" "How?" or "When?"

1. Sometimes women are discriminated against in the workplace.

Subtopic Sentence (Why? or How? or When?)

_____

_____

Specific Support (quick example)

_____

_____

_____

Specific Support (quick example)

_____

_____

_____

Subtopic Sentence (Why? or How? or When?)

_____

Specific Support (statistics)

_____

_____

_____

Specific Support (statement by authority)

_____

_____

_____

2. Computers save people time.

Subtopic Sentence (Why? or How? or When?)

_____

Specific Support (narrative example)

_____

_____

_____

_____

Subtopic Sentence (Why? or How? or When?)

_____

_____

Specific Support (statistics)

_____

_____

_____

_____

Specific Support (statement by authority)

_____

_____

_____

3. Twentieth-century medicine really works.

Subtopic Sentence (Why? or How? or When?)

_____

_____

Specific Support (statistics)

_____

_____

_____

Specific Support (statistics)

_____

_____

_____

Subtopic Sentence (Why? or How? or When?)

_____

_____

Specific Support (quick example)

_____

_____

_____

_____

Specific Support (quick example)

_____

_____

_____

B. If your instructor asks you to, outline the opposite of all the above topic sentences:

1. Women are rarely discriminated against in the workplace.
2. Too often, computers waste people's time.
3. Twentieth-century medicine sometimes causes problems.

Use whichever type of subtopic sentence ("Why?" "How?" or "When?") and whichever type of specific support (examples, statistics, statements by authorities) you wish.

C. In Exercises A and B you outlined several Stage II paragraphs. Choose the one that interests you the most and use the support you invented to write the paragraph.

D. Write a Stage II paragraph convincing us that someone you know has a positive (pleasant, good) or a negative (unpleasant, bad) characteristic. Since you're writing about someone you know, don't use invented support for this exercise.

E. Write a Stage II paragraph explaining how something you have observed impressed you. The sample paragraph in Chapter 6 about "The Nation's Attic" could have been a response to this exercise. Since you're writing about something you've observed, don't use invented support for this exercise.

F. Write a Stage II paragraph about one of these topics (using, if you wish, invented support):

birds	Native Americans
brothers or sisters	nursing homes
a building you know well	railroads
extracurricular events	restaurants
landscaping	vacation spots
losing teams	winning teams

CHECKLIST FOR THE ONE-PARAGRAPH ESSAY

Topic Sentence

_____ Does your paragraph begin with a topic sentence?

_____ Does your topic sentence have a limited subject?

_____ Does your topic sentence have a precise opinion?

Support

_____ Does your support begin with the second sentence of the paragraph?

_____ Is your support detailed enough?

_____ Do all your items of support clearly belong with the topic sentence (unity)?

_____ Do you explain your support fully so the relation to the topic sentence is clear (coherence)?

_____ Does each item of support include a reminder of the opinion in the topic sentence (coherence)?

_____ Do you have transitions at the critical locations (coherence)?

Conclusion

_____ Does the last sentence of the paragraph reword the topic sentence?

Other

_____ Is your paragraph convincing?

_____ Is your paragraph interesting?

_____ Have you checked the spelling of the words you're unsure of?

_____ Is your paper neatly done so it's easy to read?

PART THREE
The Five-Paragraph Essay

A five-paragraph essay is a handy device for learning to write longer papers. The first and last paragraphs are the introduction and conclusion, two new types of paragraphs most longer papers need. The three central paragraphs provide enough material to justify a full-length introduction and conclusion but still keep the paper short enough to be manageable—both for you and for your instructor.

You'll also begin writing about more serious topics in this part. So far you've depended on your own experiences for much of your support; you'll still present your experiences here, but you'll supplement them with occasional support from books and magazines. Of course, we don't expect you to learn the fundamentals of the multiparagraph essay and the fundamentals of documentation at the same time, so we present in this section a simplified system of documentation you can use until you study the research paper in Part Five.

8

Overview of the Five-Paragraph Essay

Are your paragraphs turning into monsters? Are they getting longer and longer, seeming more like small themes instead of one-paragraph essays?

If so, you're ready to take the next step: learning to write the *five*-paragraph essay. Actually, the five-paragraph essay is a lot like a Stage II paragraph. This diagram shows you how:

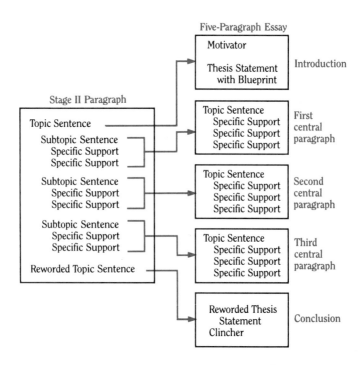

PARTS OF A FIVE-PARAGRAPH ESSAY

A five-paragraph essay has these three components:

- an introduction
- three central paragraphs
- a conclusion

Let's look at each of these briefly. (We'll discuss them in greater detail in the next few chapters.)

Introduction

An introduction is, of course, the first paragraph of the essay. In a way, the topic sentence of your one-paragraph essay served as an introduction, but now that you're about to write longer papers, you'll want something more substantial at the beginning.

Introductions have three parts: a *motivator,* a *thesis statement,* and a *blueprint.*

Motivator   A motivator is the beginning of the introductory paragraph. Its purpose is simply to get the readers interested in reading more—in other words, *motivating* the readers.

Thesis statement   A topic sentence carries the main idea of a one-paragraph essay, right? Well, a thesis statement carries the main idea of the five-paragraph essay.

Blueprint   A blueprint is simply a quick summary of the main points you are about to present in the essay. Since a five-paragraph essay has three central paragraphs, your blueprint will have three points, one for each of the central paragraphs.

Central Paragraphs

There are three central paragraphs in a five-paragraph essay, and each central paragraph supports the essay's main point (or thesis statement).

A central paragraph is like a one-paragraph essay, with a topic sentence at the beginning and specific support following. Normally, though, central paragraphs don't have reworded topic sentences.

Conclusion

Remember the reworded topic sentence at the end of a one-paragraph essay? That sentence gave your one-paragraph essay a sense of finality. The conclusion—the last paragraph of a five-paragraph essay—also gives a sense of finality. A conclusion has two parts: a *reworded thesis statement* and a *clincher.*

Reworded thesis statement   A reworded thesis statement simply does what it says: rewords the thesis statement. It's intended to be a reminder to the readers, saying, in effect, "You've just been reading my three central paragraphs. Once again, let me tell you what those three paragraphs were supporting." Then you tell them.

Clincher   A clincher is simply a finisher, a final sentence or two that leave no doubt in the readers' minds that the essay has reached its end.

A SAMPLE FIVE-PARAGRAPH ESSAY

Now let's look at a "real" five-paragraph essay. As you read it, notice the points we've been discussing: the motivator, the blueprint, and so forth.

Motivator —

Do you realize that newly born children are not even aware that parts of their bodies belong to them? I learned this fascinating fact in my psychology course from a book that says a baby "lies on his back, kicking his heels and watching the little fists flying past his face. But only very slowly does he come to know that they are attached to him and he can control them" (Mary Ann Spencer Pulaski, *Understanding Piaget*, p. 21). Children have a lot of learning to do before they can see the world—and

Thesis Statement —

themselves—through grown-up eyes. As children pass through this remarkable process of growing up, they often do some humorous things, especially

Blueprint —

in learning to speak, in discovering that all objects do not have human characteristics, and in trying to imitate others around them.

Topic Sentence —

Not surprisingly, one area in which children are often humorous is in learning to speak. I remember

Specific Support —

one time I was talking to a friend on the phone while my little sister, Betsy, seemed to be playing inattentively on the floor nearby. After I hung up, Betsy asked me, "Why is the teacher going to give Janet an old tomato?" At first I couldn't figure out what Betsy was talking about. When I asked her what she meant, she said, "You said if Janet doesn't hand in her homework, the teacher is going to give her an old tomato." Finally I caught on. The word I had used was *ultimatum!*

Topic Sentence { Children can also be funny in the way they "humanize" the objects around them. According to my

Specific Support { psychology book, "Up to four or five years old, the child believes anything may be endowed with purpose and conscious activity. A ball may refuse to be thrown straight, or a 'naughty' chair may be responsible for bumping him" (Pulaski, *Understand-*

Specific Support { *ing Piaget,* p. 45). I, myself, can still remember one vivid and scary afternoon when I was sure the sun was following me around, just waiting for the right

Specific Support { moment to get me. I can also remember a time, not scary, when Betsy stood at the top of the stairs and yelled to her shoes at the bottom, "Shoes! Get up here!"

Topic Sentence { Another way in which children are sometimes funny is in their attempts to imitate what they see

Specific Support { around them. All children look pretty silly when they dress up like their mothers and fathers and play "house." My psychology book tells of a more interesting example, though. The famous psychologist Jean Piaget wrote of the time his sixteen-month-old daughter quietly watched a visiting little boy throw a tantrum in trying to get out of his

Specific Support { playpen. Piaget's daughter thought it would be fun to try the same thing: "The next day, she herself screamed in her play-pen and tried to move it, stamping her foot lightly several times in succession. The imitation of the whole scene was most striking" (quoted in Pulaski, *Understanding Piaget,* p. 81).

Reworded Thesis { Little children are funny creatures to watch, aren't they? But as we laugh, we have to admire,

Clincher { too, because the humorous mistakes are but temporary side trips that children take on the amazingly complicated journey to maturity—a long way from the beginning, where they lay in wonder, silently watching the strange, fingered spacecraft passing, back and forth, before their infant eyes.

Now let's look at an outline of that essay:

Introduction

Motivator Children have many things to learn and adjust to as they grow up—including the awareness of the parts of their bodies.
Thesis Children often do humorous things.
Blueprint They're often humorous in learning to speak, in discovering that all objects do not have human characteristics, and in attempting to imitate others.

First Central Paragraph

Topic Sentence Children are often humorous in learning to speak.
Specific Support Betsy mistook *ultimatum* for *old tomato.*

Second Central Paragraph

Topic Sentence Children "humanize" the objects around them.
Specific Support Book says children blame balls and chairs as though the things were conscious.
Specific Support I thought the sun was out to get me.
Specific Support Betsy ordered her shoes to climb the stairs.

Third Central Paragraph

Topic Sentence Children attempt to imitate what they see.
Specific Support They dress like their parents.
Specific Support Piaget's daughter imitated a tantrum a visiting child threw.

Conclusion

Reworded Thesis Children are funny creatures to watch.
Clincher Reminder of the motivator that children have a lot of learning and adjusting to do.

MAKESHIFT DOCUMENTATION

Until now, you've been writing most of your papers based on your personal experience. Those papers can be interesting and important. At some time in your life, though, you need to learn to write about other topics—about the ideas and the words of other people. When you use the ideas and words of others, you need to let the readers know where you found them. In other words, you need to learn about documentation.

You need to document whenever you use the ideas or words of other people. However, we don't want to ask you to learn the fundamentals of the five-paragraph essay and the fundamentals of documentation all at once. On the other hand, we want you to be able to use the ideas and words of others now. As a result, we've devised what we call a "makeshift system of documentation"—a temporary and easy way for you to acknowledge your sources. Later in the book we devote Chapters 21 and 22 to a more formal way to document your writing.

Here's our makeshift system:

- Put quotation marks around all words you take directly from a source.
- At the end of every passage in which you use someone else's words or ideas, identify the source in parentheses. To identify the source, simply use the author's name (if there is one), the title of the book or article, and the page number: (Dick Francis, *Forfeit*, p. 143) or (*The Columbia-Viking Desk Encyclopedia*, pp. 45–58) or (George Miller, "The Magical Number 7, Plus or Minus 2," p. 81).

Proper documentation serves two purposes: it tells your readers that you are using the words or ideas of others; and it tells your readers where they can find your source. Our makeshift system serves only the first purpose well, because your parenthetical information simply isn't complete. As a result, your instructor may ask you to keep your sources handy.

The sample essay in this chapter has good examples of makeshift documentation. If you have any questions at all, please ask your instructor.

EXERCISE

Outline this five-paragraph essay:

> When a person thinks of that old-time, small-town doctor, he usually envisions a mannerly, dignified gentleman. However, this image did not fit my Uncle Rodney, a doctor in the small town of Bandon, Wyoming. Instead, Dr. Rodney was an obnoxious person because he had an annoying habit of speaking in crude, incoherent sentences; he had sloppy eating habits; and he was a messy smoker.
>
> Probably Dr. Rodney's most irritating trait was his crude way of speaking. For example, I recall a particularly embarrassing moment during a family reunion at my mother-in-law's house when Dr. Rodney was asked to say a blessing before dinner. He managed a "Hump, bump, grump," or so it sounded, and almost immediately added "Goddam-

mit'' as he knocked over a bowl of grated corn he was grabbing. As a result, my mother-in-law—a very religious person—was mortified. On another occasion, Dr. Rodney's nurse said, ''It's a good thing I can interpret what Dr. Rodney says and smooth over the rough feelings, or we would be out of patients.''

Additionally, Dr. Rodney bothered many people with his messy eating habits. He shoveled food into his mouth at such an alarming rate that often he could not catch his breath. My brother-in-law once remarked, ''When I see Uncle Rodney eat, I think of jackals devouring their kill.'' Furthermore, Dr. Rodney always finished his meal long before anyone else; then he would make a nauseating slurping sound by sucking air and saliva through the gaps between his top front teeth while he waited for everybody else to finish. Because of his atrocious eating habits, none of Dr. Rodney's neighbors invited him to dinner.

Dr. Rodney was also disliked because he was an inconsiderate smoker. Everywhere he went, he left a trail of ashes, a terrible stench, and wet, chewed-up cigar butts. After his death, the office cleaning lady confided that the townspeople used to bet on how many days would pass before anyone saw Dr. Rodney without a spot of tobacco juice on his shirt. Naturally, all the local children learned not to be downwind from him because no one could easily tolerate his odor of stale tobacco.

Clearly, Dr. Rodney was an obnoxious person whose talking, eating, and smoking habits alienated him from even his own family. He was indeed lucky that the town had only one doctor, or he might not have been employed.

Introduction

> *Motivator*
> *Thesis*
> *Blueprint*

First Central Paragraph

> *Topic Sentence*
>   *Specific Support*
>   *Specific Support*

Second Central Paragraph

> *Topic Sentence*
>   *Specific Support*
>   *Specific Support*
>   *Specific Support*
>   *Specific Support*

Third Central Paragraph

Topic Sentence
  Specific Support
  Specific Support
  Specific Support

Conclusion

Reworded Thesis
  Clincher

9
Thesis Statement with Blueprint

The thesis statement with blueprint is the essential part of your five-paragraph essay. As the name suggests, it has two components:

- the main idea *(thesis statement)*
- the outline of your support *(blueprint)*

Let's look at each of these two components in more detail.

THESIS STATEMENT

The thesis statement is the main idea of your five-paragraph essay, the single idea your entire essay will support.

Sound familiar? The *topic sentence* was the main idea of a one-paragraph essay. Now, the *thesis statement* is the main idea of anything larger than a one-paragraph essay—in this case, the main idea of the five-paragraph essay.

Like the topic sentence, the thesis statement can have the form of *"limited subject* is *precise opinion."* Here's the introduction to our sample five-paragraph essay—the thesis statement is highlighted:

> Do you realize that newly born children are not even aware that parts of their bodies belong to them? I learned this fascinating fact in my psychology course from a book that says a baby "lies on his back, kicking his heels and watching the little fists flying past his face. But only very slowly does he come to know that they are attached to him and he can control them" (Mary Ann Spencer Pulaski, *Understanding Piaget*, p. 21). Children have a lot of learning to do before they can see the world—and themselves—through grown-up eyes. *As children pass through this remarkable process of growing up, they often do some humorous things,* especially in learning to speak, in discovering that all objects do not have human characteristics, and in trying to imitate others around them.

The limited subject is "children as they grow up"; the precise opinion is
"humorous."

BLUEPRINT

What is a blueprint for an essay? As we mentioned in the last chapter, a blueprint is a summary of the main points you are about to present in the body of your paper. *In other words, the blueprint is a summary—in advance—of the topic sentences for your central paragraphs.*

As the name *blueprint* suggests, the blueprint is like an architect's pattern for the structure she intends to build . . . only in this case, you are the architect, and the structure you intend to build is your essay.

Suppose, for example, you have this organization in mind for your five-paragraph essay:

Thesis Statement Overly competitive sports can damage a child psychologically.
Topic Sentence They can damage a child's view of himself.
Topic Sentence They can damage a child's view of his peers.
Topic Sentence They can damage a child's view of adults.

Now to form a blueprint, simply combine the basic ideas from the three topic sentences:

Because they can damage a child's view of himself, of his peers, and of adults, . . .

Now let's combine the blueprint with the thesis statement to get the result this chapter is about—the thesis statement with blueprint:

Because they can damage a child's view of himself, of his peers, and of adults, overly competitive sports can damage a child psychologically.

Finally, let's look at the introduction to the sample essay, or theme, from the last chapter—the blueprint is highlighted:

Do you realize that newly born children are not even aware that parts of their bodies belong to them? I learned this fascinating fact in my psychology course from a book that says a baby "lies on his back, kicking his heels and watching the little fists flying past his face. But only very slowly does he come to know that they are attached to him and he can control them" (Mary Ann Spencer Pulaski, *Understanding Piaget*, p. 21). Children have a lot of learning to do before they can see the world—and themselves—through grown-up eyes. As children pass through this remarkable process of growing up, they often do some humorous things, especially *in learning to speak, in discovering that all objects do not have human characteristics, and in trying to imitate others around them.*

BLUEPRINTS ANSWERING "WHY?" "HOW?" AND "WHEN?"

The five-paragraph essay is really just an expanded Stage II paragraph, so you could use the same kind of support for both of them. Let's examine sample blueprints answering each of the questions "Why?" "How?" and "When?"

"Why?" Blueprint

If we ask "Why?" about a thesis statement, the answer will usually begin with *because*. In fact, our sample about competitive sports being psychologically damaging to children is a "Why?" blueprint, isn't it?

Let's look at another example. Why do vegetable gardens take a lot of planning?

> *Because* the soil needs to be prepared, *because* the vegetables need to be planted at the right times, and *because* the fertilizing must be done on schedule, . . .

"How?" Blueprint

A "How?" blueprint can usually begin with *by, with,* or *through*. Also, since "How?" blueprints are sometimes similar to "Why?" blueprints, they can both begin with *because*.

For example, how does Wanda distract you?

> *By* singing, eating, and talking as I try to study, . . .

or

> *With* her singing, her eating, and her talking, . . .

or

> *Through* her singing, her eating, and her talking, . . .

or

> *Because* of her singing, her eating, and her talking, . . .

"When?" Blueprint

Finally, you can usually begin a "When?" blueprint with, yes, the word *when*. When is your roommate constantly sleepy?

> *When* he gets up in the morning, sits in class, or studies in the evening, . . .

DIFFERENT FORMS OF THE THESIS WITH BLUEPRINT

So far we've showed you blueprints as part of the same sentence with the thesis and coming at the beginning of that thesis:

Because they can damage a child's view of himself, his peers, and adults, overly competitive sports can damage a child psychologically.

Actually, though, you can present the thesis with blueprint many different ways:

Overly competitive sports can damage a child psychologically because they can damage a child's view of himself, his peers, and adults.

or

Overly competitive sports can damage a child psychologically: they can damage a child's view of himself, his peers, and adults.

or

Overly competitive sports can damage a child psychologically. They can damage a child's view of himself. They can damage a child's view of his peers. They can even damage his view of adults.

Please notice, though, that for each example, each item in the blueprint has the same structure. In the last example, each was an entire sentence.

Here's a poor blueprint because the blueprint items do not have the same structure:

Overly competitive sports can damage a child psychologically. They can damage a child's view of himself and of his peers. They can even damage his view of adults.

A reader would probably be confused. Is the writer going to talk about two ideas or three? There seem to be three ideas, but, on the other hand, there are just two sentences.

You can avoid confusing your reader, then, by using the same structure—sentences, clauses, phrases—for each of your blueprint items. If you want more information, see Chapter 34, "Parallelism."

EXERCISES

A. Combine the thesis statement and ideas for topic sentences to produce a thesis with blueprint.

1. **Thesis** Amusement parks have a variety of attractions.
   Idea for Topic Sentence rides
   Idea for Topic Sentence shows
   Idea for Topic Sentence food

   Thesis with Blueprint _____

   _____

   _____

2. **Thesis** Magazine advertisers use several ways to get your attention.
   Idea for Topic Sentence large print
   Idea for Topic Sentence eye-catching color
   Idea for Topic Sentence beautiful people

   Thesis with Blueprint _____

   _____

   _____

3. **Thesis** Yard care is demanding.
   Idea for Topic Sentence mowing
   Idea for Topic Sentence trimming
   Idea for Topic Sentence watering

   Thesis with Blueprint _____

   _____

   _____

4. **Thesis** American "hard-boiled" mysteries have many things in common.
   Idea for Topic Sentence tough private eyes
   Idea for Topic Sentence uncooperative police
   Idea for Topic Sentence lying clients

   Thesis with Blueprint _____

   _____

   _____

   _____

5. **Thesis** Beach vacations are ideal for relaxing.
   Idea for Topic Sentence watching waves
   Idea for Topic Sentence lying in the sun
   Idea for Topic Sentence reading long books

Thesis with Blueprint _____

_____

_____

B. Choose any one of the items above and write a thesis statement with blueprint three different ways. See the last section of the chapter, "Different Forms of the Thesis with Blueprint," for some ideas.

C. Each item below gives you a thesis statement. Invent three ideas for topic sentences. Then combine those ideas with the thesis statement to produce a thesis statement with blueprint.

1. **Thesis** Hot-air balloons have practical uses.

    Topic Sentence _____

    Topic Sentence _____

    Topic Sentence _____

    Thesis with Blueprint _____

    _____

    _____

2. **Thesis** Finding a part-time job is frustrating.

    Topic Sentence _____

    Topic Sentence _____

    Topic Sentence _____

    Thesis with Blueprint _____

    _____

    _____

3. **Thesis** Winter is the best season here for having fun.

    Topic Sentence _____

    Topic Sentence _____

    Topic Sentence _____

    Thesis with Blueprint _____

    _____

    _____

    _____

    _____

10
Central Paragraphs

Because your purpose in a theme is always to persuade the reader to accept your thesis, you need space to argue your point. Generally, the more fully you develop the evidence that supports your thesis, the more persuasive you'll be. Central paragraphs, which form the body of your theme, provide the needed space.

Each central paragraph, which is like a Stage I or Stage II paragraph, develops an opinion that in turn helps develop the thesis statement. Specific evidence in a central paragraph supports the paragraph's topic sentence, and the topic sentences, taken together, support the thesis. Therefore, if each central paragraph supports its own topic sentence, and if the topic sentences are properly related to each other and to the thesis, then the central paragraphs should persuade the readers to accept that thesis statement.

Three of the paragraphs of a five-paragraph essay are central paragraphs. Similarly, all but two paragraphs of any multiparagraph essay are central, or body, paragraphs. The two exceptions, introduction and conclusion, are discussed in Chapters 11 and 12; until you study these chapters, the thesis statement with blueprint will suffice for both the introduction and conclusion. For the moment, then, consider the form of the five-paragraph essay to be the following:

Thesis Statement with Blueprint

> First Central Paragraph

> Second Central Paragraph

> Third Central Paragraph

Thesis Statement with Blueprint

A central, or body, paragraph is very similar to a one-paragraph essay; that is, each one presents a topic sentence followed by specific support. You already know, for the most part, how to write this type of paragraph. This chapter deals with two differences: *omission of the reworded topic sentence* and *additions to the topic sentence.*

OMISSION OF THE REWORDED TOPIC SENTENCE

Every Stage I and Stage II paragraph essay, a unit complete in itself, has three basic parts: topic sentence, specific support, and reworded topic sentence. The reworded topic sentence provides a mark of finality to the argument. Think how frustrated you would feel if someone told you most of a story but failed to complete it. In the same way, essays are more satisfying, and therefore more convincing, if the readers feel a sense of completion at the end.

A central paragraph, however, does not require this same mark of finality. Remember that a central paragraph does not present the entire argument of the theme. Instead, the development of the thesis is complete only after all central paragraphs are presented. Therefore, the mark of completion is one of the special functions of the concluding paragraph. Each central paragraph, then, ends *without* a reworded topic sentence; when the last item of specific support of a central paragraph is finished, so is that paragraph.

ADDITIONS TO THE TOPIC SENTENCE

Like a topic sentence for a one-paragraph essay, the topic sentence for a central paragraph presents the *main idea of the paragraph* in the basic form of *"limited subject* is *precise opinion."* However, the central-paragraph topic sentence has two additions—a *transition* from the preceding paragraph and a *reminder of the thesis.*

The first addition, the *transition*, provides theme coherence. Just as sentences within any paragraph must move smoothly from one to another, paragraphs within a theme must also flow together. The pieces of the total argument will not seem to combine unless the paragraphs that contain the pieces of argument also combine.

The second addition to the topic sentence, the *reminder of the thesis*, helps fit the central paragraph's main idea to the theme's main idea. The total argument will come together more easily if each central paragraph's idea (its topic sentence) connects to the theme's idea (the thesis statement). This addition, then, helps provide both coherence and unity.

Therefore, the topic sentence for a central paragraph should have these three parts:

- a transition
- a reminder of the thesis statement
- the main idea of the paragraph

EXAMPLES OF CENTRAL PARAGRAPHS

Let's look at some examples of central paragraphs. Here's the *first* central paragraph from the sample theme in Chapter 8. Can you find the three parts of the topic sentence?

> *Not surprisingly, one area in which children are often humorous is in learning to speak.* I remember one time I was talking to a friend on the phone while my little sister, Betsy, seemed to be playing inattentively on the floor nearby. After I hung up, Betsy asked me, "Why is the teacher going to give Janet an old tomato?" At first I couldn't figure out what Betsy was talking about. When I asked her what she meant, she said, "You said if Janet doesn't hand in her homework, the teacher is going to give her an old tomato." Finally I caught on. The word I had used was *ultimatum*!

Here are the three parts:

Transition "one area . . ."
Reminder "children are often humorous"
Main idea "learning to speak"

Notice also the specific support for the topic sentence: a narrative example telling the brief story of Betsy's funny question. A central paragraph should have the same detailed support as a one-paragraph essay.

Now let's look at the *second* central paragraph from the sample theme:

> *Children can also be funny in the way they "humanize" the objects around them.* According to my psychology book, "Up to four or five years old, the child believes anything may be endowed with purpose and conscious activity. A ball may refuse to be thrown straight, or a 'naughty' chair may be responsible for bumping him" (Pulaski, *Understanding Piaget*, p. 45). I, myself, can still remember one vivid and scary afternoon when I was sure the sun was following me around, just waiting for the right moment to get me. I can also remember a time, not scary, when Betsy stood at the top of the stairs and yelled to her shoes at the bottom, "Shoes! Get up here!"

Here are the three parts of the topic sentence:

Transition "also"
Reminder "children can . . . be funny"
Main idea "the way they 'humanize' objects"

This paragraph has a variety of support: a statement by an authority and two quick examples.

Finally, let's look at the *third* central paragraph:

> *Another way in which children are sometimes funny is in their attempts to imitate what they see around them.* All children look pretty silly when they dress

up like their mothers and fathers and play "house." My psychology book tells of a more interesting example, though. The famous psychologist Jean Piaget wrote of the time his sixteen-month-old daughter quietly watched a visiting little boy throw a tantrum in trying to get out of his playpen. Piaget's daughter thought it would be fun to try the same thing: "The next day, she herself screamed in her play-pen and tried to move it, stamping her foot lightly several times in succession. The imitation of the whole scene was most striking" (quoted in Pulaski, *Understanding Piaget*, p. 81).

Here are the three parts of the topic sentence:

Transition "Another way"
Reminder "children are sometimes funny"
Main idea "their attempts to imitate what they see around them"

This paragraph has an interesting form of support: a narrative example that's stated by an authority—Piaget.

Because you must have space to develop your argument, you break it into parts—the arguments of the central paragraphs. Yet, like a jigsaw puzzle, a theme will never seem complete unless you connect the pieces. The additions to the topic sentence of each central paragraph help you to fit the central-paragraph main ideas to each other and to the thesis statement, creating a whole, the body of your theme.

EXERCISES

A. Let's say you're writing a five-paragraph essay with this thesis statement:

Thesis Installing carpets requires expertise.

For each topic sentence below, identify the transition, the reminder of the thesis, and the main idea.

First Topic Sentence For one thing, measuring the rooms where the carpet will go requires expertise.

Transition _____

Reminder _____

Main Idea _____

_____

Second Topic Sentence Also, cutting the carpet into exact dimensions requires skill.

Transition _____

Reminder _____

Main Idea _____

_____

Third Topic Sentence Finally, laying the carpet in odd-sized spaces requires special techniques.

Transition _____

Reminder _____

Main Idea _____

_____

B. Do the same thing for this thesis statement:

Thesis The linebacker position on a football team requires a versatile athlete.

First Topic Sentence As a play begins, the linebacker must be intelligent enough to diagnose the offensive team's plan.

Transition _____

Reminder _____

Main Idea _____

_____

Second Topic Sentence As the play develops, the linebacker must be agile enough to move in any direction.

Transition _____

Reminder _____

Main Idea _____

_____

Third Topic Sentence And to end the play successfully for his team, he must be strong enough to stop the ball carrier.

Transition _____

Reminder _____

Main Idea _____

_____

C. Do the same thing for this thesis statement:

Thesis Meteorologists—more commonly known as weather forecasters—have important technical advantages today.

First Topic Sentence For one thing, historical records kept on computers tell seasonal patterns.

Transition _____

Reminder _____

Main Idea _____

_____

Second Topic Sentence Also, satellite photography tracks wind and cloud
movements.

Transition _____

Reminder _____

Main Idea _____

_____

Third Topic Sentence Furthermore, modern communications give immediate
access to weather data from all over the world.

Transition _____

Reminder _____

Main Idea _____

_____

D. Here's a thesis statement and three main ideas for central paragraphs. Use
these main ideas to write complete topic sentences—including transitions and
reminders of the thesis:

Thesis Restoring old houses is rewarding.
Main Idea Discovering the original interior is exciting.
Main Idea Working with one's hands is relaxing.
Main Idea Viewing the completed project is satisfying.

First Topic Sentence _____

_____

Transition _____

Reminder _____

Second Topic Sentence _____

_____

Transition _____

Reminder _____

Third Topic Sentence _____

_____

Transition _____

Reminder _____

E. Do the same with this thesis and three main ideas:

Thesis Numbers in advertisements can seduce the consumer.
Main Idea Digits in the product's name lure the consumer.
Main Idea Statistics from surveys tempt the buyer.
Main Idea Other numbers sprinkled throughout the advertisements awe the
consumer.

First Topic Sentence _____

_____

Transition _____

Reminder _____

Second Topic Sentence _____

_____

Transition _____

Reminder _____

Third Topic Sentence _____

_____

Transition _____

Reminder _____

F. For Exercises A–E, you've written topic sentences for a number of central paragraphs. Choose the one that interests you the most, and—inventing the support—write one central paragraph.

G. Recall for a minute the sample theme in Chapter 8 on the humorous things
children do. In a way, the writer of that theme was an "expert" on children's
funny behavior: she had been a child herself, and she had observed her sister
(and undoubtedly many other children) growing up. She did not depend in
that theme on any expertise in psychology, only on the behavior of children
she had observed. The expertise she did use—from the book on Piaget—was
highly interesting, of course, but it was not an essential part of the thesis
statement, nor was it the only support.

You, too, are probably an "expert" in something. Perhaps you play golf well
or understand how to tune an automobile engine or know every record the
Beatles (remember them?) recorded. Choose something you know well and
say something *significant* about it. Once you have something significant to say
about your topic, turn that statement into a thesis statement with blueprint.
Then, letting the thesis statement with blueprint serve as both the introduction and the conclusion, write the three central paragraphs of the five-para-

graph essay (you'll write the full-length introduction and conclusion later as exercises for Chapters 11 and 12).

Be sure to use the same kind of detailed support for each central paragraph that you would use for a one-paragraph essay, and be sure that each of your topic sentences contains a transition from the previous paragraph, a reminder of the thesis statement, and the main idea of the paragraph.

If you use outside sources, use them only to find support, not to find a thesis. Otherwise, you'll merely be paraphrasing someone else. Also, be sure to place quotation marks around all words you borrow directly. At the end of every sentence containing borrowed words or ideas, acknowledge your source in parentheses (look again at Chapter 8 if you've forgotten the rules for the makeshift documentation system).

11
Introduction

Your introduction serves two important purposes: it gets your readers' attention, and it tells them what your main idea is (and how you will develop it).

The part of your introduction that gets your readers' attention is called a *motivator*. The part that tells them what your main point is (and how you will develop it) is called the *thesis statement with blueprint*. Since we discussed thesis statements with blueprints in Chapter 9, we'll concentrate on motivators in this chapter.

Here's the introduction from our sample theme in Chapter 8. Can you find the motivator—the part that gets the readers' attention?

> Do you realize that newly born children are not even aware that parts of their bodies belong to them? I learned this fascinating fact in my psychology course from a book that says a baby "lies on his back, kicking his heels and watching the little fists flying past his face. But only very slowly does he come to know that they are attached to him and he can control them" (Mary Ann Spencer Pulaski, *Understanding Piaget,* p. 21). Children have a lot of learning to do before they can see the world—and themselves—through grown-up eyes. As children pass through this remarkable process of growing up, they often do some humorous things, especially in learning to speak, in discovering that all objects do not have human characteristics, and in trying to imitate others around them.

The motivator is all but the last sentence, isn't it? The writer hopes to interest you by telling you something intriguing—that infants don't know that parts of their bodies belong to them.

As you practice writing and look carefully at the writing of others, you'll find many good ways to motivate your readers. Here are three good ways— which we'll discuss in this chapter:

- the opposite opinion
- a brief story
- an interesting statement

THE OPPOSITE OPINION

A really easy way to begin your paper is to state the opinion your paper opposes and then make a transition to your thesis statement with blueprint. Basically, you state what the "poor, misguided people" believe; then you state your opinion:

- what the opposition says
- transition
- what you say

The transition is particularly important in this kind of introduction because you must move clearly from the position you oppose to the position you support.

Here is a sample introduction to an essay showing that smoking is not a good habit:

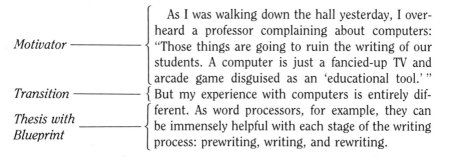

Motivator — Some people think that smoking makes them appear sophisticated and mysterious, perhaps even seductive. They become Humphrey Bogart in *Casablanca* or Lauren Bacall in *To Have and Have Not.*

Transition — Those people, however, are wrong. As far as I am concerned, smoking is really a disgusting habit—

Thesis with Blueprint — messy, irritating to others, and even harmful to nonsmokers.

See that the motivator states the opposite opinion? And notice that the thesis statement and blueprint are obvious. The readers know clearly they have read the main idea of the paper and how it will be developed.

Here is another introduction using the opposite opinion as the motivator:

Motivator — As I was walking down the hall yesterday, I overheard a professor complaining about computers: "Those things are going to ruin the writing of our students. A computer is just a fancied-up TV and arcade game disguised as an 'educational tool.'"

Transition — But my experience with computers is entirely different. As word processors, for example, they can be immensely helpful with each stage of the writing process: prewriting, writing, and rewriting.

Thesis with Blueprint

82 A BRIEF STORY

We all enjoy stories, so one of the most interesting ways to begin a paper is to tell your readers a brief story somehow related to your thesis statement. That way you've engaged their attention right from the start, and by the time they've finished the story, sheer momentum carries them into the rest of your paper.

Here's a sample introduction that begins with a brief story:

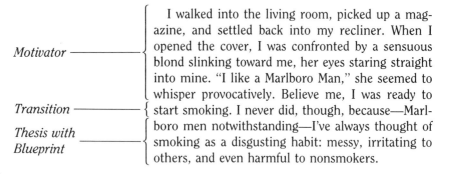

Motivator — I walked into the living room, picked up a magazine, and settled back into my recliner. When I opened the cover, I was confronted by a sensuous blond slinking toward me, her eyes staring straight into mine. "I like a Marlboro Man," she seemed to whisper provocatively. Believe me, I was ready to

Transition — start smoking. I never did, though, because—Marl-

Thesis with Blueprint — boro men notwithstanding—I've always thought of smoking as a disgusting habit: messy, irritating to others, and even harmful to nonsmokers.

Notice that the introduction has a transition ("I never did, though . . . .") between the motivator and thesis with blueprint. Some introductions need a transition—like the one above and all those that begin with opposite opinions—while others move smoothly from the motivator to the thesis with blueprint without any explicit transition words:

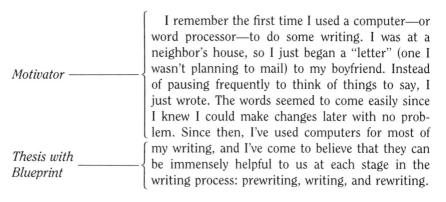

Motivator — I remember the first time I used a computer—or word processor—to do some writing. I was at a neighbor's house, so I just began a "letter" (one I wasn't planning to mail) to my boyfriend. Instead of pausing frequently to think of things to say, I just wrote. The words seemed to come easily since I knew I could make changes later with no problem. Since then, I've used computers for most of

Thesis with Blueprint — my writing, and I've come to believe that they can be immensely helpful to us at each stage in the writing process: prewriting, writing, and rewriting.

AN INTERESTING STATEMENT

Another easy way to get your readers' attention is to begin with a statement that's interesting, either because the idea is intriguing or because, perhaps, the tone is angry. The introduction to the five-paragraph essay in Chapter 8 begins with an interesting statement, one that's intriguing: "Do you realize that newly born children are not even aware that parts of their bodies belong to them?"

The next example is a motivator that's interesting because the tone is angry (after all, if we're walking along and hear somebody yelling, we would probably stop because we are curious):

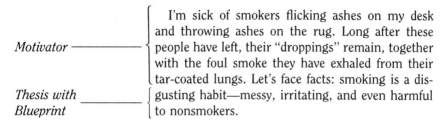

Motivator ⎯⎯⎯⎯⎯ ⎰ I'm sick of smokers flicking ashes on my desk and throwing ashes on the rug. Long after these people have left, their "droppings" remain, together with the foul smoke they have exhaled from their tar-coated lungs. Let's face facts: smoking is a dis-

Thesis with ⎯⎯⎯⎯ ⎰ gusting habit—messy, irritating, and even harmful
Blueprint ⎱ to nonsmokers.

The last example is only two sentences long, showing that an introduction can be effective even if it's fairly short:

Motivator ⎯⎯⎯⎯⎯ ⎰ Computers can *really* make a difference in how quickly and how easily you can get words on paper.

Thesis with ⎰ In fact, computers—used as word processors—can
Blueprint ⎯⎯⎯ ⎱ be immensely helpful with each stage of the process: prewriting, writing, and rewriting.

The motivator for this introduction is interesting because the writer seems enthusiastic. If you convey your enthusiasm for your topic, your beginning will often be interesting, too.

When you are writing an introduction—whether you choose the opposite opinion, a brief story, or an interesting statement—be sure you fulfill the two important purposes of all introductions: interest your readers, and tell them the main idea of your essay (and how you will develop it).

EXERCISES

A. For Exercise A in Chapter 9 ("Thesis Statement with Blueprint"), you wrote five thesis statements with blueprints. Choose one and write three introductions for it: one with the opposite opinion, one with a brief story, and one with an interesting statement.

B. For Exercise G in Chapter 10 ("Central Paragraphs"), you wrote a thesis statement with blueprint followed by three central paragraphs. Now, using any of the three types of motivators we just discussed, write a full-length introduction. You may need to change the wording of the original thesis statement with blueprint for it to fit smoothly with your motivator, but be sure not to change the essential meaning.

12
Conclusion

The conclusion, like the introduction, serves two purposes: it reminds the readers of the main point of your essay, and it gives them a sense of finality.

The part that reminds your readers of the main point is the *reworded thesis statement*. The part that gives finality is the *clincher*.

Let's look at the conclusion to the sample five-paragraph essay in Chapter 8. Can you find the reworded thesis and the clincher?

> Little children are funny creatures to watch, aren't they? But as we laugh, we have to admire, too, because the humorous mistakes are but temporary side trips that children take on the amazingly complicated journey to maturity—a long way from the beginning, where they lay in wonder, silently watching the strange, fingered spacecraft passing, back and forth, before their infant eyes.

The reworded thesis is the first sentence; the clincher is the last one.

You already know how to write a reworded thesis statement: it resembles the reworded topic sentence that you worked with on the one-paragraph essays. Therefore, this chapter concentrates on the clincher. We'll discuss two types:

- the reference to the motivator
- an interesting statement

THE REFERENCE TO THE MOTIVATOR

The simplest—and most common—clincher reminds the readers of the motivator you used in your introduction. This clincher has the advantage of bringing the paper full circle, an unmistakable signal that it is over.

The last chapter showed you three sample introductions with the thesis that smoking is disgusting. Here are those introductions again, each followed by a conclusion that refers to the motivator:

INTRODUCTION

Some people think that smoking makes them appear sophisticated and mysterious, perhaps even seductive. They become Humphrey Bogart in *Casablanca* or Lauren Bacall in *To Have and Have Not.* Those people, however, are wrong. As far as I am concerned, smoking is really a disgusting habit—messy, irritating to others, and even harmful to nonsmokers.

CONCLUSION

Reworded Thesis

Clincher

I am glad I never began such a disgusting habit, and I wish others had not started, either. I hope my sophisticated friends soon find out that Humphrey Bogart and Lauren Bacall were mysterious and appealing in spite of their habit, not because of it.

INTRODUCTION

I walked into the living room, picked up a magazine, and settled back into my recliner. When I opened the cover, I was confronted by a sensuous blond slinking toward me, her eyes staring straight into mine. "I like a Marlboro Man," she seemed to whisper provocatively. Believe me, I was ready to start smoking. I never did, though, because—Marlboro men notwithstanding—I've always thought of smoking as a disgusting habit: messy, irritating to others, and even harmful to nonsmokers.

CONCLUSION

Reworded Thesis

Clincher

I am glad I never began such a disgusting habit, and I wish others had not started, either. I no longer have the magazine with the sexy blond. Even though I miss her, I've never missed cigarettes.

INTRODUCTION

I'm sick of smokers flicking ashes on my desk and throwing ashes on the rug. Long after these people have left, their "droppings" remain, together with the foul smoke they have exhaled from their tar-coated lungs. Let's face facts: smoking is a disgusting habit—messy, irritating, and even harmful to nonsmokers.

CONCLUSION

Reworded _____ { I'm glad I never began such a disgusting habit. If
Thesis   other people had not started smoking, then neither
Clincher —————— their houses nor mine would be littered with smok-
                   ers' "droppings," and we would all be healthier.

AN INTERESTING STATEMENT

The last chapter showed you how to *begin* papers with interesting statements; an interesting statement is a good way to *end* a paper, too.

Your statement might be interesting because of the information or because of the tone. Here's a conclusion that has an interesting statement because of the information:

Reworded _____ { I am glad I never began such a disgusting habit,
Thesis   and I wish others had not started, either. I hope my
                sophisticated friends soon find out that Humphrey
Clincher —————— Bogart, mysterious and appealing though he might
                have been, unfortunately died of cancer of the
                throat—probably caused by smoking!

And here's a conclusion with an interesting—an angry—tone:

Reworded _____ { I am glad I never began such a disgusting habit,
Thesis   and I wish others had not started, either. Then the
                only smoking would take place at the fire-eater's
Clincher —————— show at the carnival—a spectacle that would give
                smoking the kind of dignity it deserves.

So to finish your five-paragraph essay, simply reword the thesis statement and end with unmistakable finality: the clincher.

EXERCISES

A. Chapter 11 presents three introductions to a paper about computers as word processors. Using the *reference to the motivator* as a clincher, write a conclusion to each one.

B. Again, for the sample introductions in Chapter 11 on computers, choose one introduction and write a conclusion that has an *interesting statement* as your clincher.

C. For Exercise B in Chapter 11 you wrote an introduction to the three paragraphs you had written for Exercise G in Chapter 10. Now finish your five-paragraph essay by writing the conclusion. Use either type of clincher.

CHECKLIST FOR THE FIVE-PARAGRAPH ESSAY

Introduction

_____ Does your introduction begin with a motivator?

_____ Does your introduction have a thesis statement with blueprint?

_____ Does your thesis statement have a limited subject?

_____ Does your thesis statement have a precise opinion?

_____ Are the items in your blueprint in the same order as your central paragraphs?

_____ Do the items in your blueprint all answer the same question "Why?" "How?" or "When?"

Central Paragraphs

_____ Does each central paragraph begin with a topic sentence?

_____ Does each topic sentence have a transition from the previous paragraph?

_____ Does each topic sentence have a reminder of the thesis?

_____ Does each topic sentence state the main idea of the paragraph?

_____ Is your support specific enough to be convincing?

_____ Do all your items of support clearly support the topic sentence (unity)?

_____ Do you explain your support fully so the relation to the topic sentence is clear (coherence)?

_____ Does each item of support include a reminder of the opinion in the topic sentence (coherence)?

_____ Do you have transitions at the critical locations (coherence)?

Conclusion

_____ Does your conclusion have a reworded thesis statement?

_____ Does your conclusion end with a clincher?

Other

_____ Is your essay convincing?

_____ Is your essay interesting?

_____ Have you checked the spelling of the words you're unsure of?

_____ Is your paper neatly done so it's easy to read?

BEYOND THE MODEL ESSAY

PART FOUR

More Patterns of Development

In Part Three you began your transition to the research paper by learning both how to write longer papers and how to use a simple method of documentation. You'll continue the transition here, again learning two important skills. First, you'll examine four different methods of developing a paper: *process, classification, comparison and contrast,* and *cause and effect.* You may discover that you have been using some of these methods already, but now you can study how they work and learn how to avoid possible pitfalls. The second skill you'll learn in this part is how to vary from the model five-paragraph essay that you've just learned. In each of the following four chapters, our sample theme differs slightly from our earlier model. At the end of each chapter, we point out and explain those differences.

13
Process

You are already familiar with process kinds of papers. This whole book so far has really been one kind of process writing. It has been telling (and showing) you how to do something. That is the first kind of process paper we'll talk about: how to tell some*one* how to do something (like how to serve a tennis ball). The other kind tells how some*thing* does something (like how a furnace works).

The first, how some*one* should do something, is commonly called a set of "instructions"; the second, how some*thing* does something, is commonly called—in technical writing—a "description of a mechanism in operation." But the usefulness of this last pattern is not limited to technical writing about man-made machinery. The "mechanism" that operates may be a natural one, such as a plant performing photosynthesis or a volcano erupting, or it may be an abstract one like the appeals court system handling cases sent from lower courts. The mechanism may also be a historical and social one, like Hitler's army invading Poland.

You will probably find the "how something does something" pattern more useful for your other classes, but at other times and other places, you may also need to write instructions. Fortunately, both kinds of process descriptions are relatively easy to write.

INSTRUCTIONS

Let's focus first on the kind of process paper that tells how someone does something: instructions.

Have you ever struggled through a badly written computer manual trying to figure out how to do something? Computer manuals today are notorious for being almost impossible to figure out. But a computer manual is, essentially, a set of *instructions*. It's unfortunate these manuals are so badly written, because writing them clearly would not be that difficult.

In fact, let's look at some "instructions" on how to give instructions—in the form of a sample paper:

How to Write Instructions

One of the most important things to keep in mind while writing instructions is simply this: "Don't waste your readers' time!" Everything in a set of instructions should follow this advice. So let's begin by looking at a brief paragraph of terrible instructions (from, of course, a computer manual) that wastes just about everybody's time. This excerpt is from a manual on a word-processing program:

> Attributes may be assigned to the elements of a document either directly or indirectly; these two ways of assigning attributes are referred to as "direct formatting" and "styles." Direct formatting has a direct effect on document layout. Assigning a style tells [the word processor] to look on a style sheet to acquire direct formatting.

"Unfair," you say? "That's taken out of context." Not really—the author of the software manual intends this to be readable as is.

So now let's look at a better way to write instructions. Here are the specifics:

1. <u>Organize the instructions into a step-by-step procedure</u>. If you truly understand the

instructions you are about to give, this should be easy for you to do. One of the main reasons instructions fail is that the writers don't fully understand the instructions themselves.

2. <u>Present the individual steps by starting with verbs, as this sentence does</u>. If you'll notice, these leading verbs are imperatives; that is, the word <u>you</u> is understood: "[You] organize . . ." and "[You] present. . . ." By using imperatives, you are talking <u>to the readers</u> rather than <u>about the subject</u> (as the mistaken excerpt above does). Good instructions, obviously, talk to the readers.

3. <u>Use an appealing layout on the page to make the instructions easier to read</u>. That is, number your steps; indent those numbered paragraphs to set them off even further; perhaps even underline or italicize the key sentence in each step. The underlining or italics take the eye to the most important sentence. And indenting and numbering paragraphs creates "white space" that makes writing much more inviting to the readers. What if, for example, we'd eliminated all of the white space in this paper and jammed all of the steps—the ones in 1 to 4—into one bulky paragraph? Even though the words would have been the same, the effect on readers (<u>you</u>, in this case) would have been much different.

4. <u>At the end of the instructions, just stop</u>. There's seldom any need for a conclusion in this

type of paper. The purpose of the paper, after
all, is simply to convey information as
efficiently as possible. This last step is all
the "finality" you need.

Here's a model of a typical process paper that gives instructions:

INTRODUCTION

BACKGROUND (if necessary)

FIRST STEP

SECOND STEP

LAST STEP

CONCLUSION (if necessary)

Now take a look at this sample paper, which gives instructions for preparing a room for painting:

Getting Ready to Paint

Nearly everyone has to paint a room at some
time or another. Whether it is your room at home,
your dorm room in college, or your first apartment,
preparing the room properly can make the actual
painting relatively simple and the cleanup
afterward easy.

Preliminaries

Clearly the easiest time to paint a room is
when the room is empty. If you're in that fortunate
position, skip directly to the next paragraph; if

your room has furnishings in it, your <u>preliminary</u> step to getting ready is to protect the furnishings. First, move all the furniture away from the walls and into the center of the room, stacking wherever possible to use as little floor space as you can. If the carpet is not fastened down, roll it up from each end toward the middle of the room. If it is fastened down or if you have a hardwood or tile floor, you will need to use a fabric drop cloth (more about that later). Once the furniture and carpet are moved away from the walls toward the room's center, you must cover them with drop cloths. The cheap, lightweight, disposable plastic sheets are best. Use as many of the 9' × 12' sheets as you need to protect the furniture and carpet. Use masking tape to fasten loose plastic so you don't trip over it and to keep out stray paint spatters.

<u>Remove Electrical Covers</u>

The next step is to remove the cover plates for electrical wall switches and outlets. The covers are usually held in place with one or two screws; unscrew them and remove the covers. Put all the covers and screws in a sealable plastic bag and store the bag safely out of the way. If the room has a ceiling light fixture, either loosen it so you can paint under it or mask it with tape so you can paint closely around it.

<u>Mask Where Needed</u>

The second major step is to mask with paper

masking tape anything you want to stay free of
paint. That means, mask around windows and
woodwork. If the room has a door, it will look
better if you don't paint the hinges and knob, so
mask them, too. You will need a sharp knife to make
precise cuts of the masking tape rather than just
tearing it. Though it takes time at this stage, a
carefully masked hinge or window will be much
quicker to clean after you paint, and the painting
itself will go faster because you won't have to be
quite so precise with your brush or roller.

Use Drop Cloths

The third step, after everything is masked, is
to get a drop cloth in place on the floor. Do <u>not</u>
use a cheap plastic drop cloth on the floor: if you
drip paint on plastic, the paint won't dry. You can
easily step on it and track paint spots in places
you don't want. Instead, use a fabric drop cloth,
one that absorbs dropped and splattered paint. The
best kinds are those with cloth on one side and
rubber or plastic backing on the other; that way
paint can't leak through to the floor. An old
sheet, doubled, can serve as a reasonable
substitute, but you will have to move it
frequently. Regardless of what you use, position it
in the area you'll paint first. Be sure all the
exposed floor is covered and be prepared to move
the drop cloth often. The little extra time it
takes will be far less than required for removing
dried paint splatters afterward.

Precautions

Have a damp cloth handy to wipe up latex paint
drops that manage to evade your precautions. (Use a
cloth and paint thinner if you're using oil-based
enamel.) Be careful to put the paint tray or can in
a place where you can't step on it, upset it, or
spill it. If you must use a ladder, be sure the
tray or can is firmly attached; no drop cloth can
protect a floor from a full tray of paint.

Rewards

With these simple preparations and
precautions, even a first-time painter can make an
old room look new--with very little cleanup
afterward.

DESCRIPTION OF A MECHANISM IN OPERATION

The second kind of process paper tells how something works. Technical
writers call this a "description of a mechanism in operation." And a mechanism can be almost anything that has parts to it and does something: from a
jet engine to a rubber-band motor, from a reflecting telescope to an overhead
projector.

To write a description of a mechanism in operation, you follow basically
the same guidelines as for writing instructions: organize the process into
steps, use an appealing layout on the page, and just stop when you're
through.

There are a couple of differences, however, between mechanism descriptions and instructions. First, you really cannot lead with verbs as you could
with instructions: you have to say "Step One: The jet engine . . ." rather
than "Step One: [You] *organize* the. . . ."

Also, the background section now becomes virtually mandatory. For the
sample paper on "How to Write Instructions," on page 94, we gave—as
background—an excerpt of some bad instructions from a word-processing
program. That kind of background is nice, even important, but not always
necessary. For a description of a mechanism in operation, though, you use
the background section to describe the parts of the mechanism. Then, the
way those parts function together—the way the mechanism operates—will
be the step-by-step part of your paper.

Let's consider a paper telling how a reflecting telescope operates. The introduction would, no doubt, describe the purpose of a reflecting telescope. The background section would then briefly describe the important parts of the telescope: the primary mirror, the secondary mirror, and the magnifying lens. The rest of the paper would describe how those parts operate. Here's a skeletal model of such a paper:

> ## INTRODUCTION
> The purpose of the reflecting telescope

> ## BACKGROUND
> The parts: primary mirror,
> secondary mirror, magnifying lens

> ## FIRST STEP
> The light hitting the primary mirror

> ## SECOND STEP
> The light hitting the secondary mirror

> ## THIRD STEP
> The light magnified by the lens

> ## CONCLUSION
> A summary of the telescope's operation

There's one more important difference between writing instructions and writing descriptions of mechanisms in operation: visual aids. You can see that a drawing of the telescope and how it operates—that is, the path the light takes—would be immensely helpful for the paper we just outlined. Although it's really beyond the intent of this book to go into detail on how to construct good visual aids, the main keys are these: *keep visual aids simple* and *label everything*. Here's a sample visual for the paper we just outlined:

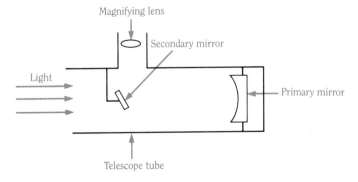

Here is a sample paper about ceiling fans. Note how the visuals fit into the text as an integral part of the paper. Putting them close to the writing that refers to them is a convenience for your readers.

How a Ceiling Fan Works

The ceiling fan--familiar from films like Casablanca and from increasing popularity in recent years--is not quite the simple device it appears. A well-designed ceiling fan does more than just add atmosphere and simply stir the air. Savings in utility costs and an increase in personal comfort result from use of a good fan.

In this description, the reader is assumed to need no explanation of ways to install the fan or to connect the fan to the electrical circuits. Furthermore, an explanation of the principles of electric motors is beyond the scope of this description.

1. The Parts. To understand how a ceiling fan works, we must first look at the parts that constitute it (see Figure 1).

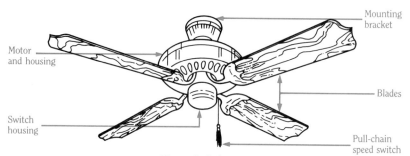

Figure 1: Ceiling Fan

a. Mounting bracket. Beginning at the top, nearest the ceiling, the first part is the mounting bracket and covering canopy. The mounting bracket

connects the fan to the ceiling electrical outlet;
the canopy covers the bracket and wires and makes
the fan look better.

b. <u>Motor, housing, and blades</u>. The second part—
and key to the fan's operation—is the motor, its
housing, and the fan blades.

(1) The electric motor normally weighs about
14 pounds and uses 75 watts of power at its highest
speed. Since the fan often is mounted in
inaccessible places, the motor will usually have
permanently lubricated bearings that require no
maintenance.

(2) Covering the motor assembly is the motor
housing. The design of the housing varies from
highly ornate embossed brass to painted sheet
metal. Since its function is largely decorative,
selection is a matter of taste for the purchaser.
Regardless of design, however, the fan housing also
serves to dampen noise and to keep dirt out of the
motor.

(3) Mounted on the lower, outer edge of the
rotating motor are the fan blades, made of wood or
plastic (see Figure 2). Usually four blades, with a
diameter of 30 to 52 inches, provide enough force
to move the air, although fans installed in small
areas sometimes have six blades. The crucial factor
in blade mounting is the pitch of the blade, the
angle it is turned from absolutely flat horizontal.
The most common pitch for a good fan is 12 degrees,
although some larger ones have a pitch of 14

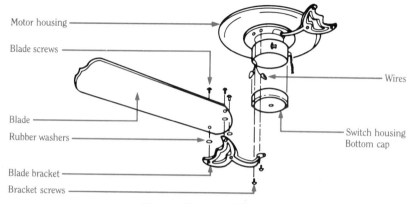

Motor housing

Blade screws

Wires

Blade

Rubber washers

Switch housing
Bottom cap

Blade bracket

Bracket screws

Figure 2: Blades and Mounting

degrees. Any pitch less than 8 degrees will not move enough air to make the fan worthwhile. Such a low pitch is the mark of a cheap fan that will merely look good and have little positive effect on cooling.

c. <u>Switches</u>. The third important part of the fan is made up of the directional and speed switches, and their housing (see Figure 3).

(1) Although it's merely a simple slide switch, the directional switch makes the fan an energy-saving device, for it changes the flow of air during warm or cold weather. More details appear below.

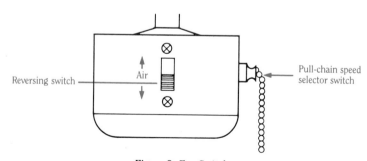

Reversing switch

Air

Pull-chain speed
selector switch

Figure 3: Fan Switches

(2) The pull-chain switch controls the speed of the fan's operation. Most fans have three speeds, from about 95 revolutions per minute to about 350 rpm. Simply pulling the chain moves the switch through the three speeds one after the other—low, medium, high.

2. <u>Operation of the Ceiling Fan</u>

a. <u>Summer operation</u>. During warm weather, the fan's switch should be set to direct air downward to create a cooling breeze. This cooling results from the phenomenon known as windchill; as air moves across the skin, we sense a chill factor of 6 degrees to 8 degrees.

For best cooling effect, the fan's speed should be set at medium or high. However, in a bedroom the speed is usually set at low because a gentle breeze is all that is needed to provide cooling all night long.

b. <u>Winter operation</u>. In cold weather, adjust the fan so the air moves upward. Because heat rises, the temperature in the area near the ceiling may be as much as 15 degrees higher than at floor level. By pulling the air upward, the ceiling fan gently pushes the warm air from the ceiling, down along the walls, and back to the floor where the people are. In circulating the heated air trapped at the ceiling, the fan reduces the temperature differential to about 2 degrees. Thus, the furnace or other heater will have to come on less frequently, thereby reducing heating costs. The fan should be run at medium or low speeds in cool weather to avoid creating a draft.

When the world watched <u>Casablanca</u> in the 1940s, the ceiling fans added to the exotic atmosphere. That the contemporary world uses fans to be energy efficient suggests that we are interested not only in their decorative suitability but also in their capability of providing lower utility bills and greater personal comfort.

VARYING FROM THE MODEL THEME

Both types of process papers are closely allied to the model theme we have been following all along. The introduction would necessarily tell that you're going to give certain instructions or that you're going to describe how a particular mechanism operates. Whether you have an explicit thesis statement is entirely up to you. If you'll look again at the sample paper we showed you at the beginning of this chapter, the thesis is *implied* throughout the introduction, but the only place it's stated *explicitly* is in the title: "How to Write Instructions." That's an approach you can take, too.

And what about topic sentences? Our sample paper on "How to Write Instructions" certainly had them: the first sentence of each step (*"Organize the instructions into a step-by-step procedure,"* etc.) was underscored for even more clarity. But there was no necessity for explicit transitions or references to the thesis statement. Numbering the steps was transition enough.

The paper describing a mechanism in operation added visuals—always useful when you're trying to describe something physical in words.

Finally, the process paper is dependent, perhaps more than any other type of paper, on a clear structure and on clear transitions. But because the structure is so obvious and so similar regardless of the subject, process papers are among the easiest to write.

If only we could convince the computer people. . . .

EXERCISES

A. Let's say you're going to give instructions on how to change a tire. Without writing the paper, simply list the various steps, in order, that you think someone should follow. If you don't know anything about changing tires, then list the steps for making a left turn in a car at a four-way stop (i.e., an intersection with stop signs at all four entrances to the intersection).

B. Now let's say you're going to describe how a simple mechanism—a mercury thermometer—operates. You'll probably have to look in an encyclopedia for this one, if you don't know offhand. Then list the parts (which would be the material for the background paragraph) and outline how it operates. Just list and outline—you don't actually have to write the paper.

C. Now write the paper for Exercise A.

D. And now write the paper for Exercise B.

E. We all know things other people don't know but might be interested in. Perhaps you're good at golf or computers or gardening. Choose something you know how to do and write a clear, concise set of instructions that tells your readers how to do it. You might try out these instructions on a friend before you hand in your paper. It's amazing how easily people (including all of us, of course) can go wrong unless the instructions are absolutely unambiguous.

F. Part of the special knowledge we all possess includes mechanisms others may know little about: the golf ball washer, the computer disk drive, the lawn sprinkler. Choose something you know about and write a clear description of how it operates. Again, you might read your description to a friend just to be sure you've been clear: often, we know exactly what we mean while others (our readers or our listeners) are just confused. By the way, you might include a simple visual aid or two, just to be even clearer.

14
Classification

Often we find ourselves with a long list of items we'd like to talk about but with no simple way to discuss them. We do know we could handle the items if we put them into three or four groups. This process of grouping a long list into categories is *classification*.

Consider this example. At the end of classes on Friday you look for a way to tackle all the studying you need to do over the weekend. Some of the work is so simple that you can do it right away before you go to a movie. You want to save some of the assignments for Sunday so the lessons will be fresh in your mind on Monday morning. And there are a couple of small research projects that would be good for a library session on Saturday. To cope with the amount of studying you have to do, you classify the assignments under these headings:

Things to Study Friday

Things to Study Saturday

Things to Study Sunday

Now you've reduced a long list to three groups. But the important idea is that the groups all answer the same question: When is a good time to do this work? In other words, you've classified according to *one* characteristic related to all the items in the list.

If you classify on the basis of a different characteristic related to the items, you'll get a different listing. For example, as usual you don't study as hard over the weekend as you planned to on Friday afternoon; late Sunday night you find yourself with most of the work to do. Perhaps you make a new list, like this:

Put Off Until Next Weekend

Put Off Until Final Exams

Put Off Forever

Now the groupings are based on how long you can avoid doing the work, so this listing will not be identical with the one you made on Friday afternoon.

Dozens of times each week we organize items by classification. We classify when we sort laundry into piles for machine wash, hand wash, or dry clean; or when we put the machine wash into piles for hot water, cold water, or medium temperature. We think of automobiles in groupings by size (subcompact, compact, intermediate, and so on), by cost (under $8,000, $8,000 to $10,000, and so on), or by expected use (individual, family, or commercial). Because classification is such a common way of thinking, it is also a popular type of theme development. The groupings automatically provide us with the theme's *organization* and help us see what we want to say about the groups, our *thesis*.

ORGANIZATION

Since it breaks a topic into packages, classification results in a simple pattern that matches the model for the multiparagraph essay. Each category forms a central paragraph:

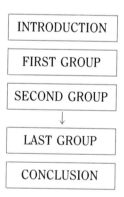

INTRODUCTION

FIRST GROUP

SECOND GROUP

LAST GROUP

CONCLUSION

You'll see a theme using a pattern similar to this one later in the chapter.

Yet, easy as the pattern of development is, you need to avoid its three potential pitfalls. You can tumble into any one of them if you're not careful when you classify.

The first problem is limiting the subject you intend to classify. A subject that is too broad could contain hundreds of items. You could put these hundreds into two or three groups, but the groups probably wouldn't be useful since each would still include a long list of items. On the other hand, you could classify hundreds of items into a large number of groups (say, fifteen), but then you'd have to write a theme with fifteen central paragraphs. In either case you might as well not classify. Instead, limit the subject until it includes a workable number of items. For example, you choose "Ethnic Groups" as your subject. The world has too many ethnic groups for you to work with. You limit to "Major Ethnic Groups in the United States," but the number of items still seems endless. Limiting the subject to "Major Ethnic Groups in San Francisco" should solve the problem.

The second and most common problem is related to unity. Remember that to classify is to group on the basis of *one* characteristic related to each item. If more than one kind of grouping shows up in your theme, you've failed to maintain unity; and readers who are troubled by the groupings themselves probably will not be convinced by your argument. Consider this list of categories for types of car:

American	Italian
Japanese	Luxury
German	

"Luxury" is not a country of origin. The grouping is unacceptable.

Finally, you need to realize that many classifications that work well for grouping items actually have minor flaws. For instance, we often put motorized passenger vehicles that run on land into three convenient groups: cars, trucks, and buses. Yet this classification does not cover the special vehicle that looks like a large station wagon (a car) but is built on a truck chassis (a truck) and can carry nine adults (a small bus). There's no simple rule for dealing with this problem; however, there is a reasonable procedure to follow when you find an exception to your classes. First, judge the importance of the exception. If the exception destroys the point you are trying to make (the thesis of your argument), then rethink your groupings. And if a single exception brings to mind dozens more, then again you must regroup. Finally, if the exception remains a minor flaw, you may want to acknowledge the complication somewhere in your paper. Or you may be able to exclude the exception by the way you word your subject. For example, if you write about "Religions on My Campus," you'll have to deal with all of them, including that of the single student who has made an idol of the oak tree on the campus mall; but if you write about "Major Religions on My Campus," you've eliminated the minor exceptions to your categories.

THESIS

Classification leads logically to one of two types of thesis. The classification may itself be the thesis. Or the classification may be only the means of organizing the argument that persuades the readers to accept a thesis. The first is easier to write, but the second generally makes a better theme.

If your classification reveals striking groupings, the classification itself may be the thesis. Such a thesis takes the general form of "There are *(number of groups)* for *(topic)*." For example, "There are three types of teacher," or "There are two types of politician." Not very interesting, really. Still, sometimes the groupings themselves reveal your stand on the topic. Then the "there are" thesis may work. Consider this example:

> Today there are two types of politician: the dishonest and the half-honest.

Implicit in these classes is the thesis that no politician today is completely honest.

Often, however, the "there are" thesis is not satisfying by itself. The readers yawn and mutter, "So what?" What they are really asking is why the writer bothered to classify items. Consider this thesis:

> There are four types of door lock available for home use.

If your readers happen to be interested in locks, the thesis may work. Probably more interesting would be a theme that uses the types of door lock to make a more important point, such as this:

> Although there are four types of door lock available for home use, an expert burglar can fool any of them.

Now the thesis is that the locks are not foolproof; the writer will develop his theme with a central paragraph for each type of lock, but he'll be showing in each case that the locks will not stop a determined burglar.

When you develop a subject by classification, you'll have to judge the value of your classification. Will the readers care that you've identified groups? Or do the groups merely help reveal something more important?

Here's a sample theme (a four-paragraph essay) in which classification serves as an organizational stepping-stone to get to the thesis idea.

The Waistland of TV Advertisements

Like thousands of Americans, my compulsive drive to eat keeps me continually on a diet. When I told a friend that I eat if I'm happy, sad, or just sort of blah, he said I need to occupy my mind. He suggested that when I'm hungry I should watch television. This solution seemed particularly appropriate, for I enjoy television when I'm happy, when I'm sad, and when my mind is too dull to feel much of anything. My friend was right about the

television shows; even the worst of them draws my
attention away from food. But my friend forgot
about the advertisements. Whether commercials for
food in restaurants or for food to take home, these
television advertisements represent cruel and all-
too-usual punishment for the dieter.

Numerous restaurant ads provide seemingly
continuous reminders of a world of eating
enjoyment, all of it forbidden on my 1,200-calorie
diet. There are so many restaurant ads that I can
turn from channel to channel during commercial time
and usually be assaulted with only one laundry
detergent ad, one pet food ad, but four ads for
restaurants. After a week on my diet, I'm jealous
of the kitten in the cat chow commercial; imagine
what the barrage of restaurant ads does to me.
There are commercials for steak (with salad,
potato, and toast), pizza (thick or thin crust,
with dozens of toppings to choose from), fish or
clams, chicken (with fixin's), hamburgers (with or
without cheese, decorated with catsup and mustard,
sprinkled with chopped onions and lettuce, topped
with a pickle, stuffed in a lightly toasted bun),
roast beef or ham sandwiches (for a change from the
hamburger habit), and tacos or burritos (as well as
related Mexican foods that I've never heard of but
begin to crave anyway when I see them on TV). Need
I go on? Probably by now even your stomach has
started to rumble, and you've had more for supper
than my spoonful of cottage cheese on half a small
peach (made more appetizing by a scrap of wilting
lettuce for decoration).

Less numerous than restaurant ads but more
enticing are the commercials for the foods I can
buy to take home. When I've been starved for
carbohydrates for a few days, the convenience of
the take-home foods appeals to the remnants of my
ability to reason. You see, if my willpower wavers
and I go to a restaurant--even a quick-order
place--someone who knows I'm dieting may catch me,
but it's easy to dart into a grocery store,

ice-cream parlor, or doughnut shop and dash home without being seen. Besides, the TV ads for foods to take home are so inviting. For example, you may remember seeing the advertisement for one of the doughnut shops in town. As the TV camera pans slowly across a counter laden with bakery goodies, I begin to drool. The commercial's sound track broadcasts a man calling to his wife to run to the TV to see the panorama of food laid out before his—and my—impressionable eyes. He says that the sight of the doughnuts will "drive him crazy," and his voice sounds as though he's already slightly deranged because of what he sees. He proclaims the scene "heavenly," but I know it's a dieter's hell. I've always assumed he demands that his wife give him her car keys so he can rush to the doughnut shop; I say "assumed" because I've never stayed at my TV set long enough to hear the end of the commercial. I'm on my way out the door to beat that crazy fool to the best of the doughnuts.

    You're reading the rantings of a dieter too often distracted by hunger and too long provoked by TV commercials for food. Yes, I confess—stop the torture—the ads are obviously effective. I salivate right on cue for all the food advertisers. But in my few remaining rational moments I can still judge those advertisements for restaurants and take-home foods. To the dieter they're cruel. They play on the dieter's weakness, his compulsion to eat. But I'll have my revenge, in my own limited way. My friend has invited me to his apartment tomorrow to watch TV, as he puts it, "to relieve the depression" of my latest diet. I'll sit calmly in his favorite chair; I'll stare innocently at his television. But when the first commercial for food comes on, I'm going to cut the plug off his set. While he's paralyzed by shock, I'll go into his kitchen to make myself a sandwich.

Don't be fooled by this writer's pretension of insanity; behind the writer's humorous mask is a pattern of development dependent upon classification.

Because he recognizes that there are too many different food ads to deal with individually, the writer has classified them into two groups—foods to eat in restaurants and foods to eat at home. Are you bothered by the fact that some of the foods he classifies as restaurant foods could be taken home? Probably not, because the inconsistency will not damage his thesis. And besides, for him the classification may well be valid; some types of foods he consistently eats at restaurants (though he could take them home) and some types he buys for his pantry. What we should recognize is this: Classifications are arbitrary, but they do allow us a reasonable means to organize material. All in all, the classification in this theme is reasonable. It allows the writer to package his support material so that he can get to his thesis.

VARYING FROM THE MODEL THEME

Did you notice the minor differences in the sample theme for this chapter? For one, the thesis is not a simple statement of "limited subject is precise opinion," but we could still tell that the writer would need to show that the food ads are numerous and that they are "cruel." You may have noticed that the first central paragraph is the Stage I type, whereas the second central paragraph, which uses subtopic sentences, is a Stage II type. Finally, in the conclusion no single sentence fully restates the thesis; nevertheless, the first five sentences of the conclusion as a whole do remind us of the thesis. As you can see, the general pattern of the multiparagraph essay remains, even though there are deviations from the model.

EXERCISES

A. Circle the class in each list below that breaks the unity of the classification.

1. **Topic**   Books

   Classes   fiction

   poetry

   paperbacks

   history

2. **Topic**   Students

   Classes   sophomores

   gymnasts

   juniors

   freshmen

3. **Topic**   Furniture

   Classes   rugs

   chairs

   tables

   desks

4. **Topic**   Buildings

   Classes   sheds

   barns

   garages

   apartments

B. Each subject below is too broad to classify easily. First limit the subject and then name at least three classes.

Example: Topic   Music

   Limited topic   classical music

   Classes   Early Renaissance

   Late Renaissance   Solo

   Eighteenth Century   OR   Small group

   Romantic   Symphonic

   Early Modern

1. **Topic**   Politics

   Limited topic _____

   Classes _____

   _____

   _____

   _____

   _____

   _____

   _____

2. **Topic**   Television

   Limited topic _____

Classes _____

_____

_____

_____

_____

3. **Topic**   Shoes

   Limited topic _____

   Classes _____

   _____

   _____

   _____

   _____

4. **Topic**   Doors

   Limited topic _____

   Classes _____

   _____

   _____

   _____

   _____

C. Choose one of the limited topics from Exercise B and write a multiparagraph essay that you organize by classification. Remember that you can make your writing more interesting if you use classification to develop a thesis other than the classification itself.

D. Use classification to develop a multiparagraph essay about one of the following topics. You'll need to limit the topic before you attempt to classify it, just as you did in Exercise B.

   Advertising

   Books

   Clothes

   Trees

   Stores

   Of course you may vary from the model theme, but list your variations on a separate page at the end of your paper. If you use outside sources for support, be sure to document them with the makeshift system you learned in Chapter 8.

15
Comparison and Contrast

Comparison and contrast aren't new to you; they are extremely common ways of thinking. Whenever you examine how things are similar, you compare them. And when you look at their differences, you contrast them.

Sometimes you use comparison and contrast to talk about something new: by telling your readers how a thing is similar to or different from something they know, you can help them understand the new thing. For instance, to explain a rotary automobile engine, you'd probably compare and contrast it to the conventional automobile engine.

However, besides explaining something new, comparison and contrast also appear frequently in decision making: because A and B share some characteristics but differ in others, one is better. You compare and contrast brands when you shop for groceries, stereos, automobiles, and so forth. When you chose the college you're attending, you probably compared and contrasted available schools, and you're likely to use comparison and contrast again when you choose your major. The list of examples could be endless. The comparison-and-contrast theme, then, is really quite practical.

THESIS

Comparison and contrast lead logically to a thesis because you usually won't bother to compare and contrast unless you have some purpose in mind. You could, of course, stop once you note that A is like B or C is different from D. But your readers will probably want to know what the similarity or difference amounts to. You could write this for a thesis:

The rotary automobile engine is different from the conventional automobile engine.

117

However, once you've noted the difference, the readers will see that you've merely stated the obvious. Much more useful would be one of the following:

> Although the mechanical structure of the rotary automobile engine is obviously different from that of the conventional automobile engine, the rotary engine offers little worthwhile improvement.

or

> Although they both depend on internal combustion, the rotary automobile engine is a significant improvement over the conventional automobile engine.

Thus, comparison or contrast for its own sake is generally pointless, but both are extremely useful to develop support for a thesis.

APPROACHES TO COMPARISON AND CONTRAST

As you may have noticed in the preceding sample thesis statements, there are two general approaches to the comparison-and-contrast paper. First, you can note the difference between items but *concentrate on their similarity* (comparison).

> Although the mechanical structure of the rotary automobile engine is obviously different from that of the conventional automobile engine, the rotary engine offers little worthwhile improvement.

Here the writer acknowledges that the engine types are different. Does the difference mean that the newer one—the rotary engine—is better? The writer says it isn't; the engines are really comparable. We can expect the theme to concentrate on the similarities of the engines.

For the second approach you can note the similarity between items but *concentrate on their difference* (contrast).

> Although they both depend on internal combustion, the rotary automobile engine is a significant improvement over the conventional automobile engine.

Now the writer acknowledges one similarity—that the two engines have the same type of combustion—but he is concerned with showing that the rotary engine is better than the conventional engine.

Notice that with either similarity or difference you acknowledge the opposite. Why? You need to establish a reason for bringing items together. Noting that items seem different gives you a reason for comparing them, and noting that items appear to be similar establishes a reason for contrasting them. In both cases the opposite can provide the motivator section of your theme's introduction.

At the same time, you must decide where in the theme you're going to discuss the similarities and differences. The thesis establishes your primary purpose, which you'll concentrate on; you'll obviously discuss that side in the central paragraphs. Yet how will you deal with the opposite? You have two choices. If the opposite is well known, let the introduction handle it. But if the opposite is not generally understood, you may need to develop it in the body of the theme. In that case cover it *first* in your central paragraphs. Doing it this way leaves the primary idea in the position of emphasis, the end of the theme.

CENTRAL PARAGRAPH ORGANIZATION

When you've decided whether to concentrate on comparison or contrast, you still must decide how to do it. Suppose you want to contrast two brands of automobile to decide which to buy; you'll consider such subtopics as price, miles per gallon, and maintenance record. You must decide whether to devote the central paragraphs to whole items (the cars) or to their various elements (price, miles per gallon, and maintenance record). The chart shows the two most likely organizational types (we've used two items with three elements per item, but other combinations are certainly possible):

TYPE I	TYPE II
Introduction	Introduction

Item A
  Element 1
  Element 2
  Element 3
	Element 1
	  Item A
	  Item B

Item B
  Element 1
  Element 2
  Element 3
	Element 2
	  Item A
	  Item B

	Element 3
	  Item A
	  Item B

Conclusion	Conclusion

Whether you choose the Type I or Type II organization for the central paragraphs of your theme, make sure that you always cover the same subtopics in the same order. As with parallelism within a sentence (see Chapter 34), this paragraphing symmetry will clearly show the relationships that are important for your ideas.

Which pattern is preferable? Well, notice that the Type I organization gives a sense of each item as a whole; however, the readers may have difficulty relating the elements. For example, suppose you compare a Nissan and a Toyota on the basis of seven elements. By the time the readers get to element five of the second car, the Toyota, they've forgotten what they read about element five of the Nissan. As a result, Type I organization is better for short papers dealing with only a few items and elements. On the other hand, Type II organization destroys the sense of the whole item as it builds the relationships of the elements. Still, Type II development can handle more items and more elements, so it's more useful than Type I for a longer comparison or contrast paper. So which type is better? There's no absolute answer, but you'll see more papers using Type II organization, probably because people are more concerned with element-by-element similarities and differences.

Type I

To demonstrate the difference, we've included a Type I essay comparing kinds of school classes. Note how the writer, one of our students, deals first with one kind of class and its elements (teacher, students, results), then another. The essay is short enough that we as readers don't get lost in all the differences.

Learning or Not: Active and Passive Classes

Everyone who has gone to school knows that some classes are better, more interesting, livelier than others. We have all sat through classes where we learned little, except the facts and to be quiet. We also have been part of classes where we actively learned by being challenged by teachers and the subject to learn for ourselves. Although classes often seem outwardly alike in having a teacher, in having some students, and in producing some results, the differences between passive and active classes are enormous.

The passive kind of class usually has a teacher who lectures, puts outlines and terms on the chalkboard, and dispenses information to the students. Like my sophomore biology teacher, Mrs. Noguida, who rarely looked up from the orange notebook in which she had carefully typed all her lectures, teachers in a passive classroom simply dictate information and answers. They tell the

students how to think and what to think. They pour
facts into the students like water into a sieve.
The students are forced, usually by the teacher's
authority, to sit, listen, take notes, and
regurgitate only what the teacher has said. The
only kinds of questions are about form: "What is
the work in subpoint 3,a,(1)?" or "How do you spell
photosynthesis?" The results in such a class are
measured by multiple-choice or true-false
questions, or questions that require memorized
answers: "What is Newton's First Law?" "What are
the three causes of the American Civil War?" The
results in such classes are also measured by the
quickness with which students forget the facts they
had poured into them.

The other kind of class, the active kind,
usually has a teacher who stimulates students to
learn for themselves by asking questions, by posing
problems, and most of all by being a student, too.
Such a teacher might plan the outline of a course,
but doesn't force the class in only one direction.
Instead, like Ms. Cerrillo, my junior history
teacher, a teacher in an active class uses the
discussion to lead to learning. Instead of
lecturing on the causes of the Civil War, Ms.
Cerrillo gave us a list of books and articles and
said, "Find out what caused the Civil War." We had
to search for ourselves, find some answers, then
discuss what we found in class. From the
discussions, we all learned more than just the
facts; we learned the facts but we also learned how
complex the causes were. Students in active classes
like that become more involved in their learning;
they ask questions about why and how. The results
in the active class are usually measured by essay
answers, individual projects, and a change in
attitude on the students' part. Learning becomes
fun; although students may forget the facts just as
quickly, their attitudes toward learning and their
excitement in developing answers for themselves
don't end with the last class.

We all remember having to learn that "4 × 9 = 36" and having to memorize dates like 1914–1918, 1776, and 1492. And those kinds of classes are important for laying some groundwork, but not much true learning takes place there. There is a difference between knowing a fact and understanding it. Despite their outward similarities, the passive kind of class is clearly inferior to the active one for helping students understand the world around them.

Type II

Here's a sample theme that compares two characters in literature. We've selected this theme because English instructors sometimes ask you to write about literature; as you'll see, a theme comparing two fictional characters is fairly easy to organize. You'll also see how well the Type II organization works for comparing a large number of subtopic elements, even though there are only two items.

Holmes and Dupin

Although Sir Arthur Conan Doyle created Sherlock Holmes in 1886, Holmes remains one of the most popular of detective characters. Moreover, Holmes' personality influenced the characterizations of other fictional detectives, both in Doyle's time and later. For example, Agatha Christie's Hercule Poirot is similar to Holmes. Yet many readers of the Holmes stories don't realize that Holmes isn't entirely original. Holmes is very much like Chevalier C. Auguste Dupin, a character Edgar Allan Poe introduced in 1841. Of course, Holmes and Dupin have their differences; Holmes himself calls Dupin "a very inferior fellow" (Doyle, A Study in Scarlet and The Sign of Four, p. 25). Nevertheless, pushing aside Holmes' criticism of Dupin, we can find numerous similarities between the two characters. Both in professional situation and in personality, Holmes is a copy of Dupin.

The conditions under which Dupin and Holmes

work are alike. Both Dupin and Holmes are "consulting detectives," to use Holmes' name for the
profession (Doyle, p. 23). This may not seem
important, but we should notice that most other
detective characters take cases on their own. On
the other hand, Dupin works on cases for Monsieur
G——, Prefect of the Parisian police, and Holmes (at
least when he first appears) works on cases that
have stumped Scotland Yard detectives. In addition,
both characters dislike the policemen they work
for, and for the same reason. In "The Purloined
Letter" Dupin says that the police are "persever-
ing, ingenious, cunning, and thoroughly versed in
the knowledge which their duties seem chiefly to
demand" but that they fail because they cannot
adapt their methods "to the case and to the man"
(Poe, Great Tales and Poems of Edgar Allan Poe, pp.
208—09). Similarly, Holmes says the Scotland Yard
detectives are "both quick and energetic, but
conventional—shockingly so" (Doyle, p. 28). Still,
Dupin and Holmes somehow control their scorn while
they solve cases for the police. The "consulting
detectives" have the satisfaction of solving
puzzles, but let the police steal the glory.

Holmes' personality also matches Dupin's. Both
characters are loners; they accept the company of
the narrators of their stories, but of no one else.
Poe writes in "The Murders in the Rue Morgue" that
Dupin is "enamored of the night for her own sake";
in fact, Dupin and the narrator close the shutters
of their house during the day and usually go out
only at night (Poe, pp. 106—07). This love of
darkness emphasizes Dupin's physical withdrawal
from society. In Holmes' case, the withdrawal and
gloominess lead to cocaine addiction; when Holmes
isn't on a case, he withdraws from ordinary life as
well as from society. Of course, the detectives
become active in society to solve cases, but each
withdraws again when his case is over. At the
opening of the second Dupin story, the narrator

says that after his first case Dupin "relapsed into his old habits of moody revery" (Poe, p. 144). And Holmes at the end of The Sign of Four calls for his cocaine so he, too, can withdraw.

Even when Dupin and Holmes actually enter society to solve puzzles, they remain mentally separate from other men. On a case, both Dupin and Holmes show energy unknown to most people. This energy involves them in society, but it doesn't mean that they actually join society. Instead, each stays separate by remaining unemotional; unlike ordinary men, they appear to be minds without feelings. In "The Murders in the Rue Morgue" the narrator describes the working Dupin as "frigid and abstract," with eyes "vacant in expression" (Poe, p. 107). Doyle is more obvious about Holmes. In The Sign of Four Holmes says that "detection is, or ought to be, an exact science and should be treated in the same cold and unemotional manner" (Doyle, p. 137). Like Dupin, then, Holmes prefers to have a mind free of emotions.

Thus, the number of similarities between the two characters shows that the 1886 Holmes is a copy of the 1841 Dupin. They take their cases for the same reason and handle them with the same dislike for their police associates. Neither character can stand the world of normal men, choosing instead to withdraw into a secret shell. And even when they work with ordinary men, they remain aloof, emotionless. These similarities are too numerous to be accidental. Clearly Doyle owes a large debt to Poe.

VARYING FROM THE MODEL THEME

As you read in the introduction to Part Four, the sample themes in this set of chapters will sometimes vary from the model five-paragraph essay. Did you see the differences in the Holmes and Dupin essay?

First, the paragraph divisions are different from what you may have expected after you read the essay's introduction. The blueprint shows only two topic divisions, but the essay uses three central paragraphs. You might have expected this organization:

Introduction

Similarities in Professional Situation

Similarities in Personality

Conclusion

You saw this instead:

Introduction

Similarities in Professional Situation

Similarities in Personality

Similarities in Personality (continued)

Conclusion

Because he had too much to discuss in one paragraph per major topic, the writer broke up the second topic into two logical groups. Thus, what began in his mind as a four-paragraph essay became (out of necessity) a five-paragraph essay.

Second, the topic sentences do not always fit exactly the model you studied earlier. The topic sentences of paragraphs two and three connect directly to the thesis. These two topic sentences begin major divisions of the support, so their topic ideas are vital for the thesis. However, paragraph four merely continues the idea of the previous paragraph. Therefore, the topic sentence contains a transition and the main idea of the paragraph, but not a reminder of the thesis.

Still, it is worth noting that the writer *could* have strictly followed the model for the multiparagraph essay. Why didn't he? He didn't need to. You, too, have developed in your writing skills; your judgment about writing has also developed. You are moving beyond simple topics dealing with only your experiences and imagination; you can also move beyond the model essay. But as the sample themes for this chapter show, the general idea of the model can help you handle a sophisticated topic. Therefore, let the needs of your topic determine the final pattern of your essay, but keep the model in your mind as a ready—and effective—guide.

EXERCISES

A. For each of the two topics below, first limit the topic and then write *two* thesis statements, one for each approach to a comparison-and-contrast paper.

Example: **Topic** Emotions

Limited topic Emotional responses _____

Acknowledge the difference and concentrate on the similarity

Although the intensity of emotional response to pleasure and to pain are obviously different, the chemical and physical effects are very much alike.

Acknowledge the similarity and concentrate on the difference

Although all emotions are very much alike in their physical and chemical effects, the responses to pain and pleasure differ in intensity.

1. **Topic** Movie theaters

Limited topic _____

Acknowledge the difference and concentrate on the similarity _____

_____

_____

_____

_____

_____

Acknowledge the similarity and concentrate on the difference _____

_____

_____

_____

_____

_____

2. **Topic** Students

Limited topic _____

Acknowledge the difference and concentrate on the similarity _____

_____

_____

_____

_____

_____

Acknowledge the similarity and concentrate on the difference _____

_____

_____

_____

_____

B. Choose one of the thesis statements you developed for Exercise A and outline the central paragraphs for a theme to support the thesis. Make your outline conform to either the Type I or the Type II central-paragraph organization: for each central paragraph you will need to show a topic item with subtopic elements (Type I) or a topic element with subtopic items (Type II).

C. Here are some possible topics for comparison-and-contrast papers:

Commercial products	Music
Computers	Radio
Emotions	Relatives or friends
Literature	Schools

First limit the topic; then write a thesis that concentrates on comparison or contrast. Organize your support with the Type I or Type II pattern, and then write the theme. If you wish to vary from the model theme, do so, but list your variations on a separate page at the end of your paper. And if you use outside sources for support, be sure to document them (you can use the makeshift system, as the second sample theme in the chapter does).

16
Cause and Effect

Remember the "Why?" subtopic sentences you studied in Chapter 7? Maybe you didn't realize it at the time, but you were studying one kind of cause-and-effect paper. We'll examine cause-effect papers more closely in this chapter.

A *cause* is a reason something happens; an *effect*, then, is whatever happens. As a simple example, we might say, "Because the television set is unplugged, it doesn't work." The *cause* is that the set is unplugged; the *effect* is that the set doesn't work.

You can write three kinds of cause-effect papers: you can state that the effect is true and examine the *cause* in detail; you can state that the cause is true and examine the *effect* in detail; or you can attempt to show that the *entire cause-effect statement* is true.

EXAMINING THE CAUSES

Sometimes the controversial part of a cause-effect statement is the cause, so your paper will naturally examine that part in detail. Let's say you've decided to write about this thesis: "The aggravated assault rate here at Gila Monster Maximum Security Prison has decreased dramatically because of the warden's innovations." The effect—that the aggravated assault rate has dropped—shouldn't be controversial, so take care of that part quickly with a statistic or two in your introduction: "In the last year, the aggravated assault rate at Gila Monster Maximum Security Prison has plummeted from nineteen per month to only four per month." After dispensing with the effect, spend the rest of your paper telling us about the warden's policies and why they work.

How? Write a paragraph about each of the warden's important policies. Your outline might look something like this:

Thesis Because of the warden's innovations, the aggravated assault rate at Gila Monster Maximum Security Prison has decreased dramatically.

> *Topic Sentence* The warden's new leathercraft shop allows inmates a constructive way to spend their time.
>
> *Topic Sentence* The warden has started an intramural sports program that permits the prisoners a physical outlet for their pent-up emotions.
>
> *Topic Sentence* The new coed jail cells allow the inmates the chance to discuss relevant social issues with members of the opposite sex.

Did you notice that the thesis begins with *Because*? That word clearly established that the essay will examine cause and effect. Another way of saying it is this: if you want to write a cause-and-effect paper, you must have the word *because* somewhere in the thesis statement.

Of course, you don't need to have exactly three central paragraphs. Two especially well-developed paragraphs or four or five shorter ones could work also.

EXAMINING THE EFFECTS

Sometimes the cause is fairly straightforward, but the effect needs elaboration. What if your thesis is that "Because Napoleon's wars killed many young men who otherwise could have worked a lifetime, Europe's standard of living dropped markedly"? Not many people would doubt that the wars killed many young men who could have done a lot of work, but people still might doubt that the standard of living actually did drop. You need to state the cause as a fact and then elaborate upon the effect.

You could then begin the theme by mentioning in the introduction (perhaps using the "striking statement" motivator) how many young men were slaughtered. Then you could develop the theme by discussing the effect ("Europe's standard of living dropped markedly") in three or four European countries. Here's a possible outline:

Thesis Because Napoleon's wars killed many young men who otherwise could have worked a lifetime, Europe's standard of living dropped markedly.

> *Topic Sentence* After Napoleon's wars, Russia had a lower standard of living.
>
> *Topic Sentence* Austria also had a lower standard of living.
>
> *Topic Sentence* Even Napoleon's home, France, had a lower standard of living.

Sometimes you have to deal with ideas that require a little more complexity. The cause may be a general assertion, but the effects are real and often complicated. In this sample paper by one of our students, though it deals

with technical matters and borrowed ideas, you will find a thesis and three
topic sentences.

The Search for Extraterrestrial Life

When the first hominid stood upright, we
speculate that it must have looked up to the
heavens in wonder, for we find ourselves doing so
today. As we look at the nighttime sky with all its
stars and spaces, we can't help wondering about
life out there. Perhaps the curiosity, the need to
know, which motivated our ancestors to explore this
planet, to go into the most forbidding jungles, or
to sail the most hazardous seas, also motivates us.
We think that what happened here on Earth might
have happened elsewhere in the cosmos, and we
follow our interest to press farther into the
universe searching for life. Because of our endur-
ing quest to know the unknown, our search for
extraterrestrial life, a search that has already
taken people to the moon, will grow in the years
ahead. Whether in the form of interstellar probes,
radio and radar signals in outer space, or
interstellar travel, the human race will continue
to look up to the heavens looking for life beyond
this Earth.
　"The search for extraterrestrial life,"
according to Isaac Asimov, "took its first flying
leap in 1969 when man walked on the moon" (Extraterrestrial Civilization, p. 183). This great step
proved that we were not destined to spend the rest
of our existence earthbound. Subsequent successful
moon landings demonstrated our race's ability to
traverse space to the moon and return safely. More
distant planets were also out there to be explored.
Viking I and II, for example, were sent to Mars in
1975 to test the planet for the possibility for
life. Landing in 1976, they found Martian soil not
unlike Earth's "but richer in iron and less rich in
aluminum" (Asimov, p. 59). The bad news was the
absence of carbon, which is essential for life as
we know it. Consequently, the search for life

beyond Earth turned to other planets and other means—long-distance radio and interstellar travel.

Attempts at interstellar communication have been going on for many years, but they take a long time. Because radio waves travel at the speed of light, it would take over a hundred years for a question to be asked and answered from a near star only fifty light-years away. And when we send out radio signals we have no way of knowing if anyone is even listening. But despite the long delays, astronomers have been sending radio signals for almost twenty years using "single or arrayed radio techniques, sensitive radio detectors, advanced computers for processing received information, and the imagination and skill of dedicated scientists" (Carl Sagan, "The Quest for Extraterrestrial Life," Smithsonian, May 1978, p. 39). They listen for meaningful sounds from outer space because scientists theorize that any civilization akin to ours would learn to use radio signals most readily. The largest listening dish in the world—in the Russian Caucasus—is devoted to this search for intelligent life beyond our planet (Sagan, p. 43).

An even more dramatic attempt to find life in space will come with interstellar travel. Both the United States and the USSR have put crews in space for months at a time. However, the barriers to interstellar exploration are enormous, both technically and humanly. For example, according to NASA, an interstellar spacecraft would need a totally efficient fuel, one that hasn't been developed yet. It may even have to wait for the discovery of antimatter. Almost certainly such a fuel would require metal alloys to withstand heat beyond anything we now know (NASA, Interstellar Communications, 1963, pp. 144-50).

Both these problems likely will be overcome; human intelligence and the quest for knowing probably will meet those challenges as we have in the past. The real barrier to interstellar travel, however, is that same human being. We do not know if humans can endure the extreme durations of space travel. Not only would travelers be confined to cramped quarters with limited exercise and have little variety to see, but also the crew might well suffer mentally from the confinement. Furthermore, if Einstein's theory of relativity is correct, the phenomenon of "time delation" will mean that the Earth from which travelers leave will be far different from the one to which they return. "Time delation" means that the rate at which time seems to progress slows with increased speed; this phenomenon would mean that a traveler hurtling through space would live what seemed to him or her a normal lifetime, while 5,000 years elapsed on Earth (Asimov, pp. 231–32). Thus, a traveler searching for life on other stars would return to an Earth that had no family, or friends, perhaps not even the nation that sent out the explorer.

Despite the barriers (and the limited success), the search for extraterrestrial life will continue. The chances seem too great that somewhere in the estimated 280 billion planetary systems in our galaxy (Asimov, p. 109) intelligent creatures also have developed. With the technological advances we already have made united with the never-ending quest to explore the unknown, our search for extraterrestrial life in the great expanse of space will go on. It must, just as much as it was inevitable that the first hominid looked up to the heavens so long ago.

EXAMINING THE ENTIRE CAUSE-EFFECT STATEMENT

Sometimes cause-effect papers examine the entire statement instead of only half of it. Perhaps both cause and effect are controversial, or perhaps neither is controversial but the fact that they have a cause-effect relationship is.

Let's look first at a cause-effect statement in which both parts are controversial and need elaboration. What if we say that "Because Colorado land developers have no long-term stake in the development they sell, customers often end up with property they cannot inhabit"? We'll have to persuade the readers of two ideas: that the developers do not have any long-term interests in development and that the new landowners can't live on their property. Both parts need support.

One simple way to organize the support is to write a paragraph on the cause and a paragraph on the effect. We could show in the first central paragraph that Colorado developers do not have any long-term interests in the land; in the next paragraph, then, we could show that the new owners often cannot use their property.

However, we could probably write a better paper by examining both parts of the cause-effect statement in the same paragraph. How? We could use examples. We'll make each central paragraph a narrative example of the entire cause-effect statement. One paragraph might be about Pyrite Acres, a development bulldozed out of the desert at the base of the Sangre de Cristo mountains. The developer, after selling the last site, disappeared into Arizona with all the money. He had not found time to tell the new owners that the underground water supply was so low it could last for only another year or two. Then—if our thesis is really valid—we should be able to present a paragraph on each of two or three similar situations with other developers. Extended examples can be effective any time both the cause and effect need support.

Extended examples can help in another case—one in which both the cause and the effect are fairly straightforward, but their relationship is not. Consider this statement: "Because many mountain climbers are elated after a difficult climb, they are in danger from carelessness after the difficulty is past." We can accept easily that climbers are elated after a difficult ascent; we can accept also that climbers who are careless afterward are in danger. We would probably like to see support for the idea that the elation from a difficult climb produces that carelessness. The following sample theme uses extended examples to provide such support. As you read this theme, you might also try to discover how it differs from the model for a five-paragraph essay we presented in Part Three. We'll come back to this point at the end of the chapter.

The Matterhorn Effect

Only a little over a century ago, some people in Europe thought that the Matterhorn—that awesome, beautiful pinnacle—was the highest mountain in the world. Many climbers from many nations had raced to climb it, but none had succeeded. Then in 1865, an Englishman, Edward Whymper, and six others reached the summit, but only Whymper and two others lived to tell about it. The rest, careless from elation and fatigue, died when one climber slipped on a relatively easy part of the descent and carried three others over a 4,000-foot cliff. That carelessness, a mental letdown that climbers tend to experience after succeeding at something hard, is called the "Matterhorn effect." I've seen it myself.

I remember how pleased I was when I first climbed Borderline, a hard route up a 150-foot spire in the Garden of the Gods, Colorado. Only six others had ever climbed it. My forearms were so cramped from exertion that I could barely pull the rope up as my climbing partner, Leonard Coyne, seconded the route. After reaching the top, Leonard mentioned that he knew the descent route was fairly hard, though the previous climbers had disdained using a rope for it. Filled with overconfidence, I simply tossed the rope to the ground below. We had just done the tough ascent, so surely we did not need a rope either. Then I started down the nearly vertical face. Suddenly Leonard yelled, "Your handhold is loose! Grab my leg!" There I was—unroped, 150 feet above the ground, and apprehensively holding a couple of loose flakes of rock—when my foothold broke. I still don't know what kept me on the rock, but apparently as my foothold gave way, my foot slipped onto a barely visible toehold. I didn't fall, but if I hadn't been overconfident from the hard ascent, I would never have ventured into that dangerous position without a rope.

I've seen the Matterhorn effect almost claim Leonard, too. Last summer, he, Gary Campbell, and I had just finished climbing the northwest face of Half Dome, a magnificent 2,000-foot vertical cliff in Yosemite, California. We'd been climbing, eating, and sleeping on the face for three days, and finally we were on top—well, almost. Actually, we were about 30 feet from the top, but that part was really easy. We untied, coiled the ropes, and stowed our climbing hardware. Leonard slung on one of the packs—a rather unwieldy thing with a sleeping bag tied precariously to the outside—and started up the last 30 feet. As he began to haul himself onto a five-foot shelf, the pack shifted on his back, almost jerking him off the rock. Two

thousand feet above the ground, he balanced—like a
turtle about to flip on its back—for what seemed
like a minute before he rolled slowly forward onto
the shelf. Three days of numbing fatigue and the
elation of doing such a hard climb had caused us
all to have a mental letdown; we had put away the
ropes too soon. That letdown almost cost Leonard
his life.

The point is clear to me: the Matterhorn
effect is real for anybody who has just done
something hard, but especially for climbers. I've
seen it in myself too many times and too many times
in others. But—so far, at least—I've been
fortunate not to learn about it in the way Edward
Whymper and his companions did.

Each extended example in this sample theme presents the entire cause-
effect relationship. The cause (the author's elation and fatigue on Borderline
and Leonard's on Half Dome) seems to lead quite naturally to the effect (the
near-accidents).

PITFALLS OF THE CAUSE-EFFECT THEME

In Chapter 14 you learned not to choose a subject that is too general for
your classification paper. That advice is also true for cause-effect papers. In a
theme, you could never hope to convince disbelievers of this thesis: "Because
the United States wanted to ensure the freedom of South Vietnam, it went to
war against North Vietnam." You'd need a book, or a substantial chapter in
one, to support that statement.

You must also be careful that your cause-effect statement presents the important cause and not just a secondary one. We'd be foolish to blame a field-
goal kicker for losing an important game just because he missed a thirty-two-
yard attempt during the last five seconds. The team may have lost in part
because of that missed attempt, but what about the quarterback who threw
an interception during the first quarter, the defensive lineman who missed a
key tackle, or the coach who canceled practice last Wednesday? Be sure, in
other words, that your cause is really the main cause.

VARYING FROM THE MODEL THEME

As you saw in the preceding chapters, one of our purposes in Part Four is
to help you learn how to vary from the model theme. How does our sample
about the Matterhorn effect differ from the model five-paragraph essay you

learned in Part Three? Before we discuss the differences, look back at that sample and underline the thesis, blueprint, and topic sentences. Then read on.

You probably noticed immediately that the sample has only four paragraphs. An extra central paragraph would have been too much, tacked on just to fill out the model. This theme didn't need another central paragraph for two reasons: both central paragraphs are very fully developed and—more important—the introduction contains another example already.

You probably underlined this sentence as the thesis: "That carelessness, a mental letdown that climbers tend to experience after succeeding at something hard, is called the 'Matterhorn effect.' " It doesn't exactly state the main idea of the paper (that the Matterhorn effect is real), but certainly it implies it. Readers expect the rest of the paper to convince them that the Matterhorn effect exists.

Did you find a blueprint? The last sentence of the first paragraph—"I've seen it myself"—is not really a blueprint of the topic ideas for each paragraph, but it certainly *implies* the development. We know we are about to read some examples.

The topic sentence for the first central paragraph is also implied, not by any one sentence but by the entire paragraph. A stated topic sentence isn't nearly as important as unified support and coherence. As long as you could write a topic sentence for a paragraph—the paragraph, in other words, is unified—and as long as the readers have no doubt what they are reading and why, a topic sentence is not necessary.

EXERCISES

A. Use these topics to answer the items below:

> Airline safety
> Drug education in elementary grades
> Educating children at home
> Farm subsidies
> Public school system
> Seat belts
> Sex education

1. Write a cause-effect thesis with a cause that is controversial but an effect that isn't. Then write three proposed topic sentences to show how you could develop your thesis.

   Thesis _____

   _____

Topic Sentence _____

_____

Topic Sentence _____

_____

Topic Sentence _____

_____

2. Write a cause-effect thesis with an effect that is controversial but a cause that isn't. Again write the topic sentences you would use.

Thesis _____

_____

    Topic Sentence _____

_____

    Topic Sentence _____

_____

    Topic Sentence _____

_____

3. Write a cause-effect thesis that has both a controversial cause and a controversial effect. Write the proposed topic sentences.

Thesis _____

_____

    Topic Sentence _____

_____

    Topic Sentence _____

_____

    Topic Sentence _____

_____

B. Find your own support and write a cause-effect theme using this thesis: "Because they try to dupe me, I object to car advertisements in magazines." Choose some other kind of advertisement if you like, but attach the advertisements to your paper when you hand it in. If you wish to vary from the model theme, do so, but list your variations on a separate page at the end of your paper.

C. Choose something that had a significant effect on you and write a cause-effect paper. Again, if you wish to vary from the model theme, list your variations on a separate page. If you use outside sources for support, be sure to document them. You can use the makeshift system you learned in Chapter 8.

D. Choose one of the topics in Exercise A (not necessarily one you outlined) and write the theme. If you wish to vary from the model theme, list your variations on a separate page. If you use outside sources for support, be sure to document them. You can use the makeshift system you learned in Chapter 8.

PART FIVE

The Research Paper

You've probably been having nightmares about the research paper ever since we first mentioned it. Actually, you already know most of the skills involved. You know the fundamentals of organization and support, and you may have looked at the punctuation and expression chapters. You've even used some outside sources and a simple method of documentation. The only new skills you need to learn are efficient ways to find your support in the library, organize it, use it in the paper, and document it. You'll find these new skills demand more time and patience than you needed for your earlier papers, but they are not difficult to learn.

17

Overview of the Research Paper

Sooner or later the longer paper comes to us all, usually because it's assigned or perhaps because we find ourselves interested in a subject. But regardless of the reason, we're all faced with the same problem. How do we say anything intelligent for five or ten pages or more?

Either we write about a subject we know intimately, or we go to some other source—an interview with an eyewitness, perhaps, or a book in the library. When we must use sources outside our own minds or experience, we rely on research.

Unlike some of the earlier exercises and paragraphs in this book, the research paper has *no invented evidence*. You must find the specific support for your research paper by consulting real sources, not imaginary ones.

By now you may be worried because of stories you've heard about research papers. A research paper can be long, and it can be a lot of work, especially if you put it off until the day before it's due. But you may also have heard some wrong statements about the long paper; let's get rid of those ideas now.

WHAT IT'S NOT

The research paper is not

- a rehash of encyclopedia articles
- a string of quotations one after the other like sausages
- a mass of invented support
- a mystical kind of writing that is more difficult than the kind you have been doing

WHAT IT IS

The research paper is

- an organized statement about a subject, using support from sources out-side your experience
- one that credits sources with thorough documentation
- a normal requirement in many college courses and professional jobs
- the next step in your development as a writer

This chapter and the ones to follow will help you take that step. They will show you what a research paper looks like, how to organize it, how to present your research in a paper, and how to give credit for ideas and words you borrow. In addition, the Appendix at the back of the book provides tips on such format conventions as types of paper, margins, spacing, and pagination.

THE SHAPE OF THE RESEARCH PAPER

Like the writing you did for Part Four, the research paper is an expanded form of the five-paragraph essay. Of course it's longer, but the basic structure is still the same. Let's look at the relationship between a five-paragraph essay and a longer research paper. Study the chart on the next page.

Not every paragraph must have exactly three items of specific support, nor must every main idea have exactly three paragraphs of support. Some may have more and some less. Whatever the number, the support paragraphs help persuade your readers to accept one of the major topic sentences in the same way specific support helps persuade them to accept the topic sentences in a five-paragraph essay. And the major topic sentences in the research paper help convince your readers of the thesis. By now you've learned that a model is simply a guide, a handy way to begin thinking about your paper. Treat this model the same way.

RESEARCH PAPER: PURPOSE AND PROCESS

But, you may ask, now that we know the basic shape of a research paper, what is a research paper anyway? The basic purpose of a longer paper could be to explore a particular problem (the major cause of the British defeat at Singapore in World War II, for example), or to inform your readers of a development (the effects of an increase in the minimum wage), or to trace the history of a particular situation (how America became involved in the Panama Canal). Keep in mind that the research paper is not just a classroom exercise; it has many practical uses, too. Businesses use research papers as marketing studies or as reports to stockholders; the military services call them staff studies; doctors call them case studies; professors sometimes call them monographs.

Regardless of the term we use, the important thing to note is that the *process* is the same: study the problem, gather the facts, assemble the facts, write a draft, revise it, and prepare the final version.

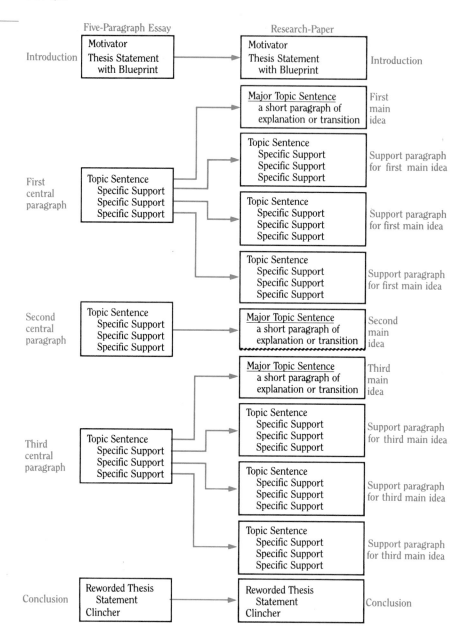

Five-Paragraph Essay   Research-Paper

Introduction
| Motivator
| Thesis Statement
| with Blueprint
→
| Motivator
| Thesis Statement
| with Blueprint
Introduction

| Major Topic Sentence
| a short paragraph of
| explanation or transition
First
main
idea

First
central
paragraph
| Topic Sentence
| Specific Support
| Specific Support
| Specific Support
| Topic Sentence
| Specific Support
| Specific Support
| Specific Support
Support paragraph
for first main idea

| Topic Sentence
| Specific Support
| Specific Support
| Specific Support
Support paragraph
for first main idea

| Topic Sentence
| Specific Support
| Specific Support
| Specific Support
Support paragraph
for first main idea

Second
central
paragraph
| Topic Sentence
| Specific Support
| Specific Support
| Specific Support
| Major Topic Sentence
| a short paragraph of
| explanation or transition
Second
main
idea

| Major Topic Sentence
| a short paragraph of
| explanation or transition
Third
main
idea

Third
central
paragraph
| Topic Sentence
| Specific Support
| Specific Support
| Specific Support
| Topic Sentence
| Specific Support
| Specific Support
| Specific Support
Support paragraph
for third main idea

| Topic Sentence
| Specific Support
| Specific Support
| Specific Support
Support paragraph
for third main idea

| Topic Sentence
| Specific Support
| Specific Support
| Specific Support
Support paragraph
for third main idea

Conclusion
| Reworded Thesis
| Statement
| Clincher
→
| Reworded Thesis
| Statement
| Clincher
Conclusion

A SAMPLE RESEARCH PAPER AND ITS OUTLINE

To see what can be done in about 1,500 words, look at the sample research paper one of our students wrote. To help you see the skeleton of organization, we've also included a formal sentence outline for the paper.

James i

Hostages of Testing

Minimum competency tests are of questionable value for students; they hold at risk the quality of education of all students--not just those who fail one or more times--making them hostages to the testing system.

I. Minimum competency tests should be viewed against the background that led to their creation: the need for simple measures of quality that would restore public confidence in American education and the standardized tests of minimum skills that resulted.

   A. Public distrust in American education led to demands for simple measures of quality.

   1. In the 1960s and early 1970s, the American public felt that the quality of education was inadequate.

   a. Employers claimed high school diplomas were meaningless.

   b. The public interpreted the decline of Scholastic Aptitude Test scores as proof that secondary schools were failing.

   c. Meanwhile education costs rose, prompting calls for proof that tax dollars were buying quality in education.

   2. The public desire for simple, easy-to-understand proof of quality led to standardized tests of minimum skills.

    a.   After complex reporting to parents failed to restore public confidence in education, testing appealed for its simplicity.

    b.   Standardized tests offered apparently scientific, unbiased measures of quality.

    c.   Standardized tests offered decision makers a convenient, cost-effective way both to improve education and satisfy public demands.

B.   The tests that resulted measure development of minimal skills, or minimum competency.

    1.   Minimum competency tests are standardized examinations of development of minimal skills, primarily in reading, writing, and math.

    2.   Usually the tests are connected to serious consequences, such as promotion to a higher grade or graduation from high school.

    3.   By 1984, 40 states had adopted some type of minimum competency testing, about half connected to high school graduation.

II. Standardized testing of minimum competencies leads to three major drawbacks of mass testing: class time lost to coaching, narrowing of the curriculum, and deflection in the overall curriculum.

A.   Minimum competency tests result in significant amounts of time being devoted to coaching students for the test, time taken from other classroom activites.

James iii

    1. The New Jersey department of education admitted
providing local districts with testing material used
for extensive coaching.

    2. Maryland's citizenship competency test can lead to a
student's being taken out of regular social science
classes for up to 15 weeks for remedial coaching.

B. Minimum competency tests lead to narrowing, or
trivialization, of the curriculum.

    1. Maryland's citizenship competency test reduces
citizenship to a trivia test.

    2. Multiple-choice questions reduce writing to rules of
grammar and punctuation.

    3. Testing science competency reduces science from a
process of investigation to identification of basic
facts.

C. Minimum competency tests lead to deflection in the
overall curriculum.

    1. Deflection results from emphasis on tested material
rather than on other curriculum areas not tested.

    2. A survey of testing in Florida in 1977 showed that
emphasis on basic skills deflected from literature,
language, and composition.

    3. Virginia's math competency testing of recognition of
parallel lines resulted in reduced student ability
to recognize perpendicular lines.

III. The effects of minimum competency testing that are used as
justification by advocates suffer under scrutiny.

James iv

A. Improvements in test scores are an overly simplistic measure of success.

   1. Minimum competency test scores for a number of states show improvements.

   2. Improvements in scores can be interpreted as a natural reaction to the high stakes connected to the tests.

B. Use of minimum competency tests both to determine curriculum and judge whether teachers comply holds students hostage.

   1. Minimum competency testing can determine what and how teachers teach.

   2. High-stakes testing to judge whether teachers are teaching as they are directed places students at risk.

C. Minimum competency tests have no demonstrated connection to success in life.

   1. For students not attending college, two studies comparing test scores and earnings show no connection.

   2. Research shows a significant connection between unemployment and lack of a high school diploma.

   3. For most students attending college, tests of minimum competency are meaningless.

Although minimum competency testing appears to offer simple, satisfying statistical evidence of the usefulness of the tests,

James v

behind this evidence are serious impacts that hold hostage the
quality of education of American students.

Jennifer James

Professor Wilson

English 111

April 15, 1988

Hostages of Testing

The school system my sisters attend uses standardized tests
for final examinations. Last year, two weeks before my younger
sister took her seventh-grade history final, her teacher drilled
the students on lists of names, dates, and places that would be
on the test. The teacher even told them that if they saw
certain questions, to provide certain answers. I've learned
since that this is called "teaching to the test," although
"cramming to the test" would seem more appropriate. The problem
is a typical result when schools use standardized tests for
large numbers of students and the stakes are high for students
and teachers. But when my tenth-grade sister took her minimum
competency test to qualify for eventual high school graduation,
I realized how serious testing could be. Across the United
States, thousands of students are subject to minimum competency
tests, yet those tests lead to a number of problems, among them
"teaching to the test." Despite their appeal to the public,
minimum competency tests are of questionable value for the
students. They hold at risk the quality of education of all
students--not just those who fail one or more times--making them
hostages to the testing system. A look at what minimum

James 2

competency tests are and why they have been adopted, at problems
generated by the tests, and at the effects of minimum competency
tests will show why this is true.

Minimum competency tests make the most sense if we
understand the setting in which they were created. In the 1960s
and early 1970s, the public became convinced that the quality of
education in the United States was inadequate. Employers
claimed high school diplomas were meaningless. News of declines
in Scholastic Aptitude Test scores convinced many that schools
weren't doing their jobs. And, of course, education costs
continued to rise (Madaus 614). The public wanted proof that
youth were being prepared for life and that tax dollars weren't
being wasted.

Attempts in the 1960s to develop detailed activity plans
and report progress to parents proved too complex for most
parents (Salganik 608). What the public wanted was simplicity:
scores they could understand and proof that money spent on
education brought improvement. As Laura Salganik notes:

> In the new climate of uncertainty about the adequacy
> of the schools (and thus about the competence of
> educators), testing introduced a welcome simplicity
> to the task of restoring both educational quality and
> public confidence in the schools. Few people were
> willing to argue with the use of tests as a means of
> insuring quality control (608).

To policy makers, standardized testing appeared to offer
accurate, unbiased assessment tools. The tests were

"objective," because they were scored by machine rather than by a person, and to many that equated to "scientific" (Strenio 63-65, 192-94). To policy makers and school administrators, the standardized tests appeared to offer a convenient, cost-effective way of improving education and especially of pleasing the public. And if you're trying to demonstrate that students graduate from high school with at least minimal skills, what better way to show it than to administer a minimum competency test?

Minimum competency tests are standardized examinations, almost always multiple-choice, developed to ensure that students have developed minimal proficiencies. In most states the tests are on reading, writing, and math, with a few adding other skills. Usually the tests are connected to some serious consequence, such as promotion to a higher grade; the most common connection is to high school graduation. Karen Klein reports that by 1984, 40 states had some type of minimum competency testing program, about half of them a requirement for graduation (565).

The American Association of School Administrators noted the most serious drawback of the minimum competency movement: "its almost total reliance on testing. Testing alone cannot guarantee that students will become more competent" (8). What the testing does, however, is create serious problems for the educational process in the classroom. Critics of minimum competency testing point out these problems: time lost in coaching students, narrowing of the material taught, and

James 4

deflection in the curriculum overall.

When a test has serious consequences for either students or teachers, significant classroom time goes into preparing the students, time taken away from other studies. This is "teaching to the test." For example, the department of education in New Jersey admitted providing local districts with the previous year's test and that some teachers coached students for weeks or even months (Madaus 616). For students who fail a minimum competency test, the loss of normal class time can be greater. Michael Henry reports that 33 to 50 percent of the Maryland students fail the citizenship competency test at least once, and that a student who hasn't passed by the end of the junior year can have been taken out of 15 weeks of normal classroom work in world geography, world history, and U.S. history (11).

Teachers also report that the tests lead to narrowing, or trivialization, of the curriculum. Michael Henry charges that the Maryland competency test has reduced the concept of citizenship to "an exercise in trivia": "The test requires a commitment to memory of hundreds of details--information probably forgotten before the last test booklet has been packed and shipped back to the state board of education" (11). The problem results because test makers have difficulty designing multiple-choice questions that go beyond identification of correct rules or facts or of simple computations. Thus, composition becomes rules of grammar and punctuation, not actual writing. As Gerald Bracey notes, "It is difficult to present science as an ongoing process of discovery, as a detective story, when test items converge on the recall of a single right answer" (686).

The third major effect of minimum competency testing is deflection in the curriculum. Deflection results when emphasis is placed on preparing students for the test material rather than on other curriculum areas of equal or greater merit. Most competency tests focus on reading, writing, and math; that leaves the arts and social sciences, for instance, without emphasis. It even ignores courses such as shop and home economics that are designed to prepare students for later life. Charles Suhor cites a survey of the effects of testing in Florida in 1977; results showed that because of the focus on basic skills, there had been reduced emphasis on literature, language, and composition (639). Gerald Bracey provides a particularly apt example: the Virginia math competency test assessed recognition of parallel lines, but not of perpendicular lines. One version of the test, however, included a question on perpendicular lines, and student performance on that question dropped significantly (685). The conclusion is simple: if the test covers an item, it receives classroom attention, yet other, even closely related areas may be ignored.

The problems we have just covered are likely to result to some degree from any standardized testing. Without doubt, however, they become more acute when the stakes are high, as they are with minimum competency testing. How, then, can these tests be defended? Advocates and the public seem to be convinced by increases in scores. James Popham provides these

James 6

figures of improvement associated with competency testing:

Locale	Subjects	Grade	Period	Percent Improvement
Alabama	Reading, Writing, Math	11	1983-85	4-8
Connecticut	Reading, Writing, Math	9	1980-84	6-16
Detroit	Reading, Writing, Math	12	1981-86	19
Maryland	Reading, Writing, Math	9	1980-86	13-25
	Citizenship	9	1983-86	23
New Jersey	Reading, Math	9	1977-85	16-19
	Reading, Math	10	1982-85	8-11

Source: Phi Delta Kappan 68 (1987): 682.

Gerald Bracey argues against a simple interpretation of such data. He points out that when students are threatened with failure and teachers with loss of jobs, "it is something less than miraculous to find that test scores rise" (686).

James Popham, a vocal advocate of minimum competency testing, accepts that the tests affect teaching and wants to push things further. He advocates using tests with serious consequences to drive curriculum, to determine what teachers will teach. This, he feels, will overcome mediocre teaching in the classroom (680-81). But let's consider what he's asking for. So that teachers will teach certain things in certain ways, their students should be held at risk; then outsiders can

be assured the teachers are doing what is required of them.
This is a hostage situation.

Finally, we should consider research about the effect of
minimum competency testing on earnings after high school
graduation, especially since the tests were adopted partially
because of employer complaints about student quality. Karen
Klein cites two studies of the relationship between math and
reading scores of students not attending college to their
earnings after leaving high school. Those studies showed that
scores and earnings were totally unrelated. However, other
research shows that people between 16 and 21 are twice as likely
to be unemployed if they have no diploma. And as Klein notes,
for most students who are going to college, the minimum
competency tests are just a "formality" (566). So whom do the
tests really help?

The minimum competency tests, it seems, provide simple
statistics that appear to "prove" the usefulness of the tests.
Yet, when we go behind those statistics to see what the impact
is on the classroom and on the preparation of students for life,
the results are very different. The tests indeed appear to
force students to learn bits of information, and, not
surprisingly, overall improvement on retaining bits of
information has improved as a result. But do those bits equate
to learning? Many educators say no. At the same time, the cost
to all students is severe. Time that could be spent on
developing thinking and reasoning is spent on memorization.
Vital subjects are reduced to bare minimums that can be tested

easily, so that the minimum level for competency becomes the maximum level for teaching. Courses and activities that do not lead to test preparation begin to be ignored. In this way, the quality of education of American students is held hostage by the minimum competency testing process.

James 9

Works Cited

American Association of School Administrators. <u>The Competency</u>
    <u>Movement: Problems and Solutions</u>. By Shirley Boes Neill.
    AASA Critical Issues Report. Sacramento: Education News
    Service, 1978.

Bracey, Gerald W. "Measurement-Driven Instruction: Catchy
    Phrase, Dangerous Practice." <u>Phi Delta Kappan</u> 68 (1987):
    683-86.

Henry, Michael. "A True Test or a Trivia Game?" <u>Newsweek</u> 22
    Jun. 1987: 10-11.

Klein, Karen. "Minimum Competency Testing: Shaping and
    Reflecting Curricula." <u>Phi Delta Kappan</u> 65 (1984): 565-67.

Madaus, George F. "Test Scores as Administrative Mechanisms in
    Educational Policy." <u>Phi Delta Kappan</u> 66 (1985): 611-17.

Popham, James W. "The Merits of Measurement-Driven
    Instruction." <u>Phi Delta Kappan</u> 68 (1987): 679-82.

Salganik, Laura Hersh. "Why Testing Reforms Are So Popular and
    How They Are Changing Education." <u>Phi Delta Kappan</u> 66
    (1985): 607-10.

Strenio, Andrew J., Jr. <u>The Testing Trap</u>. New York: Ransom,
    1981.

Suhor, Charles. "Objective Tests and Writing Samples: How Do
    They Affect Instruction in Composition?" <u>Phi Delta Kappan</u>
    66 (1985): 635-39.

ABOUT THE SAMPLE PAPER

You can learn several things from the sample paper to help you write a good research paper. First, the writer narrowed the topic from the broad subject of *testing* to *minimum competency testing* to *the negative impact of minimum competency testing on the quality of education.* By developing an effective thesis, the writer helped you understand something you probably didn't know before, although you may have taken a minimum competency test before graduating from high school.

Another positive point about this paper is that the writer used transitions skillfully to help readers follow the discussion. Note how each paragraph seems to lead logically into the next. In this manner, the transitions provide effective signposts to guide our reading.

Finally, the writer was careful to introduce quotations and borrowed ideas so that readers can know where the borrowed material began and ended. That's important for two reasons: it gives authority to what the author says, and it provides credit to the original sources. We'll talk more about ways to introduce material in Chapter 20, and in Chapters 21 and 22 we'll show you how to prepare the in-text documentation references and the Works Cited listing the sample research paper illustrates.

PREVIEWING THE PROCESS

You already know what a good thesis looks like—a precise opinion about a limited topic. Research papers, too, require a good thesis, but because the research paper is longer and uses other people's ideas, we might call the thesis a thoughtful assertion about the limited topic. That means the research thesis is more than just an opinion; it is opinion supported by facts, ideas, and words of other authorities. To help you devise a good thesis, we'll preview the research process here.

Although you might be an intuitive writer and settle immediately on the exact thesis statement you'll use in writing your paper, that would be very unusual. If you're an ordinary mortal like most of us, this will be more common: You pick a topic, narrow it enough to make the scale of research reasonable, and only slowly move toward the final thesis statement as your research goes along. In the next chapters we'll go into more details, but here's the procedure we recommend to start you on your way:

- Select a general topic that interests you.
- Do some preliminary reading in handy and reliable sources to find out whether your topic and your ideas about it seem to be based on accurate assumptions and whether enough sources appear to be available. If you are unhappy about your topic at this point, choose something else.
- Develop a working thesis statement to set a reasonable scope for re-

search. As you find sources and think about what you've learned, constantly refine your thesis by checking to see whether the subject is sufficiently narrow and your opinion or assertion is precise. Keep your mind open so that you can refine the working thesis when necessary.

POSSIBLE TOPICS

Now we'll take a look at some topics that may stir your imagination. Any of these broad topics could lead to a good narrow topic and thesis, or they may suggest similar topics that interest you. All, however, need to be narrowed carefully. Moreover, you'll do yourself and your readers a real favor if you stay away from some kinds of topics. Avoid writing about politics or about religion. Such topics are both too broad and often too personal to write a research paper about. Thus, they are frequently ineffective from the beginning.

Remember, the topics that follow all need deliberate limiting, and, of course, before you can develop a thesis, each needs a thoughtful assertion—a precise opinion—made about it.

Acid Rain	Endangered Animals	Poisons
Adoption	Environmental Legislation	Pollution
AIDS Research	Espionage	Prison Overcrowding
Airline Deregulation	Flemish Painting	Rain Forests
Auto Safety	Gambling	Sharks
Ballet	Hazardous Wastes	Social Customs
Bicycling	Hospices	Speech Disorders
Cable Television	Insulation	Strip-mining
Censorship	International Terrorism	Tax Reform
Chemical Fertilizers	Iran-Iraq War	Teen Alcoholism
Child Abuse	Islamic Movement	Trojan War
Child Custody	Marathons	Urban Transportation
Commercial Satellites	Midwives	Vegetarianism
Digital Technology	Minoans	Volcanoes
Drugs in Sports	Missing Children	Worker Productivity
Drug Testing	Organ Donation	Yoga

18
Finding Support

Many times when you have to write a research paper, you won't know much about the subject, so you won't know what you want to say until you've studied the subject enough to narrow it to something manageable, to a thesis. For example, from the broad subject of *driving* you might narrow to *drunk drivers* and even further to the narrower thesis that *drivers who drink are a hazard to themselves and others.*

WHERE TO BEGIN

One way both to narrow your topic and to get a lead on the information is to do some preliminary research in general reference tools such as encyclopedias. At this point, begin to keep an informal record of your research by listing briefly the title and the headings or subjects you looked under. This step is especially important if you later want to return to pick up that bit of information you remember reading but didn't write down.

As you continue in your research, you may well be in for some surprises, for what you find may take you in new directions. Despite your earlier belief, for example, you might find that drunk drivers are really careless people who have little respect for themselves and little understanding of the serious physiological effect of one drink too many. When such a change happens, you must revise your thesis; in this case, you might say something like "Despite contrary opinion, people who drive after drinking alcohol are ignorant and inhumane."

Once you have a thesis, you are ready to begin the more formal research process. The problem is to know where to begin to find the best written support for your subject. You may begin with either books or periodicals. Let's say you decide to start with books.

The primary guide to a library's book collection traditionally has been called the "card catalog." This made sense because all the library's books were listed on index cards filed in long, narrow drawers. Today the library you use may not have such cards, but it will have a catalog of some sort—in microform or in a computer file, and perhaps called "catalog of books," "catalog of documents," or simply "catalog." Whatever the form and name, however, it will provide basically the same information as does the traditional card catalog, so let's deal with that first.

Cards come in three kinds: author, title, and subject. If you know a book's author or title, look for one of those. But sometimes—especially as you look for support for your research paper—you know only a general subject, say, architecture. Then you can look at cards under that heading.

The information on the card catalog cards will save you time. All three kinds of cards start as author cards. A title card has the title typed across the top so it can be alphabetized by title easily, and a subject card has the subject typed on top so it can be alphabetized by subject. Beyond that top line, however, the contents of the cards are the same. If you were trying to find out something about building styles of ancient civilizations, you could look for books on architecture, specifically on the history of architecture. In the card catalog under the subject heading "Architecture—History" you might find this card:

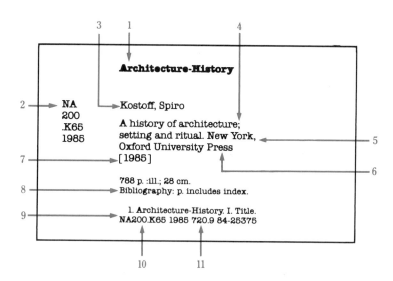

1. Subject heading. A title card would have the book's title instead. The basic author card would have nothing in this position.
2. Call number. The library where we found this card uses the Library of Congress classification system for filing its books. If it had used the Dewey decimal classification system, "720.9" would have appeared in this position.
3. Author's name.
4. Title.

5. Place of publication.

6. Publisher.
7. Publication date.
8. Notes on special contents. The book is illustrated, has a bibliography, and is indexed. Information about the number of pages may prove useful in evaluating the potential value of the book. The bibliography is especially important, for it can lead to other related books.
9. Recommended subject headings.
10. Recommended Library of Congress number.
11. Recommended Dewey decimal number.

Besides finding this card under "Architecture—History," you also would find it under the author's name and the book's title. Depending on how a library files its cards, the three card types may be integrated in the same catalog or filed separately.

As we indicated earlier, the library you use may hold similar information about its books in microform or in a computer file. In either case you'll probably find basically the same information as on the card catalog card, listed in the same three ways: author, title, subject. For example, a large public library system in northern Virginia catalogs the document holdings of all its regional and branch libraries on microfiche, with copies of the microfiche in each library. In that system the Spiro Kostof book above appears three times: under the subject heading, the author, and the book's title—just as it would if the library had a traditional card catalog. Here's the entry under "Architecture–History":

Kostof, Spiro. A history of
architecture: New York: Oxford
University Press, c1985. 788 p.
720.9K GFxTyRrSPo

Notice that this library system files books under the Dewey decimal classification system. The final series of letters—"GFxTyRrSPo"—indicates which of the regional and branch libraries hold copies of the book, in this case six of them. This entry is not quite as helpful as the full contents of the card catalog card: it doesn't, for example, include all the notes on special contents, so you wouldn't know whether the book includes a bibliography until you actually examined it. However, the entry does include the information you need to locate the book.

As you consult your library's book catalog, whatever form it's in, be sure to jot down the exact call number, the author's name, and a brief version of the book's title. This information helps you find the book on the shelf or gives you the basic data for requesting a recall of the book if it's out of the library (and if your library recalls books).

PERIODICALS

The card catalog, however, isn't the only way to find support you need for your research. Periodicals, which include popular magazines and professional journals, are also basic sources—and you should remember that even the most recent book is at least a year out of date by the time it appears, and the information in it may be several years old. As a result, if your topic requires last-minute, up-to-date information, you may need to use some periodicals.

How do you find what you need? You could, of course, go to the library stacks and start leafing through all the bound volumes of *Time* or *Psychology Today* in hope you'd find the article you need. But even just looking at the table of contents in each issue would take more time than you can afford. So what do you do? Find a shortcut to get to the information quickly. That's where reference tools come in. They help you find the right article, as the card catalog helped you find the right book. The problem is that there is more than one "card catalog" for periodicals.

Let's say, for example, that you want to write about *drug abuse*. That's too big a topic, so you narrow it to *the problems of drugs in the workplace,* which is still pretty broad. You go further to decide on the more limited topic of *drug abuse testing programs in business, industry, government, and sports.* That may need more limiting and will require the focus of a thesis, but *drug abuse testing programs* is narrow enough to set reasonable bounds on research. After checking the card catalog for books, you decide to try your hand at periodicals. You check one of the most widely known periodical indexes, the *Readers' Guide to Periodical Literature.* On page 193 of the May 1987 issue (covering January 17 to April 17, 1987) under the major heading of *Drug abuse,* you find the subheading *Testing:*

> **Testing**
> Air traffic controllers sue to block FAA drug testing. C. Preble. *Aviat Week Space Technol* 126:32-3 Mr 2 '87
> Big John [guidelines for administering drug tests to federal workers] il *Time* 129:19 Mr 2 '87
> Drug testing OK with most black pilots, execs say. *Jet* 71:32 F 23 '87
> Drug tests may explain why Vida Blue retired. por *Jet* 71:50 Mr 23 '87
> Free enterprise rushes to fill a delicate need [mail order urine samples circumvent drug testing regulations] D. Collins. il *U S News World Rep* 102:10 F 23 '87
> Maury Wills favors drug testing for all players. il por *Jet* 71:46 Mr 2 '87
> On-the-job drug tests: what to know. C. Kitch. il *Good Housekeep* 204:145 Ja '87
> Urine tests can be misleading [views of Roger P. Maickel] *USA Today (Periodical)* 115:13 F '87

What do these entries tell us? We find entries for eight articles: two related to employee reactions to drug testing in aviation, two related to drugs in sports, one about a mail order scheme to circumvent testing, one about the accuracy of some tests, one about federal testing, and one general article about on-the-job drug testing. We also can see that most of the articles appeared in magazines that are generally available in public or university libraries. Note that each entry gives a volume or issue number, followed after the colon by the page numbers and the abbreviated date. For three articles, commentaries in brackets expand on the articles' contents because the titles aren't self-explanatory. Of course, we can't be sure these articles will be useful until we read them.

The *Readers' Guide* covers some 180 magazines and journals considered to contain articles of general (or "popular") interest: *Time, Newsweek, U.S. News & World Report, Jet, Good Housekeeping, Popular Mechanics,* and the like. Since it doesn't cover professional or scholarly journals, it may not help much with scholarly topics, but as the sample above shows, it's certainly worth checking if you're working on a topic that would be covered by general-interest magazines.

Don't stop here. Try another index. The *Public Affairs Information Service Bulletin* (or *PAIS Bulletin*) is like the *Readers' Guide,* but it may be more helpful because it covers some 1,400 periodicals, as well as some books and government documents. Here's an excerpt from pages 130–31 of the December 1986 issue (covering October to December 1986) under the major heading of *DRUG ABUSE,* subheading *Testing:*

Testing

The drug problem: fighting back. il *Police Chief 53:21-2 +* O '86
> Law enforcement responses to drug abuse, including demand reduction, employee drug testing, and cooperative efforts; U.S.; 12 articles.

Fost, Norman. Banning drugs in sports: a skeptical view. *Hastings Center Rept 16:5-10 Ag '86*
> Performance-enhancing and recreational drugs: ethical aspects of recent proposals to punish athletes for taking drugs or to impose mandatory drug testing: U.S.

Hartsfield, William E. Medical examinations as a method of investigating employee wrongdoing. *Labor Law J 37:692-702* O. 767-79 N '86
> Excerpts from his forthcoming book, ''Investigating employees: a guide for employers and employees.''
> Legal constraints on the use of mandatory blood tests for alcoholism and urine tests for drugs: privacy rights: U.S.

Muczyk, Jan P. and Brian P. Heshizer. Managing in an era of substance abuse. *Personnel Administrator 31:91-2 +* Ag '86
> Legality of, and problems associated with, screening and testing for alcohol and other drugs: U.S.

New Jersey. Gen. Assembly. Labor Com. Public hearing on Assembly Bill 2850 (The Workplace Drug Abuse Testing Act): Trenton, New Jersey, September 4, 1986. '86 131 + 56p il pa—*State House, Trenton, NJ 08625*

Reagan, Ronald. Drug-free federal workplace: Executive Order 12564, September 15, 1986. *W Comp Pres Docs 22:1188-92* S 22 '86

Rust, Mark. Drug testing: the legal dilemma. *ABA (Am Bar Assn) J p 50-4 N 1 '86*
> Includes some court decisions on employee drug abuse testing programs; U.S.

The format of the entries is similar to that in the *Readers' Guide.* Again there's a brief summary of the article if the title isn't self-explanatory. Notice the fifth item in the *PAIS Bulletin* extract, the one marked with the # sign:

this is a government document. Though you may be looking for periodicals, don't pass up the books and government documents that are indexed as well.

You probably recognize almost all the magazine titles in the extract from the *Readers' Guide,* but probably few if any in the extract from the *PAIS Bulletin.* Right? This is a reflection of our exposure to popular magazines, of course, but it also reflects the relative availability of the publications in libraries. Large public libraries will have many of the magazines indexed by the *Readers' Guide* but only a few covered by the *PAIS Bulletin.* Your college library will have a mixture of popular magazines (particularly the news magazines) and professional and scholarly journals. How can you tell what a library holds? Usually a library has a list of all the periodicals available there. It could be a short list posted on a wall. Often, though, it is a large computer listing lying conspicuously on a table in the reference area (where the indexes are kept) or near the periodical shelves. Check this list for the periodical title you need, and for the volumes or issues held by the library.

As useful as the *Readers' Guide* and the *PAIS Bulletin* are, they index a total of only about 2 percent of the published articles. Another kind of reference tool, an abstract, may also help. There are thousands of abstracts, covering hundreds of topics. You must consult the specialized index for abstracts for your subject: *Psychological Abstracts, Biological Abstracts,* or *Chemical Abstracts,* for example. An abstract summarizes the contents of a technical or scholarly article, but the abstract is much longer than the brief summaries you saw in the *PAIS Bulletin.*

Let's say that you become interested in the psychological aspects of controlling drug abuse. You might, therefore, find *Psychological Abstracts* useful. On page 2030 of the July 1987 issue you could find this abstract of an article dealing with the attitudes of law enforcement officers toward fighting drug trafficking:

> 20571. **Wachtel, Julius.** (US Treasury Dept. Bureau of Alcohol, Tobacco & Firearms, Helena, MT) **Production and craftsmanship in police narcotics enforcement.** *Journal of Police Science & Administration,* 1985(Dec), Vol 13(4), 263–274. —Explored the hypothesized conflict between production and craftsmanship by interviewing and administering questionnaires to 45 narcotics officers of 7 units. Data indicate that (1) making arrests was one of the most important activities of the Ss, and (2) routine narcotics work was placed on a much higher plane than initially supposed. Findings support the proposition that given limited resources, narcotics police will focus on petty drug offenders because going after the ''bigger'' dealers has a high opportunity cost (i.e., produces fewer arrests) and yields fewer individual and organizational rewards. (24 ref)—*V. Levy.*

Like the periodical indexes, the abstract provides bibliographic information that you'll need to find the work the abstract covers. Again, check your library's list of holdings of periodicals to see if the journal and issue are available.

This abstract is not an article, but a summary only. So what can you use? First, the abstract is useful as an indicator of the content of the article it summarizes. But it's like a metal detector. It can only tell you it's there, not how valuable it is. To use the article, you must read it. Second, the abstract number can make it easier if you have time for the librarian to order a copy of the original. As a general rule, don't cite abstracts in your parenthetical references or Works Cited source listing. Go to the original.

What happens if you've been to all these library resources and still haven't found what you want? Don't give up, for this is where the challenge of research comes in. Your library will have many more research tools to help you get the paper written.

Among the more common reference tools, besides those we've already mentioned, you might find these in your library:

Annual Bibliography of English Language and Literature: indexes articles and books about authors and literature written in English.

Art Index: art periodicals, both professional and scholarly.

Biography Index: an index to biographical material on living and historical figures.

Biological Abstracts: abstracts covering articles on biosciences published in professional journals worldwide.

Book Review Digest: summary of book reviews for modern literature; useful for finding out how a book was received.

Business Periodicals Index: as the title indicates, index of business and economics articles.

Chemical Abstracts: abstracts of research articles in chemistry.

Education Index: for articles dealing with education research and development.

Essay and General Literature Index: author and subject index to collections of essays.

MLA International Bibliography: published annually by the Modern Language Association; covers scholarly journals and books about language and literature in English and other modern languages.

New York Times Index: a key, comprehensive index to all news events in *The New York Times;* a basic tool, good for almost any topic.

Social Sciences, Humanities, and General Sciences Indexes: a family of indexes covering scholarly and professional journals on these subjects. (The *International Index,* published 1907–65, became the *Social Sciences and Humanities Index,* which split in 1974 into the *Social Sciences Index* and the *Humanities Index;* the *General Sciences Index* joined the family in 1978.)

Other good sources of help are subject bibliographies. They list all the books and articles on a limited subject, such as G. B. Shaw, novels in the nineteenth century, or the Battle of Gettysburg. Consult an experienced librarian for help in finding a bibliography in your subject.

COMPUTER LISTINGS AND SEARCHES

As indicated in the discussion of card catalogs, in some libraries you now use a computer terminal to gain access to the catalog. The library's listing of available periodicals may be available on line as well. Some libraries also have access to computerized listings, by subject, to regional catalogs, or to other helpful resources. Because libraries differ in what is available, you'll have to talk to a reference librarian for more ideas.

One of your goals, however, should be to become self-sufficient in your library research so that you can move quickly and surely to solve the problems for yourself. To help you begin, we have prepared the following exercises.

EXERCISES

A. In April 1987, because of public complaints, the Federal Communications Commission (FCC) adopted rules changes to restrict the use of indecent language on radio, television, and telephone services. *The New York Times* described the rules changes and the reasons for the FCC action. Use library resources to answer the following:

1. How long had it been since the FCC previously had taken action against indecent programming?
2. What standard is to be used for defining indecent language?
3. What standard does the newer definition replace?
4. What issue of *The New York Times* carried the article?
5. What source did you use to answer these questions?

B. From late 1986 through early 1987, the Reagan administration was troubled by disclosures related to the Iran arms–contra aid scandal, also called Iranscam and Irangate, among other labels. For eleven weeks, ending in early August 1987, House and Senate select committees held joint hearings to investigate the matter. Use reference tools in your library to do the following:

1. List six different periodical articles that comment on the hearings. Name the reference work or works you used to find these articles.
2. List the name, date, and page number of a national newspaper article on the hearings. Name the reference work you used to find this information.
3. List the name, date, and page number for an article about the hearings in a local newspaper. What reference tool did you use to find this article?

C. In an early 1987 *Time* magazine issue is a Charles Krauthammer essay about the critical response to colorization of classic motion pictures.

   1. What is the title of the essay?
   2. What is the full date of the *Time* issue that includes the essay?
   3. On what page does the essay appear?
   4. At the end of the essay the author defines a "Hollywood Puritan" as a person who fears what?
   5. What reference work did you use to find the article?
   6. What subject heading is the article listed under?

D. In 1985 the *Environmental Law Reporter* published an article by Murray Drabkin, et al., entitled "Bankruptcy and the Cleanup of Hazardous Waste: Caveat Creditor."

   1. In what issue did the article appear, and on what pages?
   2. What *two* types of laws does the article deal with?
   3. What reference work did you use to find this information?
   4. Under what heading did the information appear in that reference work?

E. In 1985 Jurgen Schmandt and Hilliard Roderick edited a book entitled *Acid Rain and Friendly Neighbors: The Policy Dispute Between Canada and the United States*.

   1. How many pages does the book have?
   2. Who published it?
   3. Where did you find this information?

19
Taking and Organizing Notes

Let's review for a moment. You settle on a general topic and narrow it as much as you reasonably can. Your preliminary reading helps you focus the topic and at the same time reassures you that sources appear to be available for you to draw on for support material. For example, let's say you're interested in those prehistoric people who left their homes on the Asian continent and for some reason found their way to the American continent and developed new lives here. You realize that *prehistoric Indians* is too large a topic, so you reduce it to *prehistoric Indians in North America,* to *the new way of life in America.* That, you decide, still is too broad, but it's a place to start with your preliminary reading. This preliminary exploration of the topic leads you to a new, interesting idea: contrary to the popular belief you've heard for years that the prehistoric Indians wandered across the American continent struggling to survive, there is relatively recent evidence that the prehistoric Indians adapted well and produced sophisticated cultures. Your preliminary reading also suggests that your library holds enough sources to support your research, so you use the card catalog and the indexes and bibliographies of your library's reference section to make a list of books and periodical articles that look promising. Now what? Here's where the work begins.

You obviously can't remember every idea or fact you find in your reading. You could keep all the books and magazines piled up around you and then flip through them to find a bit of support when you need it. But that's the hard way. Therefore, most researchers have developed some systematic way to keep track of the research information they find.

This chapter will show you two methods for noting specific ideas and facts and keeping them organized. The most commonly taught system for keeping track of research information involves taking notes on note cards. This system, which we'll call "the traditional system," has proved its value to thousands of researchers. The second system we'll call "the copying machine system" because it relies heavily on a stack of coins and a copying machine. It

171

offers a shortcut in the notetaking process by eliminating the need to write down notes.

THE TRADITIONAL SYSTEM

Both the traditional and copying machine systems involve keeping track of *two* kinds of information. The first kind is information about the sources you use; the second kind is the information you find in those sources.

The traditional system employs two sets of index cards—one set for each kind of information. Some researchers prefer two sizes of index cards (for example, 3 × 5 cards for sources and 4 × 6 or 5 × 8 cards for notes from the sources); others use the same size cards for both kinds of information. No matter what size of index cards you choose, here's the traditional notetaking process.

Bibliography Cards

For Books

Pick the most likely-looking book and check the table of contents or index to see which parts of the book apply. (It's just not sensible to read the entire book if only Chapter 2 deals with prehistoric American Indians.)

If the book has nothing useful, put it aside to return to the library as soon as you can. Someone else may need it.

When you find a book that has information you think you might use, make out a *bibliography card.* Record only one book on each card and be careful to include all the necessary data about the book. Chapter 22, "Works Cited," explains in detail the information you'll need and shows the various formats for presenting that information for your final paper. For now, be sure your bibliography card has all the following items that apply to the book you're recording:

- Author(s) or group responsible.
- Title and subtitle of book (and volume title if part of a multivolume set).
- Title of part of the book (if you're using only a piece of the book, such as an essay in a collection).
- Translator(s).
- Editor(s).
- Edition (don't worry about the number of "printings," but do note the edition if the book is other than the first edition).
- Volume number(s).
- Series (if the work is part of a series, such as "Studies in Anthropology, No. 5").
- Place of publication (the first one listed if there are several).
- Publisher.

- Date of publication (latest copyright date, not date of printing).
- Inclusive page numbers of a part of the book (if you're using only a piece of the book, such as an essay in a collection).

You can save yourself time later by putting all the items in correct bibliographic format for your paper's Works Cited pages (Chapter 22 shows formats). Here's a sample bibliography card with the necessary information in the form required for its Works Cited entry:

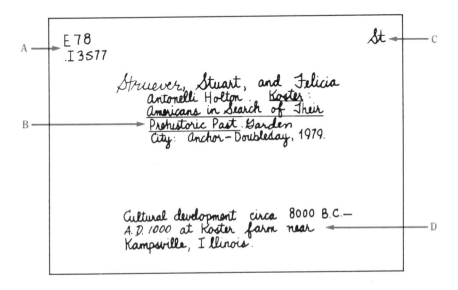

Note these things about the bibliography card:

A. Always include the *library call number;* it will save you time if you have to go back to recheck a quotation or find information you forgot to copy down.
B. Include all the applicable information (author, title, etc.) from the list above.
C. Add your own *bibliography code.* We use the first two letters of the first author's last name. But you may use any consistent system—numbering, small letters, Roman numerals. The coding system will save you time as you take notes and as you write drafts of your paper.
D. *Optional.* As a reminder, add a brief note about what the book contains.

With your first bibliography card, you've begun to compile your paper's working bibliography. As you consult the books and articles you've found, prepare a separate card for each one.

For Articles in Periodicals

For magazines, journals, and newspapers, be sure your bibliography card has all the following items that apply to the article you're recording:

- Author(s) (articles may be unsigned, and sometimes you'll find only initials for the author).
- Title of article.
- Type of article (for letters to the editor and reviews).
- Name of periodical.
- Series number (such as "old" or "new").
- Newspaper edition (if the newspaper publishes more than one edition per day).
- Volume and/or issue number(s).
- Date of publication.
- Inclusive page numbers for the article.

Also note whether the periodical is paginated continuously throughout a volume or independently by issue. For example, if issue 2 of a volume ends with page 563 and issue 3 of the same volume begins with page 564, the publication paginates continuously throughout a volume. If each issue starts with page 1, then the issues are paginated independently. This distinction won't matter for your research, but it will help you decide which format to use when you write your entries for the Works Cited pages of your final paper.

Note Cards

When you come across a fact or idea you think you can use, make a *note card*. Put only one fact or idea on each card. When you are ready to use the information for your draft, you will be much freer to move the cards if you have only one idea on each card.

Now read the following passage from page 244 of the Struever and Holton book about the archaeological diggings at the Koster farm near Kampsville, Illinois. ("Horizon 11" is the designation for a level of human occupation dating to about 6400 B.C.)

Traditionally, archaeologists have assumed that Archaic people went through a long, slow, gradual process in learning how to cope with their environment and how to extract a decent living from it. They thought it took the aborigines several thousand years, from Paleo-Indian times (circa 12,000–8000 B.C.) to 2500 B.C., to learn about various foods in eastern North America and how to exploit them.

This is simply not true. The Koster people know their food resources intimately and did a superb job of feeding their communities. During the occupation of Horizon 11, Early Archaic people had developed a highly selective exploitation pattern of subsistence. They were not just taking foods randomly from the land-

scape. Rather, they calculated how to provide the community with the most nutritious foods possible while expending the least effort. In addition to deer and
smaller mammals, they ate large quantities of fish, freshwater mussels, and nuts.
Fish and nuts—in addition to being available each year, and easy to take in large
quantities—are highly complementary components of a nutritious diet. Nuts
contain fat for high energy, which many freshwater fish lack. The kind of input-
output analysis which was taking place was worthy of the most sophisticated
culture.

Here's a sample note card for a *quotation* of an important portion of that
passage:

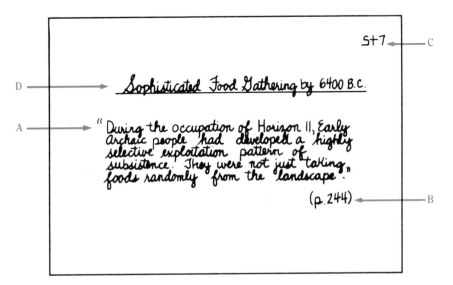

What to include on a quotation note card:

A. Put *quotation marks* around quoted material.
B. Put the page number (here, p. 244) in parentheses. If you are using a
   book that is part of a multivolume set but that doesn't have a separate
   title, include the volume number like this: (3:172).
C. The *code number* shows that this is the seventh card made from the
   Struever and Holton book. Using the bibliography code (St) from the
   bibliography card makes it unnecessary to put complete bibliographic
   information on each note card, and the number added (to make St7)
   provides a code that distinguishes this note card from others from the
   same book. In Chapter 20 we'll show you another way to use the code
   number. For now, keep all note cards from the same work together.
D. *Optional.* Use key word headings that might help you later to arrange
   the facts and ideas and to make sure you have enough support.

If you had *summarized* the entire passage, condensing the original material into a shorter version in your own words, the card would look like this:

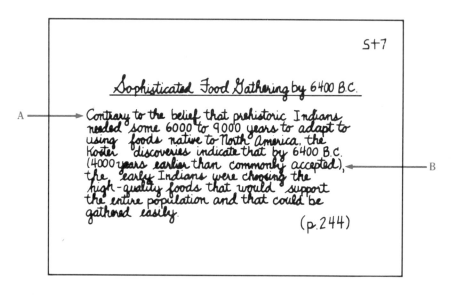

What's different about a summary note card?

A. *No quotation marks.* Of course, even though you don't borrow the exact words, you do borrow the idea, and you must give credit for it (more about this in Chapter 20).
B. Your own words but the author's ideas. More important than reducing the length of the original, with a summary you mentally "process" the material, capturing the idea or facts and making yourself more knowledgeable about your topic. Notice that the comment in parentheses within the summary above is an *interpretation* of the evidence in the original, demonstrating that the writer of the note card has processed the passage.

A *paraphrase,* too, is a retelling of the original in your own words. But a paraphrase is different from a summary: the paraphrase tends to follow the sentence-by-sentence pattern of the original more closely and also is about the same length as the original. Use paraphrase note cards sparingly. If you're going to take notes that closely follow the original, why not quote instead? Then you'll have the exact words in case you decide to quote all or part of the passage in your paper. Still, a paraphrase is useful when the original is technical or complex or when it isn't worded well—then the paraphrase can help simplify or "interpret" the original. If we paraphrase the two sentences quoted in the sample quotation note card on page 175, the paraphrase would look like this:

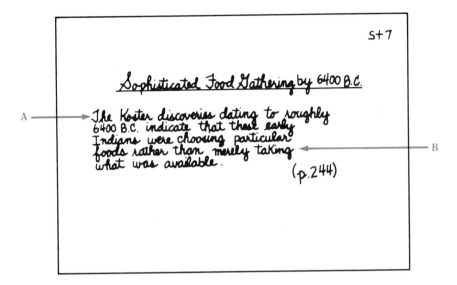

What's special about the paraphrase note card?

A. You restate the quotation in your own words, so there are no quotation marks.
B. The paraphrase interprets the technical wording from the original: "highly selective exploitation pattern of subsistence" has been simplified to "choosing particular foods."

How to Go Wrong

Most of the problems with taking notes come with paraphrases and summaries. If you're putting the original into your own words and you want to retain wording from the original, you must use quotation marks. What if you had written something like this?

> For many years archaeologists have assumed that the prehistoric Indians needed several thousand years to discover how to exploit the various foods in eastern North America, but the Koster Indians had learned to be highly selective in their food choices rather than just taking foods randomly from the landscape.

This looks like a paraphrase or summary, right? Right. It *looks* like one, but it's an unacknowledged, loose quotation. It should have looked like this:

> For many years "archaeologists have assumed" that the prehistoric Indians needed "several thousand years" to discover "how to exploit" the "various foods in eastern North America," but the Koster Indians had learned to be "highly selective" in their food choices rather than "just taking foods randomly from the landscape."

Of course, that looks peculiar. No thought has been given here to choosing effective portions of the original for a quotation—rather, the use of key words from the original appears to be accidental.

You *can* mix quotation with summary or paraphrase, but be selective in the quotation part. And keep this rule in mind: Whenever you use another author's words, put them in quotation marks. Failure to do so is dishonest.

THE COPYING MACHINE SYSTEM

As you can see, the traditional system requires considerable writing, and that can slow you down, interrupting your train of thought during research. The copying machine system offers an alternative.

When you find a portion of a book or an article that looks worthwhile, use a copying machine to make a copy. On that copy, write the complete bibliographic information (just as you would on a bibliography card in the traditional system). Then, use a *highlighting* pen to mark anything you want to be able to refer to later (the equivalent of writing down quotations in the traditional system). Please do not highlight the library copies of books and articles in periodicals.

Which system should you use? The traditional system takes time but offers two distinct advantages:

- As you take notes, you are actively involved with the material, so you will understand it better than if you had only glanced through it.
- Note cards offer flexibility: you can rearrange them to match your outline or even place them in the rough draft to save time during the writing stage.

At the same time, though, the traditional system can be tedious. Nevertheless, for many researchers the benefits of the painstaking process outweigh the cost.

For others, the pain of notetaking outweighs the benefits. If you are one of these, consider the copying machine system. You won't be able to shuffle note cards. Moreover, you'll still have to spend time processing the material you've highlighted on the copies—turning the original material from your sources into quotations, summaries, and paraphrases to integrate with your own writing. However, you'll do that processing as you write the draft of your paper, so you'll choose the form for presentation to fit your needs as you write. That offers flexibility not possible with the traditional system.

Choose the system that fits your personality. Either system can work well. What won't work is having no system at all: random reading combined with mistaken confidence in your ability to remember details from research when the time comes to write your paper.

SOME FINE POINTS IN QUOTING

Whether you use the traditional system or the copying machine system to compile detailed support from your research, you'll likely present a portion of that support as direct quotations from your sources. Be careful to quote accurately. If you need to alter a quotation, there are special techniques to show the alteration.

Omitting Words

Sometimes you'll want to omit words from something you're quoting because they're irrelevant or awkward out of their original context. In addition, you may need to alter a passage so that the edited passage fits into the grammar and sense of your own writing. The device you use to show an omission is an ellipsis (. . .)—three spaced periods with a space at the beginning and the end.

When you quote only a word or phrase, you don't need to show that material has been left out before or after the quotation; the cutting is obvious. However, when your editing results in a complete sentence (or complete line of poetry), use the ellipsis to show that you've modified the original, no matter how minor the change. Of course, it's *never* acceptable to edit the original so that you change its meaning (for example, by leaving out *not* or *never*); omissions are acceptable only as a convenience to trim unnecessary words or to fit the quotation into the pattern of your writing.

When the omission occurs *inside a sentence (or line of poetry)*, the remainder will look like this:

```
"Fish and nuts . . . are highly complementary
components of a nutritious diet."
```

If the omission occurs at the *end of a sentence,* use four spaced periods without a space in front of the first period (a period for the sentence plus the ellipsis):

```
"The Koster people knew their food resources
intimately. . . . They were not just taking foods
randomly from the landscape."
```

An ellipsis at the end of a sentence can represent omission of the end of that sentence, one or more sentences, or one or more paragraphs. At the end of a line of poetry, it would indicate omission of one or more lines of poetry.

If an omission at the end of a sentence precedes a parenthetical documentation reference, show the ellipsis before the parentheses and the sentence punctuation after:

```
"The Koster people knew their food resources
intimately . . ." (Struever and Holton 244).
```

Notice that there is a space between *intimately* and the ellipsis but not between the ellipsis and the ending quotation marks. (You'll learn how to format parenthetical references in Chapter 21.)

Adding Words

If you need to add an explanation within a quotation so that the quotation will make sense in the context of your writing, use square brackets to separate your words from those you're quoting:

```
"During the occupation of Horizon 11 [circa 6400
B.C.], Early Archaic people had developed a highly
selective exploitation pattern of subsistence."
```

Don't use parentheses instead of square brackets. If your typewriter can't make brackets, draw them neatly by hand, using black ink or pencil.

Adding Emphasis

You can emphasize a portion of a quotation by underlining (or italicizing) it. However, to ensure that readers can tell who added the emphasis, provide an explanation at the end of the quotation if the emphasis is yours (no explanation is required if the emphasis is part of the original):

```
"The kind of input—output analysis which was taking
place was worthy of the most sophisticated culture"
(emphasis added).
```

Verifying Quotation Accuracy

If you find an error, or material that may seem to be peculiar, in the quotation you want to use, add "sic" to the quotation—in square brackets if inside the quotation or in parentheses if outside. The word *sic* (Latin for "thus") tells readers you have rendered the quotation faithfully:

> "When the Imperial Air Forces of Japan attacked
> Pearl Harbor on 7 December 1940 [sic], they
> demonstrated how vulnerable ships were to surprise
> air attack."

In addition, if you quote a passage that itself contains an ellipsis or words in brackets, use "sic" to verify that you have quoted accurately.

Altering Final Punctuation

Within a quotation, punctuation must appear as in the original, unless properly modified through use of an ellipsis or an addition in square brackets. Final punctuation, however, will depend on how you integrate the quotation into your own writing. This quotation ends in a period:

> "They were not just taking foods randomly from the
> landscape."

However, you might change that period to a comma if the quotation became an internal clause in your writing:

> "They were not just taking foods randomly from the
> landscape," according to authorities Stuart
> Struever and Felicia Holton.

EXERCISES

A. The paragraph below is from page 6 of the second edition of *Pathophysiology: Clinical Concepts of Disease Processes,* by Sylvia Anderson Price and Lorraine McCarty Wilson. The second edition was published in 1982 by the McGraw-Hill Book Company of New York, New York. In the library it has call number RB113.P363.

> Another important element in the concept of disease is the recognition that disease does not involve the development of a completely new form of life but rather is an extension or distortion of the normal life processes that are present in the individual. Even in the case of an obviously infectious disease, where the body is literally invaded, the infectious agent itself does not constitute the disease but only serves to evoke the

changes in the subject that ultimately are manifested as disease. Thus, disease is actually the sum of the physiological processes which have been distorted. In order to understand and adequately treat the disease one must take into account the identity of the normal processes interfered with, the character of the disturbances, and the secondary effects of such disturbances on other vital processes.

1. Make a bibliography card for the book.

2. Select at least three lines of the paragraph and prepare a note card quoting directly from the paragraph.

3. Now prepare another note card paraphrasing the lines you quoted in Exercise A2.

4. Prepare a note card summarizing the entire paragraph; use no more than three lines of your own words to do it.

5. A final check:
   Did you put a bibliography code on the bibliography card?
   Did you use that code on the note cards?
   Is the library call number on the bibliography card?
   Did you use quotation marks where needed?

B. In the library, under call number DF221.T8W66, you find *In Search of the Trojan War* by Michael Wood. The book is a Plume Book published by the New American Library, of New York, in 1987. Following is a passage from pages 26 to 27 (all punctuation has been rendered as in the original):

In the ancient world it was the almost uniform belief that the Trojan War was an historical event: the philosopher Anaxagoras was one of only a handful known to have doubted it, on the good grounds that there was no *proof*. But then, as now, everyone knew there was no primary source for the war; equally they *knew* that it had happened! It is a paradox unique in historiography. When the 'Father of History', Herodotus, who lived in the fifth century BC, asked Egyptian priests whether the Greek story of the war was true, he was simply asking whether they had any alternative record of it, for there were no *written* sources before the epics of Homer were committed to writing, perhaps as late as the sixth century BC, hence there were no documentary sources at all available to the historians of the fifth century BC. It is interesting to see then that those historians were prepared to give total credence to the basis of the tradition in Homer.

1. Make a bibliography card for the book.

2. Select at least three lines of the paragraph and prepare a note card quoting directly from the paragraph.

3. Now prepare another note card paraphrasing the lines you quoted in Exercise B2.

4. Prepare a note card summarizing the entire paragraph; use no more than three lines of your own words to do it.

5. A final check:
   Did you put a bibliography code on the bibliography card?
   Did you use that code on the note cards?
   Is the library call number on the bibliography card?
   Did you use quotation marks where needed?

20
Using Borrowed Material in Your Paper

AN OUTLINE

As we mentioned in the last chapter, you don't need to wait until you've finished taking all your notes to begin organizing that new knowledge. Develop an outline early and revise and expand it as you learn more. The working outline helps you discover gaps in your support, thereby suggesting areas for continued research. And the research suggests ways to modify the organization. In other words, you need to work back and forth between notetaking and outlining—each influences the other.

How do you begin organizing the support? By thinking. List all the *key* ideas you've discovered about your topic; just jot down the key words. Now, does a pattern of organization suggest itself? Would chronological order work? How about cause and effect or some of the other patterns you studied in Part Four? Once you've settled on the basic arrangement, fill in this outline, using as few words as you can without sacrificing clarity. Of course, you may not need exactly three major topics with three support ideas for each one. This is just a basic model.

I. Introduction (as a minimum, write the thesis of the paper):
II. First major topic:
   A. Support idea:
   B. Support idea:
   C. Support idea:
III. Second major topic:
   A. Support idea:
   B. Support idea:
   C. Support idea:

   IV. Third major topic:
    A. Support idea:
    B. Support idea:
    C. Support idea:
  V. Conclusion:

The outline should look familiar, for it's the same basic pattern you've seen before. The outline here represents a greater amount of material, but the organizing process is the same.

What you have just done is to prepare a working outline, one that shows the way your paper looks so far. Your outline reduces a large quantity of information to its bare skeleton—just the main ideas and key support. This outline is merely a tool to show logically and clearly the relationships among the main ideas in the paper. It will help you discover gaps in support, indicating where you need to work more in research.

When you've worked out fully the major ideas, supporting ideas, *and* specific support, you'll have the complete skeletal organization for your research paper. It will look like something like the outline on pages 144–188, which shows the organization of the sample research paper in Chapter 17. And as you write the first draft of your own research paper, your outline will guide you as you fill in the details.

A TIMESAVER

Once you've prepared an outline, you're ready to assemble your detailed support. Arrange your notes (note cards or highlighted photocopy pages, depending on the research system you chose) to follow your outline. Use the floor, your desktop, your roommate's bed, whatever you need to spread the cards out so you can see how they fill out the skeleton. Don't let your outline keep you from moving notes around. That outline is not engraved in bronze; you can alter it as you need to. But laying out your notes will help you see where the outline may be incomplete or where you need more information. You probably will have more notes than you can use. Don't throw any away; you may find a place for them later.

When you are satisfied with the outline and its support, start writing. You may begin at the beginning with an introduction, then move on to the first major topic, then the second, and so on. Many writers do it this way, and it may work for you. Or you may decide to start with the first major topic, go on to the next topics, and finish writing with the conclusion—and then the introduction. Many other writers do it this way. The reason is simple: frequently you're not sure what you're going to say until you've said it. You actually discover what you think as you write because the ideas take over and lead you to new discoveries. If you have already written the introduction, you may find it has little relationship to what you finally say.

Regardless of where you start writing, you'll have to use some of your notes. If you're quoting—and if you've used the traditional system with note cards—here's a trick that can save you some work: In writing your draft, when you come to a place for a quotation, don't copy it again. Just paper-clip or tape the quotation note card in place or leave room in your draft and write in the code number for the note card (remember the code number St7 we used on page 175?). Doing it this way will save you writing and will help keep the quotations accurate, no matter how many drafts you go through. *A caution:* This trick isn't intended for use with summaries and paraphrases; those notes already are in your own words, and you should be weaving the ideas and facts into the fabric of your writing in the paper's draft.

USING BORROWED MATERIAL SKILLFULLY

Skilled use of borrowed material is one mark of an accomplished writer. You can't expect just to sprinkle it on the paper in the hope it will magically create an argument for you. Good arguments with borrowed material supporting them don't just happen; they come from careful work. To make sure your borrowed material helps your argument, you must consider two key questions: whether to quote or not, and what to quote from. Answers to these questions are closely related and depend on the paper you're writing.

USING PRIMARY SOURCES

A primary source is an original source of basic facts or opinions on your subject: eyewitness accounts, official investigations, newspaper articles of the time. The following, for example, is an excerpt from page 443 of Volume 1 of the *Personal Memoirs of U. S. Grant* (published by Charles L. Webster & Company of New York in 1885); here Ulysses S. Grant is explaining why he risked operations against Vicksburg without first setting up a protected logistics base:

> Marching across this country in the face of an enemy was impossible; navigating it proved equally impracticable. The strategical way according to the rule, therefore, would have been to go back to Memphis; establish that as a base of supplies; fortify it so that the storehouses could be held by a small garrison, and move from there along the line of railroad, repairing as we advanced, to the Yallabusha, or to Jackson, Mississippi. At this time the North had become very much discouraged. Many strong Union men believed that the war must prove a failure. The elections of 1862 had gone against the party which was for the prosecution of the war to save the Union if it took the last man and last dollar. Voluntary enlistments had ceased throughout the greater part of the North, and the draft had been resorted to to fill up our ranks. It was my judgment at the time that to make a backward movement as long as that from Vicksburg to Memphis, would be interpreted, by many of those yet full of hope for the preservation of the Union, as a defeat, and that the draft would be resisted, desertions ensue and the power to capture and punish deserters lost. There was nothing left to be done but to *go forward to a decisive victory.* This was in my mind from the moment I took command in person at Young's Point.

If you're writing a paper about the Battle of Vicksburg, or perhaps about General Grant's strategic planning of Civil War campaigns, then Grant's own words showing his thoughts about the Vicksburg campaign are particularly important. Other writers might tell you what Grant probably was thinking, but Grant on Grant's thinking provides one of the best sources. Primary sources are not always easy to find, but they're worth looking for.

There are three basic reasons for choosing to quote from a source (in preference to summarizing or paraphrasing):

- A passage is worded particularly well, providing facts or opinions phrased effectively.
- A passage is written very clearly (so that paraphrasing or summarizing would provide a poor substitute).
- A passsage provides the words of an authority (not necessarily someone famous, just someone in a position to know).

Because a primary source is the origin of facts or opinions on your subject, it is likely to fit one or more of the criteria for quoting. The excerpt from Grant's writing about the Vicksburg campaign, for example, provides clear, effective wording and, most important, provides the words of an authority on Grant's thinking at the time of the campaign.

USING SECONDARY SOURCES

A secondary source is secondhand, removed one step or more from the primary source. It uses primary sources or other secondary sources as its basis. Thus a 1987 article about Grant's Vicksburg campaign would be a secondary source, drawing perhaps from Grant's *Memoirs* but also from the writings of other people who were at Vicksburg and from other books and articles analyzing the Vicksburg operations.

Compare these two lists:

Primary Source	*Secondary Source*
• The Panama Canal Treaty printed in the *Congressional Record*	• An article about the Panama Canal Treaty in *Time*
• Shakespeare's Sonnet 73	• A critical analysis of Shakespeare's sonnets
• The transcript of a trial	• An article in *Newsweek* about that trial
• An 1865 newspaper article about Lincoln's assassination	• A 1986 book about Lincoln's assassination

The distinction isn't always clear-cut. The last primary source might have been considered a secondary source in 1865, if the writer wasn't present at the assassination. Today we'd call it a primary source because a journalist in 1865 had greater opportunities for investigating true primary sources (such as eyewitnesses) and also could capture the feelings of the time.

Secondary sources select, filter, evaluate, and analyze material from primary sources (as well as other secondary sources). That is both their value and their weakness. Primary sources are more likely to provide "unfiltered truth," but primary sources generally lack the scope provided by secondary sources, which draw on multiple primary and secondary sources. That is, secondary sources are valuable because their writers already have done a lot of work for you, but at the same time you have to be cautious and guard against the biases of the writers who selected and filtered truth for you.

As a general rule, you'll probably find fewer reasons to quote from secondary sources and more reasons to summarize or paraphrase. By no means is that an absolute rule, however.

But whether you use primary or secondary sources, whether you quote or summarize or paraphrase, you must follow three steps to use borrowed material effectively:

- *Introduce* the borrowed material.
- *Present* it.
- *Credit* the source.

INTRODUCING BORROWED MATERIAL

Perhaps the most neglected step in using borrowed material is the first one—introducing it. In this step you mention the author or title of the source before presenting the material, to signal to your readers that you are beginning the borrowed material. Here are some sample introductions:

```
As Grant explained in his Memoirs, . . .

According to the press secretary, the President
decided that. . . .

Reverend Jackson was right when he said, . . .

In his essay "Here's HUD in Your Eye," Larry
McMurtry reveals. . . .
```

The variety of introductions is almost endless, but all of them identify your source, often helping your readers judge whether the source you're citing is reputable. Without an introduction, the borrowed material seems just spliced in; look for such an example in the following paragraph:

```
        Washington's victory at Yorktown was
precarious almost up to the moment of the
British surrender. What really defeated the
British was the inability of Lord Cornwallis
to move his forces away from Yorktown. "The
secret of the British failure there was either
the ministry's neglect in immediately securing
absolute naval supremacy on this coast . . .
or the over-confidence or carelessness of the
admirals in command. It is the British naval
administration that is to be charged with the
Yorktown catastrophe" (Johnston 101). The
British under Cornwallis were occupying
Yorktown because it was the best available
naval station, and retreat by sea would have
been possible had not the French fleet kept
the British fleet away from the battle area.
```

Readers will recognize where the borrowing begins and ends because of the quotation marks, but they will wonder who Johnston is and where the quotation comes from. Annoying, isn't it? Don't annoy your readers; don't even leave them slightly frustrated from wondering about who said what. Introduce the material:

```
        Washington's victory at Yorktown was
precarious almost up to the moment of the
British surrender. What really defeated the
British was the inability of Lord Cornwallis
to move his forces away from Yorktown. In The
Yorktown Campaign and the Surrender of
Cornwallis, historian Henry P. Johnston blames
the British navy: "The secret of the British
failure there was either the ministry's
neglect in immediately securing absolute naval
supremacy on this coast . . . or the over-
confidence or carelessness of the admirals in
command. It is the British naval adminis-
tration that is to be charged with the
Yorktown catastrophe" (101). The British under
```

```
Cornwallis were occupying Yorktown because it
was the best available naval station, and
retreat by sea would have been possible had
not the French fleet kept the British fleet
away from the battle area.
```

This way, your readers know who wrote what you've quoted and where you found it. The parenthetical documentation reference, used in conjunction with the research paper's Works Cited list, gives the complete data to find the book if your readers should want to.

An introduction is even more important for a summary or paraphrase than it is for a direct quotation. Quotation marks show where a quotation begins and ends. But where does the paraphrase begin here?

```
        Washington's victory at Yorktown was
precarious almost up to the moment of the
British surrender. What really defeated the
British was the inability of Lord Cornwallis
to move his forces away from Yorktown. The
British failed because the navy did not
control the sea off the American coast or
because the British admirals blundered. The
British navy should be blamed for the Yorktown
defeat (Johnston 101). The British under
Cornwallis were occupying Yorktown because it
was the best available naval station, and
retreat by sea would have been possible had
not the French fleet keep the British fleet
away from the battle area.
```

How many of the ideas come from Johnston's book? Where does the paraphrase begin? At the first word of the paragraph? Or is it only the sentence ending with the parenthetical documentation reference? Who knows? But when you introduce the paraphrase, everyone will know:

```
        Washington's victory at Yorktown was
precarious almost up to the moment of the
British surrender. What really defeated the
British was the inability of Lord Cornwallis
to move his forces away from Yorktown. In The
Yorktown Campaign and the Surrender of
Cornwallis, historian Henry P. Johnston
```

asserts that the British failed because the navy did not control the sea off the American coast or because the British admirals blundered. The British navy should be blamed for the Yorktown defeat (101). The British under Cornwallis were occupying Yorktown because it was the best available naval station, and retreat by sea would have been possible had not the French fleet kept the British fleet away from the battle area.

With just that simple introduction readers know where the paraphrasing begins. Be sure to introduce your summaries as well.

PRESENTING BORROWED MATERIAL

Paraphrases and summaries, no matter what their length, are fully integrated with your own writing. Introduce them, of course, and credit the source with a parenthetical reference, as we'll discuss later. But no special formatting is required for the presentation. Quotations require special presentation techniques.

For a short quotation, *four or fewer lines of typing in your paper:*

- *Type the quotation along with your own writing, without special indentation or spacing.*
- *Use quotation marks to enclose your source's exact words and punctuation.*
- *Place a parenthetical reference, if required, after the quoted material and before the quotation mark, if any, that ends the sentence, clause, or phrase with the material it documents.* ("Placement in Text," page 200 in Chapter 21, provides a thorough explanation about placing parenthetical references in the text of your paper.)

For a long quotation, *more than four lines of typing,* in a paper with double-spaced text:

- *Begin the quotation on a new line.*
- *Double-space before and after the quotation.*
- *Double-space the quotation itself.*
- *Indent the quotation ten spaces from the left margin but retain the normal right margin.* Indent an extra three spaces from the left for lines that begin paragraphs in the original.
- *Place a parenthetical reference, if required, after the quoted material and before the punctuation mark that ends the long quotation.*

Here's a sample showing double-spaced text followed by a long quotation:

The integration of the Normans into the culture of England was thorough but by no means smooth and easy. In The History of England from the Accession of James the Second, Lord Macaulay describes the degree of control achieved by the Normans after the Battle of Hastings and the opposition from Saxon rebels:

> The Battle of Hastings, and the events which followed it, not only placed a Duke of Normandy on the English throne, but gave up the whole population of England to the tyranny of the Norman race. The subjugation of a nation by a nation has seldom, even in Asia, been more complete. The country was portioned out among the captains of the invaders. Strong military institutions, closely connected with the institution of property, enabled the foreign conquerors to oppress the children of the soil. A cruel penal code, cruelly enforced, guarded the privileges, and even the sports, of the alien tyrants. Yet the subject race, though beaten down and trodden underfoot, still made its sting felt. Some bold men, the favorite heroes of our oldest ballads, betook themselves to the woods, and there, in defiance of curfew laws and forest laws, waged a predatory war

against their oppressors. Assassination
was an event of daily occurrence. Many
Normans suddenly disappeared, leaving no
trace. The corpses of many were found
bearing the marks of violence. Death by
torture was denounced against the
murderers, and strict search was made for
them, but generally in vain; for the
whole nation was in a conspiracy to
screen them (14–15).

In less than two centuries, these different people
had become indistinguishable for the most part.

Notice that the block indentation of the long quotation substitutes for quotation marks. The indentation indicates that you are quoting.

But remember, like a short quotation, the long one needs an introduction, too. In fact, the introduction to a long quotation often tells readers what you expect them to notice about it, thus giving them the right perspective. In the introduction to the passage from Lord Macaulay's history, we told you to watch for Norman control and Saxon opposition.

CREDITING YOUR SOURCE

Whenever you use borrowed material, the third step also is essential: crediting your source. You must identify the printed or spoken source of your information.

Failure to credit your source is dishonest, a form of cheating called *plagiarism*. Plagiarism is presenting someone else's words or ideas without giving credit. You avoid plagiarism by documenting the words and ideas of others when you use them in your writing. Chapters 21 and 22 show you in detail the mechanics of documenting; here we're concerned with the concept of properly presenting research material in the text of your paper. The following are forms of plagiarism:

- Presenting someone else's idea but not documenting it (so the idea seems to be yours).
- Presenting someone else's words without documenting them (so they seem to be part of your writing).
- Quoting someone else's words—perhaps even documenting them—but failing to use quotation marks. This problem is most likely to arise if

your paraphrases or summaries result in the type of unacknowledged, loose quotation you studied in the last chapter (page 177). Also, you may want to look again at the special techniques used to alter quotations (beginning on page 179).

Together, the next two chapters cover documentation. Chapter 21 explains the parenthetical references that you'll place in the text of your paper. Chapter 22 tells you how to prepare the Works Cited pages, the list of sources for your research paper. In combination these in-text parenthetical references and the Works Cited list make up the parenthetical documentation system.

EXERCISES

A. Explain the difference between primary and secondary sources. Give an example of each.

_____

_____

_____

_____

_____

B. What are the three key steps for using borrowed material skillfully?

_____

_____

_____

C. In Volume 1 of his memoirs (*Personal Memoirs of U. S. Grant,* published by Charles L. Webster & Company of New York in 1885), Ulysses S. Grant described his early army service in the 1846 war between the United States and Mexico. Besides explaining his part in the war, Grant offered his personal observations of its causes. After asserting that the annexation of Texas was "a conspiracy to acquire territory out of which slave states might be formed for the American Union," Grant wrote the following:

Even if the annexation itself could be justified, the manner in which the subsequent war was forced upon Mexico cannot. The fact is, annexationists wanted more territory than they could possibly lay any claim to, as part of the new acquisition. Texas, as an independent State, never had exercised jurisdiction over the territory between the Nueces River and the Rio Grande. Mexico had never recognized the independence of Texas, and maintained that, even if independent, the State had no claim south of the Nueces. I am aware that a treaty, made by the Texans with Santa Anna while he was under duress, ceded all the territory between the Nueces and the Rio Grande; but he was a prisoner of war when the treaty was made, and his life was in jeopardy. He knew, too, that he deserved execution at the hands of the Texans, if they should capture him. The Texans, if they had taken his life, would have only followed the example set by Santa

Anna himself a few years before, when he executed the entire garrison of the Alamo and the villagers of Goliad.

In taking military possession of Texas after annexation, the army of occupation, under General Taylor, was directed to occupy the disputed territory. The army did not stop at the Nueces and offer to negotiate for a settlement of the boundary question, but went beyond, apparently in order to force Mexico to initiate war.

1. Does this material represent primary or secondary source material?

2. What would be the advantages or disadvantages of quoting part or all of this material in a research paper about the Mexican War?

3. Quote at least two sentences from Grant and provide an introduction for the quotation. Be sure to quote accurately; if you alter the original material in any way, show the alteration as you learned to do in Chapter 19. Use "(1:55)" for the parenthetical documentation reference.

D. In the revised edition of *Herculaneum: Italy's Buried Treasure* (London: Thames and Hudson, 1985), Joseph Jay Deiss describes a sort of Roman prefabricated housing that was found among the ruins of Herculaneum, a city that along with Pompeii was buried by the eruption of Vesuvius in A.D. 79. (Vitruvius, who is mentioned in the excerpt below, was a Roman writer whose work dates to 16 B.C.)

The structure is called the "House of *Opus Craticium*" (Casa a Graticcio) because the phrase is the Latin designation for the type of construction, though sometimes it is called simply the "Trellis House." It is nothing more than a wooden skeleton of square frames, with each square filled in by stones and mortar crudely thrown together. Inner partitions frequently are flimsy laths of cane, thinly plastered. The general appearance is not unlike an English halftimbered house, though the roof is not gabled. This technique was developed in response to the growing population and housing crisis which accompanied Roman expansion. In Republican times structures were firmly built of heavy stone. After Augustus, brick and marble were the preferred materials of the Empire. But an economical, fast method of construction was needed, and *opus craticium* was the result. Vitruvius takes the trouble to point out its disadvantages: lack of permanence, dampness, danger of fire. It would astonish him to know that one such house survived two thousand years.

1. Does this material represent primary or secondary source material?

2. What would be the advantages or disadvantages of quoting part or all of this material in a research paper about the building techniques of the ancient Romans?

3. Quote a sentence or two from the passage above and provide an introduction for the quotation. Be sure to quote accurately; if you alter the original material, show the alteration using the techniques covered in Chapter 19. For the parenthetical documentation reference, use "(Deiss 115)" if your introduction does not contain the author's name or "(115)" if it names the author.

4. Prepare a paraphrase of the material you quoted in Exercise D3 and introduce the paraphrase. For the parenthetical documentation reference, use "(Deiss 115)" if your introduction does not contain the author's name or "(115)" if it does.

21
Parenthetical Documentation

Whether you use quotations, paraphrases, or summaries, you must document the sources of your information. In Part Three you learned a makeshift documentation system that let readers know whenever you were using outside sources for support. This chapter introduces a better system, one that not only tells readers that you are using borrowed material, but also gives them enough information to find the source.

The formats for documentation in this chapter and the next generally follow the second edition of the *MLA Handbook for Writers of Research Papers,* published by the Modern Language Association. This handbook is an accepted standard for documentation in many academic fields, especially the humanities. Other style guides also exist, of course, and there are differences in specific entry and presentation formats from one manual to another. We've chosen to follow MLA on most points because the guidance is thorough, reasonable, and widely accepted.

Don't be too concerned about differences among style manuals. Most differences exist to accommodate the varied needs of differing academic fields. More important, however, most documentation guides differ little on what should go into a specific documentation entry for an article or book. In practical terms, then, if you learn one system well—the one in this book, for example—you can adapt easily to the particular style required in another place at another time. You'll know basically what should be in documentation entries by anybody's standard, so you'll be able to see quickly the peculiarities of the "new" system you're required to follow. When you've practiced documentation in the style shown here, you'll have in hand one good, general-purpose documentation system.

PARENTHETICAL DOCUMENTATION SYSTEM

The parenthetical documentation system depends on the interaction of material you place in two portions of your research paper:

- *General source listing.* At the end of your research paper you provide an alphabetized listing, called Works Cited, with full bibliographic information about each source document you used. The list provides a general reference to your sources but, of course, doesn't identify the specific portions you used for the quotations, summaries, and paraphrases in the body of the paper:
- *Specific portion reference.* Within the body of your paper, along with each presentation of material borrowed from your sources, you include in parentheses a documentation reference to the specific portion(s) of the source or sources supporting your text. This parenthetical information provides a reference to the data in the Works Cited listing so readers can connect the general and specific documentation portions.

When readers combine the information in parentheses in the body of your paper with the full bibliographic information in your Works Cited listing, they have the data they need to locate each source and to find the specific portion you used.

For example, readers might find this in your paper:

```
At least one western authority believes too many
skiers in the eastern United States are unaware of
the beauties and challenges that are available in
the southwest corner of Colorado (Edwards 34).
```

The *specific portion reference* is *(Edwards 34)*. *Edwards* tells readers to look for that entry in the Works Cited listing, the *general source listing,* where they'd find this:

```
Edwards, Marilou. Skiing in Colorado. Albuquerque:
    La Madera, 1982.
```

The *34* in the parenthetical reference in the body of the paper indicates that the material supporting the statement appears on page 34 of Marilou Edwards' *Skiing in Colorado.*

Clearly, then, you want to learn the conventions for both the general source and specific reference portions of the parenthetical documentation system. The next chapter focuses on format conventions for the Works Cited listing (the general source portion of parenthetical documentation). The rest of this chapter treats the specific portion references that give the system its name: the parenthetical references.

PARENTHETICAL REFERENCES

Basic Content

Parenthetical references in the text of your paper should give your readers the following information:

- *A reference to the opening of the corresponding entry in the Works Cited list.* If the Works Cited entry shows only one author, you'll give that author's last name. The reference also could be two or three last names, one person's name with "et al.," the name of a group, a shortened version of the title, or a name with the title, depending in every case on what information is necessary to identify clearly the *one* work in Works Cited that you are referring to. ("Basic Forms" below details the various possibilities.)
- *Identification of the location within that work of the material you're documenting.* Normally this will be a reference to a single page or several pages. However, when your Works Cited listing gives a multivolume work, the parenthetical reference usually will require a volume number with the page(s). If the reference is to a one-page article, to an article in an encyclopedia that alphabetizes its articles, or to a source that has no pagination (such as a film or videocassette), you'll not give a place reference.

Basic Forms

The material required for the parenthetical reference varies somewhat with the nature of the work you refer to from your Works Cited list and how much of it you are citing. (For rules on showing inclusive page numbers, see page 225.)

Work with One Name Listed

When the Works Cited listing begins with only one person's name, use the last name and the page reference: (Brown 281) or (Brown 281–83). If the name has a qualifier such as "ed." or "trans.," you still use only the last name.

Work with Two or Three Names Listed

If the Works Cited entry opens with two or three names, include those names in the parenthetical reference: (Wesson and Jones 117) or (Stockton, Avery, and Beal 63).

Work with One Name and "et al."

If the Works Cited entry begins with a name and "et al.," which means "and others," include the "et al." in your parenthetical reference: (Steinnem et al. 92–93).

Work with Group as Author

Treat the group just like another author: (President's Commission on Energy 315). A reference such as this, of course, could easily interrupt a reader's train of thought; we'll discuss on page 199 how to avoid that problem by streamlining the parenthetical references.

Work Listed by Title

If the Works Cited entry begins with a title, use the title, or a reasonable shortened version of it, in the parenthetical reference. Be careful in shortening the title, though, because readers must find the words you give in an alphabetized list; make sure the shortened title includes the word by which the work is alphabetized in your Works Cited listing. A reference to *A Short Study of Linguistics for Beginners* might look like this: (*Short Study of Linguistics* 53). Again, streamlining might be preferable.

Multivolume Work

In a reference to a multivolume work, normally you'll give a volume number with the page reference: (Martin 2:65–66). This is a reference to pages 65 to 66 of volume 2 of a multivolume work alphabetized in Works Cited under "Martin." However, if the entry in Works Cited clearly identifies only a single volume of the multivolume work, then the parenthetical reference need not include the volume number.

Multiple Works Listed for the Same Name(s)

When two or more works are alphabetized in Works Cited for the same name(s), include in the parenthetical reference the title, or a shortened version of it, of the specific work you're referring to. If two books are listed for Brian Pierce, then a reference to one of them would look like this: (Pierce, *Amateur Golfing* 27). Here's another candidate for streamlining.

Citing an Entire Work

If you need to document a textual reference to an entire work, then a page reference is inappropriate, so the parentheses would contain only the author element: (Brown). Streamlining, however, will eliminate the need for any parenthetical reference.

Indirect Reference

Although you always should attempt to find the original source for a quotation, sometimes you'll have to quote information from a source that quotes the original. If you quote or paraphrase a quotation, add "qtd. in" (for "quoted in") or "paraphrased from" to the parenthetical reference, as here:

```
John Harris calls literary critic Edmund Wilson a
"pompous, close-minded reader" for his insistence
that detective fiction is not worth reading (qtd.
in Armstrong 13).
```

Multiple Works in a Reference

To include two or more works in a single parenthetical reference, list each as you would for itself and use semicolons to separate them: (Jackson 53–54;

Morgan 15). Again, streamlining may help reduce the interruption, but if you need to show a long, disruptive list, consider using an actual footnote instead (see the section "Notes with Parenthetical Documentation" below).

Streamlining Parenthetical References

Several times we've mentioned the possibility of streamlining. The idea is to keep the information with the parentheses as short as possible so readers are not distracted. You accomplish this by giving part or all of the needed reference in the introduction to the borrowed material. If the introduction includes the name of a book's author, then the parentheses might contain only the page reference:

```
Brown notes General Grant's occasional impatience
with the progress of his attrition campaign in 1864
(281).
```

Because Brown's name is in the introduction to the material from his book, the parenthetical reference needs only the page reference.

Especially in the case where your Works Cited list has several works by the same author and you must refer to one of those works, streamlining lessens the interruption of the parenthetical reference. Without streamlining, a reference might look like this:

```
Although the Battle of the Crater, for which Union
coal miners tunneled under the Confederate
fortification lines near Petersburg, captures our
imagination today, it has been labeled a bloody
tactical blunder because of the cost in lives
(Winchester, Civil War After Gettysburg 314).
```

The version below streamlines that long parenthetical reference:

```
Although the Battle of the Crater, for which Union
coal miners tunneled under the Confederate
fortification lines near Petersburg, captures our
imagination today, in The Civil War After
Gettysburg Winchester labels it a bloody tactical
blunder because of the cost in lives (314).
```

Keep in mind that streamlining does not permit omission of required material, but it can reduce the interruption of parenthetical references.

Placement in Text

Place the parenthetical references in the text of your paper so that they interrupt the flow of thought as little as possible. Put the parentheses as close as reasonably possible after the end of the material you're documenting, but always at the end of a clause or phrase so the reference doesn't intrude. Normally, the parenthetical reference can be placed at the end of a sentence. Even with quotations, the reference doesn't have to come *immediately* after the quotation marks:

> Brown asserts that General Grant's "inability to remain patient with the pace of his attrition campaign" led to the horrendous Union losses in a mere half-hour at Cold Harbor, Virginia (281).

Of course, don't delay the parenthetical reference until the end of a sentence if readers could be confused about what material the reference documents:

> Although Brown notes Grant's occasional impatience with the progress of his attrition campaign in 1864 (281), the overall strategy of attrition--Grant against Lee's Army of Northern Virginia and Sherman against the Southern homeland supply base--brought the Union victory.

The reference here is in the middle of the sentence because only the first portion is attributable to the source. Note, however, that the parentheses do come at the end of a clause so the reference intrudes as little as possible.

Position Relative to Sentence Punctuation

Notice that the parenthetical reference in the first of the two samples above preceded the period at the end of the sentence, and the parentheses in the second sample came before the comma that ended the clause. Always place your parenthetical references before the punctuation mark, if any, that ends the sentence, clause, or phrase with the material you're documenting. If a quotation ends the sentence, clause, or phrase, place the parenthetical reference between the ending quotation marks and the punctuation for the sentence, clause, or phrase:

> The Union losses at Cold Harbor, Virginia, can be attributed to General Grant's "inability to remain patient with the pace of his attrition campaign" (Brown 281).

Notes with Parenthetical Documentation

Parenthetical references will take care of almost all documentation references, but they don't accommodate digressions from the text. Avoid long side arguments, but if you must add notes to support your text, use standard footnote or endnote entries: that is, use parenthetical references for your normal documentation, but also use notes for the explanatory digressions, like this one:

> [1]Smithson disagrees with Brown about Grant's blunder at Cold Harbor (224), but offers little support. See also Winchester 271; Souther 416–18; and Blake 76.

EXERCISES

A. Given the Works Cited entries below as the general source listing for a research paper, write parenthetical references to show the specific portion references required for the numbered exercise items that follow. (Just show the parentheses and what would go in them; don't be concerned for this exercise with placing the references into textual passages.)

> Carter, Sheila F. *Case Studies of Drugs and Business.* 2 vols. Arlington: Burning Tree, 1986.
>
> Jackson, Greg, and Rachel Brooks. *Drugs in the Workplace.* New York: Shirlington, 1987.
>
> Kendall, Oliver, ed. *Studies in Office Management.* Ann Arbor: U of Michigan P, 1987.
>
> Llosa, Julio. "Employees Object to Testing." *Productivity Issues* Dec. 1986: 105–12.
>
> Van Beck, Theresa. "Mandatory Drug Testing and the Courts." *Journal of Business Management* 12 (1986): 453–74.

1. Page 217 of *Drugs in the Workplace.*

2. Page 455 of "Mandatory Drug Testing and the Courts."

3. Pages 115 through 117 of *Studies in Office Management.*

4. Page 105 of "Employees Object to Testing."

5. Pages 34 to 35 of volume 1 of *Case Studies of Drugs and Business.*

6. Page 107 of "Employees Object to Testing" if another source by Julio Llosa appeared in the same Works Cited listing.

7. A quotation from Gayle Stein's *Drug Testing and Rehabilitation Programs* that is quoted on page 471 of Theresa Van Beck's "Mandatory Drug Testing and the Courts."

B. Rewrite the following passages to streamline their parenthetical references. In your rewritten versions, be sure to modify the material inside the parentheses to account for the information you incorporate into the introduction to the borrowed material. And be sure you've followed the rules for punctuation relative to the parenthetical reference and quotation marks.

1. According to one drug rehabilitation specialist, "when employers identify drug users early and offer rehabilitation programs that are reasonable but that also have teeth in them, employees do accept help and get well" (Merrill, "Employer-Sponsored Drug Rehabilitation Programs" 72).

2. It may be true that "mandatory drug testing is the only scheme yet devised to ensure that factory workers are alert and aware enough to perform in hazardous work environments" (Mills and Harris, *Drugs and the Factory* 144), yet employees who don't abuse drugs have every right to object to being tested as if they did.

22
Works Cited

As you saw in Chapter 21, parenthetical references in the body of your research paper are possible because they refer to a *general source listing* at the end of the paper. This chapter focuses on that source listing—first on the format of the pages for the list as a whole, then on the formats of the entries that appear in the list, and finally on a few special format rules that affect the appearance of parts of some entries.

WORKS CITED PAGE FORMAT

The usual name for the listing of works at the end of the paper is *Works Cited*. This title assumes that the listing contains all (and only) the works you cite in the text of your paper; it does not include others that you read but that did not account for ideas or data in your paper. Your instructor might ask you to include the other works you read during research, in which case you could change the title to *Works Consulted*.

For the Works Cited page(s), start the list on a new page, numbering that page in sequence with the rest of your paper. Here's how the page should look:

```
                                              Richards 9

                        Works Cited
Edwards, Marilou. Skiing in Colorado.
       Albuquerque: La Madera, 1982.
Jenkins, Barry. Looking for Powder. New York:
       Shirlington, 1983.
Kelly, Timothy P. "What's Happening to the
       Western Ski Paradises?" Sports Today 10 Feb.
       1984: 57-63.
```

- Use the same margins as for the rest of the pages of your research paper.
- Center the title one inch from the top of the page.
- Double-space after the title to find the line on which to begin the first entry.
- Double-space both within and between entries. (*Note:* Your instructor may prefer you to single-space within individual entries and double-space only between entries.)
- Begin the first line of each entry on the left margin, but for all subsequent lines of an entry indent five spaces.
- List entries in alphabetical order.

WHAT WORKS CITED ENTRIES CONTAIN

It has become commonplace to say that Works Cited documentation entries contain three basic parts: author, title, and publication information. And that's true enough for the most simple citations, which usually make up the majority of entries in a Works Cited list. Unfortunately, there are dozens of exceptions to that basic pattern. We believe, then, that the following five basic groups more accurately describe a documentation entry and will better help you understand the job ahead:

1. Person(s) or group responsible for the piece of material you're documenting
2. The title(s)
3. Amplifying information, to help identify or describe the work precisely
4. Publishing information, or similar information that will help someone find the work
5. Identification of the portion you are citing.

Here are those groups in a simple three-part citation:

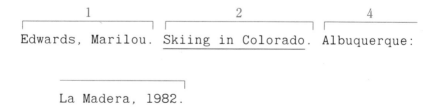

Group 3 is missing because no amplifying information is necessary to describe the book, and group 5 is unnecessary because the entry is for the entire book, not a portion of it. An entry for an essay in a collection of essays, however, might have all five basic groups, as this one does:

Clemens, Norman H. "The Ceausescu Dynasty in

Romania." Studies in East European Politics.

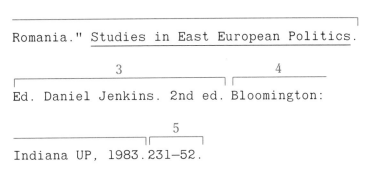

Ed. Daniel Jenkins. 2nd ed. Bloomington:

Indiana UP, 1983.231–52.

Documentation entries can be even more complex. Yet generally, despite complexities, the information required falls into the five groups.

ENTRIES FOR BOOKS

General Form: Books

Divided here into the five basic groups are the thirteen elements you may need for a book citation. Few entries actually have all thirteen; the simple citation in the previous section has only five elements, while the sample complex citation has nine. Obviously you include only those elements that are appropriate for the book you're documenting.

(1) Person(s) or Group Responsible for the Piece of Material You're Documenting

- *Name(s) of individual(s) or group.* Usually this is an author, but it can be an editor, translator, or organization. The key is identifying the people *directly responsible* for the particular piece of material you're documenting. Use names as they appear on the title page of the book. Do not include professional or educational titles, such as "M.S." or "Ph.D." If the entry is to begin with a person's name, reverse the name for alphabetizing (last-first-middle instead of first-middle-last).

(2) The Title(s)

- *Title of a part of a book.* You'll need this when you're documenting an essay, a poem, a short story, and so forth, within an anthology, or when you cite a division of a book (such as the Introduction).
- *Title of the book.* If a book has both a title and subtitle, give both with a colon and a single space between them (omit the colon if the title itself ends with punctuation, such as a question mark). (Special rules begin-

ning on page 223 give guidance for capitalization, quotation marks, and underlining in titles.)

(3) Amplifying Information, to Help Identify or Describe the Work Precisely

- *Translator(s)*. One translation is rarely like another, so it's necessary to show the translator(s) of the work.
- *Editor(s)*
- *Edition*. Readers will assume you're citing the first edition, without revisions, unless you indicate otherwise. Portions of different editions of the same book will be different, so you need to show exactly which one you used.
- *Number of volumes*. An indication of the number of volumes in a multivolume set will appear before the publication data, and a volume number also can appear with the page reference, depending on how you refer to the material.
- *Series*. If the work you're citing is part of a series, give the series name and the number of the work in the series (e.g., "Studies in Anthropology, No. 5").

(4) Publishing Information, or Similar Information That Will Help Someone Find the Work

- *Place of publication*. Look for the place of publication on the title or copyright page or at the back of the book, especially for a book published outside the United States. If several cities are listed, use the one listed first unless you have some reason for using a different one. Give the state or country along with the city if the city is not likely to be recognized or could be confused with another city with the same name.
- *Publisher*. You need not name the publisher for a book printed before 1900. For books printed since 1900, use a shortened version of the publisher's name; e.g., "Holt" rather than "Holt, Rinehart and Winston." (See pages 224–25 for special rules on dealing with publishers' names and special imprints.)
- *Date of publication*. Again, look for the publication date on the title page, on the copyright page, or at the back of the book. If no publication date appears, give the latest copyright date. Ignore dates for multiple printings; however, if you are citing a work in other than its first edition, use the publication date for the edition you're using, not the original date. For example, if a book in its third edition shows dates of 1979, 1984, and 1987, use 1987.

(5) Identification of the Portion You Are Citing

You'll use this part of an entry only when you're citing a part of a book (e.g., an essay or Introduction).

- *Volume number.* For a multivolume work, the volume indication may appear with the page number, depending on how you're referring to the material.
- *Page numbers.* Show the *inclusive* page numbers for the portion of the book you're citing. Don't be concerned if you refer to only one or a few of those pages in the text of your paper; those specific page references will be clear in your parenthetical references in the text. Here you must show the pagination for the entire piece. (See page 225 for special rules on showing inclusive page numbers.)

Sample Entries: Books

Following are samples illustrating recommended formats for citations for books. A word of caution: These samples were designed to illustrate particular portions of a book citation. They do not cover every variation you may run across. (A list of samples detailing all the variations would be unbelievably long.) If the book you're citing doesn't quite fit a sample, adapt the format to fit your needs, but be sure to include all the appropriate information you've just read about in the preceding section. *Note:* Since the samples have been listed to demonstrate points about formats, no attempt has been made to alphabetize them, except for entries under "Two or More Books by the Same 'Author(s).' " In yours Works Cited pages, of course, you'll list all works in alphabetical order.

One Author

Edwards, Marilou. Skiing in Colorado.
        Albuquerque: La Madera, 1982.

Two or Three Authors

Only the name of the person listed first is given out of normal order (last-first-middle rather than first-middle-last). Be sure to use authors' names as they appear on the book's title page. Do not include professional or educational titles, such as "M.S." or "Ph.D." Names of multiple authors may not be alphabetized on the title page; list them in the order in which they appear.

Davila, Maria, and Linda Cole. A Basic Guide
        to Spanish Grammar. New York: Holt, 1983.
Cox, Benjamin R., G. R. Blackwell, and Paul
        Cartwright, Jr. The Maghreb: Is Unity
        Possible in North Africa? Austin: U of
        Texas P, 1982.

More Than Three Authors

For more than three authors, give only the one listed first in the book and follow that with "et al." (for "and others").

> Linzy, N. A., et al. <u>Making Your Way in a World Created by Men</u>. New York: Shirlington, 1980.

Group as Author

When a group or agency is responsible for a book, treat that group as the author and list its name first, even though the group's name may appear in the book's title or may appear again as publisher. List the group or agency name in normal order. ("GPO" in this entry is the accepted abbreviation for "Government Printing Office," which prints U.S. federal publications. Note that "D.C." is omitted.)

> President's Commission on Energy. <u>Report of the President's Commission on Energy</u>. Washington: GPO, 1980.

Government and International Body Publications

Many government agency publications are simple enough to be treated as books with groups as authors, with the responsible agency serving as author, as in the entry above. Occasionally government publications show a specific person as author; you can begin with that person (as in the second sample below), or you can show the individual author after the title (as in the first sample).

For the *Congressional Record,* you need show only the full date and the inclusive pages for the portion being cited. For other congressional documents, give the government and body, house, committee (if appropriate), document title, number and session of Congress, and type and number of publication, followed by standard publication data. Congressional documents include bills (S 16; HR 63), resolutions (S. Res. 16; H. Res. 63), reports (S. Rept. 16; H. Rept. 63), and documents (S. Doc. 16; H. Doc. 63).

There are also state and local government documents, foreign government documents, and those of international bodies (such as the United Nations). Begin these as you would a U.S. federal publication, naming first the government or international body (e.g., "Indiana. Dept. of Revenue" or "United Nations. Committee for Economic Development").

> United States. Dept. of State. <u>The Pan-Arabic Movement in Africa</u>. By Louis L. Clark. Washington: GPO, 1981.

Clark, Louis L. The Pan-Arabic Movement in
Africa. U.S. Dept. of State. Washington:
GPO, 1981.

Cong. Rec. 8 May 1979: 2756-57.

United States. Cong. House. Subcommittee on
Crime of the Committee on Justice. The
Growth of Organized Crime in America.
94th Cong., 2nd sess. H. Rept. 616.
Washington: GPO, 1976.

United Nations. Committee for Economic
Development. Petroleum Resources in West
Africa. Elmsford: Pergamon, 1982.

Author Not Given

If no author is given in a book, begin the entry with the title. (When you alphabetize the entries for your Works Cited pages, you'll go by the first word in the title other than an article—that is, other than *A, An,* or *The.*) Of course, treat books with groups as authors or government and international body publications as indicated above, even though these books frequently show no individual as author.

A Collection of Neapolitan Idioms. New York:
Bantam, 1983.

Editor(s)

If your use of an edited book, for the most part, is the text of the work itself, then the name(s) of the editor(s) ("ed." or "eds.") should appear after the title, as in the first sample below. However, if the work of the editor(s)— including introductory or other extratextual comments—is being cited, begin the entry with the editor(s), as in the second sample. Moreover, if you are citing an anthology or other collection—rather than a piece within the collection—use the second format below (for a piece in a collection, see "Part of a Collection" below).

Winslow, Elijah. A Country Doctor in the Great
Rebellion. Ed. Eric Wells. Ann Arbor: U
of Michigan P, 1979.

Wells, Eric, ed. A Country Doctor in the Great
Rebellion. By Elijah Winslow. Ann Arbor:
U of Michigan P, 1979.

Translator(s)

Normally you'll show the translator(s) of a book after the title, as in the first sample below. However, as with editors, if you are citing primarily commentary by the translator(s), then begin with the translator(s), as in the second sample. If the book has both a translator and an editor, show the translator first, as in the third sample.

> Solzhenitsyn, Alexander. One Day in the Life
>   of Ivan Denisovich. Trans. Irene Mason
>   and Claude Brown. New York: Harper, 1978.
> Mason, Irene, and Claude Brown, trans. One Day
>   in the Life of Ivan Denisovich. By
>   Alexander Solzhenitsyn. New York: Harper,
>   1978.
> Kafka, Franz. Amerika. Trans. Kevin Scott. Ed.
>   Joseph P. Watson. Boston: Little, 1981.

Two or More Books by the Same "Author(s)"

Sometimes two or more entries in your Works Cited listing have *exactly* the same names at the beginning for the person(s) or group responsible for the piece you're documenting. In such a case, give the name(s) only for the first entry; in the following entries type *three hyphens* and a period in place of the name(s). *The three hyphens signify the same name(s),* so if a person named is shown in the first entry as, say, an author and in the next as a translator, you should use the three hyphens for the name in the second entry, following the hyphens with a comma and "trans." (Notice, in the samples below, that the order is determined by the alphabetical order of the titles, since the author block is the same for each.)

> Alexander, Charles. "Amethyst Visions" and
>   Other Poems. New York: Macmillan, 1977.
> ---. Collected Poems. New York: Macmillan,
>   1981.
> ---, trans. The Flowers of Evil. By Charles
>   Baudelaire. New York: Schocken, 1980.

However, if an entry with a single name is followed by an entry in which the first of multiple authors is that same name, do not use the three hyphens in the second entry. Three hyphens can stand for more than one name, but the name block in each case must be *exactly* the same.

> Mason, Irene, trans. The Cancer Ward. By
>   Alexander Solzhenitsyn. New York: Harper,
>   1980.

Mason, Irene, and Claude Brown, trans. August **211**
    1914. By Alexander Solzhenitsyn. New
    York: Harper, 1981.
———, trans. One Day in the Life of Ivan
    Denisovich. By Alexander Solzhenitsyn.
    New York: Harper, 1978.

Finally, the three hyphens also should be used when groups, governments, or international bodies serve as authors. And since government entries begin with the name of the government and the name of the body or agency sponsoring the work, you may need more than one set of three hyphens. The samples below illustrate the author blocks for several government publications.

Indiana. Dept. of Health.
———. Dept. of Revenue.
United States. Cong. House.
———. ———. Senate.
———. Dept. of Energy.

Extratextual Material

In citations for such extratextual material as an Introduction or Afterword, give the name of the author of that division of the book, followed by the name of the extratextual piece; the author of the work itself follows the book title. If the author of the extratextual material is also the author of the book, give only the last name after the book title, as in the second sample.

Knox, Christopher. Introduction. The Lure of
    the Bush. By Arthur W. Upfield. New York:
    Shirlington, 1978. i—xii.
Bourjaily, Vance. Afterword. Confessions of a
    Spent Youth. By Bourjaily. Albuquerque:
    La Madera, 1979. 450—52.

Part of a Collection

For parts of anthologies, collections of articles, and casebooks, the title of the piece precedes the title of the work. Normally the title of the piece will appear in quotation marks; however, if it was published originally as a book, underline (or italicize) it instead. Notice that as for an extratextual piece of a book discussed above, the inclusive pages for the piece of the collection end the citation.

```
Miller, Barbara. "Encounter While Jogging."
    Short Fiction for Today. Ed. Patrick S.
    O'Neal. New York: Schocken, 1983. 217–35.
```

Cross-References

If you're documenting multiple pieces from the same collection, you have a choice. You can treat each piece as a part of a collection, giving full data for the collection itself each time. Or you can give one entry for the collection and then simplify the citations for the pieces by referring to the entry for the collection. Keep in mind, however, that each specific piece of the collection that you refer to in the text of your paper requires its own entry in the Works Cited section. Thus, with cross-referencing you save repeating some information in each of the citations for a piece of the collection, but you then must add an entry for the collection itself.

```
Miller, Barbara. "Encounter While Jogging."
    O'Neal 217–35.
O'Neal, Patrick S., ed. Short Fiction for
    Today. New York: Schocken, 1983.
Richardson, Norman M. "Meeting My Karma."
    O'Neal 198–216.
```

Republished Books

If you use a republished book (a new publication of an out-of-print book or a paperback version of a book originally published in hard cover), show the original publication date before the new publication information.

```
Baker, Scott. Escape from Despair. 1955. New
    York: Avon, 1981.
```

Edition Other Than First

Readers will assume the book is a first edition unless you indicate otherwise, such as second edition ("2nd ed."), alternate edition ("Alt. ed."), revised edition ("Rev. ed."), and so on.

```
Kingston, Neil. The Art of Neapolitan Cooking.
    3rd ed. New York: Shirlington, 1982.
```

Series

If a book is part of a series, give the series name and the number of the work in the series.

Barrett, Arthur. The People of Mesa Verde. **213**
    Studies in Anthropology, No. 5.
    Albuquerque: La Madera, 1981.

Multivolume Work

Despite the various possibilities below for citations of works with two or more volumes, all include the total number of volumes as amplifying information.

For a specific page reference to a multivolume work, the parenthetical reference in the text of your paper usually will include the volume number with the page reference (e.g., 2:111–12). However, if in your paper you never need to document from more than one volume of the set, you can end the Works Cited entry with the volume number (as below) and give only page references in the text itself (e.g., 111–12 instead of 2:111–12).

Anderson, Todd. The Etruscans. 3 vols.
    Nashville: Vanderbilt UP, 1979. Vol. 2.

If the single volume you cite for your paper has its own title, include the specific volume reference between the individual and multivolume titles, as below. Again, references in the text of your paper need not include the volume number.

Payne, Heather. Roman Engineering. Vol. 2 of
    Architecture and Engineering of the Roman
    World. 3 vols. New York: Holt, 1981.

If your paper requires references to two or more volumes, then use the more general multivolume citation in your Works Cited listing (as below) and include the volume number with each parenthetical reference in the text.

Anderson, Todd. The Etruscans. 3 vols.
    Nashville: Vanderbilt UP, 1979.

If the volumes of the multivolume work were published over a period of years, then the publication date block should show the first and last years of the set.

Haines, Tracy. Indians of the American
    Southwest. 7 vols. Albuquerque: U of New
    Mexico P, 1971–83.

If the multivolume set has not been completed, include "to date" with the number of volumes and follow the publication date of the first volume with a hyphen and a space.

> West, Anita. <u>Ancient Civilizations of Latin</u>
>   <u>America</u>. 3 vols. to date. New York:
>   Shirlington, 1979– .

When you cite a piece in a multivolume collection of pieces, show the volume number with the inclusive page number for the specific part of the work.

> Levy, Nathan. "New York Bliss." <u>Twentieth</u>
>   <u>Century Short Fiction</u>. Ed. Russell S.
>   Harper. 2 vols. New York: Macmillan,
>   1980. 2:617–42.

Published Conference Proceedings

If the book title doesn't include information about the conference, provide amplifying information after the title.

> <u>Resource Planning for the 1990s</u>. Proc. of a
>   Conference of the American Engineering
>   Association. 24–26 Sept. 1984. Madison: U
>   of Wisconsin, 1984.

Pamphlet

Treat pamphlets as books.

> Hunter, Max. <u>Selling Yourself to Industry</u>.
>   Washington: Spinnaker, 1982.

Missing Publishing or Pagination Data

Use the following abbreviations for missing publication or pagination information:

no place of publication: n. p.

no publisher: n. p.

no date: n. d.

no pagination: n. pag.

The abbreviations for "no place" and "no publisher" are the same, but their positions left or right of the colon will allow readers to tell the difference.

When a book has no pagination indicated, your Works Cited entry needs to contain "N. pag." so that readers will understand why parenthetical references in the text of your paper do not show page numbers.

<u>Being Your Own Publisher</u>. N. p.: n. p., 1981.
    N. pag.

ENTRIES FOR ARTICLES IN PERIODICALS

Periodicals are publications that are issued periodically on some sort of schedule—quarterly, bimonthly, weekly, daily, and so forth. Authorities group periodicals into three classes: journals, magazines, and newspapers. Newspapers are easy to recognize, but there isn't an absolute distinction between journals and magazines.

Many journals don't have the word *journal* in their titles, and not all periodicals with *journal* in their titles are considered journals for documentation. Nevertheless, some differentiation is necessary because the data required after the publisher in a Works Cited entry differ for the various types of periodicals. Fortunately, we don't need a scholarly distinction; instead we can make fairly simple divisions based on how the periodicals paginate their issues and on how frequently they publish issues. Therefore, the sample formats for periodicals can be distinguished on the following bases:

- *A periodical paged continuously throughout a volume is treated as a "journal, with continuous pagination."* (If, for example, the first issue of a particular volume ends with page 171 and the next issue begins with page 172, the periodical uses continuous pagination.)
- *When each issue of the periodical is paginated independently it is treated as a "journal, with issues paged independently" if it is published less frequently than once every two months.* (If each issue of a periodical begins with page 1, the issues are paginated independently.)
- *All other periodicals are distinguished by frequency of publication.*

General Form: Articles in Periodicals

(1) Person(s) or Group Responsible for the Piece of Material You're Documenting

- *Author(s).* If an article is signed, the name(s) (sometimes only initials) will appear at either the beginning or the end of the article. Treat multiple authors as you would for book entries.

(2) The Title(s)

- *Title of article.* (See pages 223–24 for guidance on capitalization, quotation marks, and underlining in titles.)

(3) Amplifying Information to Help Identify or Describe the Work Precisely

• *Type of article.* You'll need this only for editorials, letters to the editor, and reviews.

(4) Publishing Information, or Similar Information That Will Help Someone Find the Work

• *Name of periodical.* The name of the periodical itself is all the publishing information that is necessary. Drop any introductory article from the title. If readers aren't likely to recognize the title by itself, insert after the title the name of the institution or, particularly for newspapers, the city, enclosing the name in brackets.

(5) Identification of the Portion You Are Citing

• *Series number.* If a journal has been published in more than one series (e.g., old and new), indicate the applicable one. Otherwise readers may have difficulty determining where to find the article you used.
• *Newspaper edition.* If a newspaper has both morning and evening or special editions, you may need to show which you used; check the masthead of the newspaper when you read it. The same article often will appear in more than one edition, but not necessarily in the same place in each.
• *Volume and/or issue number(s).* For *journals,* you'll include the volume and/or issue number for the issue you used.
• *Date.* All entries will include at least the year, but whether year only, month and year, or complete date depends on the type of periodical.
• *Page number(s).* (See page 225 for guidance on showing inclusive page numbers.)

Sample Entries: Articles in Periodicals

As with the samples for books, the following entries were designed to illustrate particular portions of documentation entries. You may need to adapt the formats to fit your needs, but be sure to include all pertinent information listed in the preceding discussion of general form. *Note:* The three-hyphen form for repeated authors (see "Two or More Books by the Same 'Author(s)' " on pages 210–11) applies to entries for articles in periodicals as well, but is not repeated below.

Journal, with Continuous Pagination

This type of entry includes the volume number followed by the year in parentheses, a colon, and then inclusive page numbers for the article.

```
Morris, Laura. "Morocco's Claim to the Western
     Sahara." African Studies 16 (1981): 218-
     34.
```

Journal, with Issues Paged Independently

After the volume number, add a period and the issue number.

Thompson, Lee. "Animal Symbolism in the Novels
    of John Irving." American Fiction 12.3
    (1982): 55–81.

Journal, with Issue Numbers Only

If a journal does not use volume numbers, use the issue number as if it
were a volume number.

Gardner, Barry. "Life Signs in Pottery
    Decorations of the Southwest American
    Indians." Indian Art 4 (1980): 23–31.

Journal, with Series

If a journal has been published in more than one series, precede the volume number with the series. Use a numerical designator such as "4th ser."
or "ns" and "os" for "new series" and "original series."

Martinelli, Luigi. "Naples' Phlegraean Fields:
    Cycle of History or Lurking Tragedy?"
    World Science ns 7 (1983): 563–79.

Monthly or Bimonthly Periodical

Instead of volume and/or issue, use month(s) and year.

Reed, Donald S. "The Significance of Black
    Holes." Space Technology Mar. 1982:
    15–30.

Weekly or Biweekly Periodical

Whether a magazine or a newspaper, for a periodical published once a week
or once every two weeks, give the complete date rather than volume and issue
numbers.

Berry, Edmund. "Endangered Species in·
    America." American Wildlife 13 Jan. 1984:
    47–54.

Daily Newspaper

Show the newspaper's name as it appears at the top of the first page, omit-
ting any beginning article (e.g., *The Washington Post* becomes *Washington
Post*), except for *The New York Times,* which retains the article. If the news-

paper title doesn't name the city, give the city and state in brackets after the title, as in the first sample below. The first sample also illustrates how to indicate the edition for a newspaper that prints more than one edition a day (again, check the masthead on the first page to see if an edition is given).

For inclusive page numbers, check the pagination system of the newspaper carefully. If the newspaper doesn't have sections or if it numbers continuously through the edition, you'll need only the page number(s) after the date (e.g., 13 Mar. 1984: 38). If the newspaper includes the section number with the page number(s), the appropriate section-number combination can follow the date (e.g., 13 Mar. 1984: A12–A13). But if the section designator is not combined with the page number(s), then show the section designator between the date and the page number(s) (e.g., 13 Mar. 1984, sec. 3: 12).

> Davis, Raymond. "Is That Really Mud in the
> River?" Star–Herald [St. Louis, MO] 13
> Mar. 1984, early morning ed.: A12–A13.
> Washington, Keith. "Inflation Versus
> Modernization in NATO." Washington Post
> 12 May 1984: B10.

Author Unknown

Whatever the type of periodical, if no author is given, begin with the article's title. The format for the rest of the entry, of course, depends on the type of periodical in which the article appears; the sample below is for a monthly magazine.

> "Making Fitness Fun." Sports and You Oct.
> 1985: 36–45.

Editorial

Begin with the author if named, otherwise with the editorial's title, and follow the title with "Editorial." The rest of the entry depends on the source; our sample uses a daily newspaper.

> "Why Mine the Red Sea?" Editorial. Washington
> Post 29 Aug. 1984: A17.

Letter to the Editor

Since letters to editors can appear in any type of periodical, the portion after the title depends on the type of publication in which the letter appears. We show a journal (with continuous pagination).

> Bradley, Dan. Letter. Engineering Review 15
> (1980): 561.

Review

Reviews may be signed or unsigned and titled or untitled, and they may appear in any type of periodical. For a signed review, use the name(s) of the reviewer(s), the review title (if there is one), and then "Rev. of . . . ." For an unsigned review, give the title (if there is one); if not, begin with "Rev. of . . . ." The first entry below shows a signed and titled review in a monthly magazine; the second sample is for an unsigned, untitled review in a daily newspaper.

> Donner, L. Michael. "Blues on Wall Street."
> Rev. of The Bonfire of the Vanities, by
> Tom Wolfe. Review of Fiction Dec. 1987:
> 15-18.
> Rev. of Blue Highway: A Journey into America,
> by William Least Heat Moon. Washington
> Post 15 Dec. 1982: D8.

ENTRIES FOR OTHER SOURCES

General Form: Other Sources

This mixed group of reference types lacks a "standard form." Still, the general idea for all documentation entries applies: (1) person(s) or group responsible for the piece of material you're documenting; (2) the title(s); (3) amplifying information, to help identify or describe the work precisely; (4) publishing information, or similar information that will help someone find the work; and (5) identification of the portion you are citing.

Sample Entries: Other Sources

If you can't find a sample that fits your needs exactly, adapt entries or create a format, but keep the general guidelines in mind.

Speech

Use the speech title, if known; when it isn't, use in its place a designator such as Address, Keynote speech, or Lecture (titles, as below, go in quotation marks, of course, but the descriptive designators would be used without quotation marks).

> Petrikonius, Jennifer. "Managing Both Home and
> Business." Conference of the Association
> of Single Parents. Washington, 5 Dec.
> 1983.

Class Handout or Lecture

Show class, place, and date; as appropriate and available, give speaker and title.

"Aspects of Criticism." English 112 handout.
    Ticonderoga College, 1985.
Hall, Cathy. Math 210 lecture. Miami U, 17
    Oct. 1984.

Reference Work

Entries for items in standard reference works require less information than do basic entries for books. For a signed encyclopedia article (the first entry below), give the author, article title, encyclopedia title, and edition. For an unsigned article, begin with the article title. If citations are for encyclopedias or dictionaries that alphabetize articles, volume and page references are unnecessary. Of course, if the encyclopedia has separate major divisions, each of which has articles in alphabetical order, include the division title with the encyclopedia title (e.g., *Encyclopaedia Britannica: Macropaedia).* For other standard reference works, such as one of the *Who's Who* series, give only the edition, if applicable, and publication year after the title (e.g., 12th ed. 1982–83.) However, treat an article in a less common reference work as a piece in a book collection (see "Part of a Collection," page 211), and give full publication information.

Burrows, T. L. "Mexican War." Funk and
    Wagnalls New Encyclopedia. 1985 ed.
"Stonehenge." Encyclopedia Americana. 1986 ed.

Computer Software

For commercially produced computer software, begin with the writer of the program, if available; if not, begin with the title. Label with the term "Computer software" and give as a minimum the distributor and publication year. Optional information may be added at the end of the entry—such as the computer for which the program is designed, the operating system, and the type of medium the program is recorded on (cartridge, cassette, or disk).

Wordload Word Processing. Computer software.
    Scienobyte, 1983. CP/M 2.2, disk.

Material from a Computer or Information Service

Material from a computer service (such as DIALOG, Mead, or BRS) or an information service (such as ERIC or NTIS) is like other printed material, but after the publishing information you need to add a reference to the service,

giving its name and the accession or order number for the material you're
citing. Thus, most of the sample entry below corresponds to a document that
is part of a series, while the end of the entry refers to the information service.

>   Stephens, Harold. An Argument for Sectioning
>   by Ability. Classroom Education
>   Techniques, No. 3. Syracuse: Syracuse UP,
>   1975. ERIC ED 041 216.

Unpublished Thesis or Dissertation

When a thesis or dissertation has been published, treat it as a book. However, if you use an unpublished form, show the type of work, the institution
for which it was prepared, and the year it was accepted. Note that the title
appears in quotation marks because the work is unpublished.

>   Koslowski, Edward E. "The Migrations and
>   Impact of the Athapaskan—Speaking
>   Indians." Diss. U of Colorado, 1980.

Unpublished Letter

Treat a published letter as a part of a book collection or as a letter in a
periodical. The first entry below shows the format for a letter you yourself
have received. The second illustrates an unpublished letter in an archive.

>   Mitford, Jessica. Letter to the author. 13
>   Jan. 1982.
>   Freeman, Lloyd. Letter to James R.
>   Livingstone. 2 Oct. 1862. James
>   Livingstone Papers. Antietam Memorial
>   Library. Sharpsburg, MD.

Interview

To document an interview you have conducted, begin with the name of the
person interviewed, show the type of interview (personal or telephone), and
give the date it was held.

>   Latham, Jerry. Personal interview. 21 Apr.
>   1984.

Film, Filmstrip, Slide Program, or Videocassette

For a film usually you'll begin with the title, followed by the director,
distributor, and year released. Other information (stars, writers, etc.) is optional but should be included if it bears on how you discuss the film in your

paper; put this information as amplification after the director. However, if your paper deals with the work of a particular individual connected with the film, begin with that person. For a filmstrip, slide program, or videocassette, show the type of medium after the title and then follow the format for a film citation.

> The Morning After. Dir. Roy Baxter. Panorama, 1983.
> Using Hand Tools. Videocassette. Dir. Sam Riley. Video Concepts, 1984.

Radio or Television Program

As a minimum, give the program title, the network that aired it, the local station and city for the broadcast that you viewed or heard, and the broadcast date. An episode title, if available, can be shown in quotation marks preceding the program title (as in our sample), and a series title, with no special markings, can be shown after the program title. Other information may be added for amplification, and if your paper deals with the work of a particular person connected with the broadcast, begin the entry with that individual's name.

> "Does Anybody Care?" News Closeup. NBC. WGAR, Chicago. 1 Mar. 1984.

Record or Tape

Begin the entry with the person you want to emphasize (speaker, author, composer, producer, etc.); then give the title and follow it with "Audiotape" if your source is a tape rather than a record. Show the artist(s) (along with any appropriate amplification), manufacturer, identification number, and release year.

> Alexander, Charles. Poetry of Charles Alexander. Read by Mark S. Taber. Vox, SRP 63217, 1982.

Legal Citation

Complex legal citations are beyond the scope of this volume. Consult the Harvard Law Review Association's *A Uniform System of Citation* for help. The sample entries below are for federal statutory material; both use section references rather than page references. Use similar entries for state constitutions and statutes.

> 5 US Code. Sec 522a. 1974.
> US Const. Art. 3, sec. 1.

Citations for law cases show the names of first plaintiff and first defendant, the volume of the report being cited, the name of the report, the page of the report, the name of the court where the case was decided, and the year decided.

> Jefferson v. Sommers. 153 AS 613. Ind. Ct.
>   App. 1978.

SPECIAL RULES FOR TITLES

Capitalization

Do use capital letters for the *first letters* of the following types of words in titles:

- Each important word in the title (see below for "unimportant" words)
- The first word in a title (e.g., "*A* House on Tatum Hill")
- The first word after a colon that joins a title and a subtitle (e.g., "Faulkner's 'Delta Autumn': *T*he Fall of Idealism")
- Parts of compound words that would be capitalized if they appeared by themselves (e.g., "School Declares *A*ll-*O*ut War on Misspelling")

Don't use capital letters for the following "unimportant" words:

- The articles *a, an,* and *the*
- Short prepositions such as *at, by, for, in, of, on, to, up*
- The conjunctions *and, as, but, if, nor, or, for, so, yet*
- The second element of a compound numeral (e.g., "Twenty-*f*ive Years of Tyranny")

Neither Quotation Marks nor Underlining

Don't use either quotation marks or underlining (or italics) for the following:

- The Bible, the books of the Bible, and other sacred works such as the Talmud or the Koran
- Legal references (such as acts, laws, and court cases)
- Extratextual material in a book (such as the Introduction or Foreword)

Underlining

Printers usually use italics, but in typing you use underlining (or italics if your typing system, such as a word processor, has this capability) for certain types of titles. Underline the title of works published separately—such as novels and poems that are entire books or pamphlets—and the titles of periodicals (magazines, journals, and newspapers). Also underline the titles of movies and radio or television programs.

Quotation Marks

Use quotation marks to enclose titles of works published as parts of other works—such as short stories, most poems, and essays. Also, enclose titles of speeches and class lectures in quotation marks.

If, however, a work that has been published separately appears as part of a larger work—such as a novel as part of an anthology—underline the title. For example, underline Voltaire's *Candide* even when it is a part of an anthology entitled *Great Works of World Literature.*

Mixed Quotation Marks and Underlining

You have to adapt the rules somewhat when one title appears within another. The following samples illustrate the markings for the four possible combinations of titles with quotation marks and titles with underlining (or italics):

- "Faulkner's 'Delta Autumn': The Fall of Idealism" (a short-story title within an essay title: each title without the other would have double quotation marks, but here the title within a title has single quotation marks)
- Faulkner's "Delta Autumn" and the Myth of the Wilderness (a short-story title within a book title: each title has its normal markings)
- "Laertes as Foil in *Hamlet*" (a play title within an essay title: each title has its normal markings)
- Shakespeare's "Hamlet": Action Versus Contemplation (a play title within a book title: the title within a title, which by itself would be underlined, here has double quotation marks)

SPECIAL RULES FOR PUBLISHERS' NAMES
Shortening

Follow these rules in shortening publishers' names for your Works Cited entries:

- Omit the articles *a, and,* and *the.*
- Omit business designators such as *Co., Inc.,* or *Ltd.*
- Omit labels such as *Books, Press,* or *Publishers. Note:* University presses create an exception. Since both universities and their presses may pub-

lish independently, use *P* for *Press* when the publisher is a university press (thus, *Indiana U* is distinct from *Indiana UP*).

- If the publisher's name includes the name of one person, use only the last name (*Alfred A. Knopf, Inc.* becomes *Knopf*).
- If the name includes several people, use only the first name (*Holt, Rinehart and Winston* becomes *Holt*).
- Use the following standard abbreviations: *UP* for University Press; *GPO* for Government Printing Office; *HMSO* for Her (His) Majesty's Stationery Office; *MLA* for The Modern Language Association of America; *NAL* for The New American Library; *NCTE* for the National Council of Teachers of English; and *NEA* for The National Education Association.

Imprints

When the title page or copyright page of a book shows a publisher's special imprint, combine the imprint with a shortened version of the publisher's name: for example, a Sentry Edition published by Houghton Mifflin Company becomes Sentry-Houghton; a Mentor Book published by The New American Library becomes Mentor-NAL.

SPECIAL RULES FOR INCLUSIVE PAGE NUMBERS

When you indicate inclusive page references, often you can shorten the second number. Up to 100, show all digits (e.g., 3–4, 54–55). Thereafter, reduce the second number of a set to two digits (e.g., 253–54, 304–05, 2614–15) *unless* the hundred or thousand changes (e.g., 499–501, 2998–3002).

EXERCISE

Prepare a Works Cited page to include entries for the works below:

1. A book entitled *Critical Care Unit Management.* It was written by Nancy Ulrich, R.N.; Deborah Prichart, R.N., B.S.N.; David Ely, R.N., B.S.N.; and Susan Bartosch, R.N., C.C.R.N. It was published by Shirlington Press of New York in 1985.

2. Another book by the same set of authors as in exercise item 1. This one is entitled *Critical Care* and is subtitled *A Basic Text.* It, too, was published by Shirlington Press of New York, but in 1987.

3. An article entitled "Care of Cardiac Patients in the ICU Setting," which is found on pages 78 through 93 of a collection of articles entitled *Essays in Nursing.* The article was written by Ed Fleming, R.N., B.S.N., M.S.N., C.C.R.N., while the collection was edited by Jennifer Berry. The book of articles was published by Holt, Rinehart and Winston of New York in 1987.

4. A three-volume work entitled *The Complete Guide to Critical Care,* by Jim Blevins. All three volumes were published in 1987 by the Indiana University Press of Bloomington, Indiana.

5. An unsigned editorial on page A17 of the June 24, 1987, issue of the *Washington Post;* the editorial is entitled "Why Does Getting Well Cost So Much?"

6. A book entitled *Nursing Diagnosis in Critical Care,* written by the Committee to Standardize Nursing Diagnoses, and published in 1986 by the American Society of Nursing in Washington, D.C.

7. A journal article by Judy Buskirk. The article—"Is Critical Care Nursing for You?"—appeared on pages 415 to 438 of volume 8, the Winter 1987 issue, of *Critical Clinician,* a journal that paginates continuously throughout a volume.

8. An article appearing on pages 68 to 75 of the August 14, 1987, issue of *The Senior Citizen,* a weekly magazine. The magazine showed no author for the article, which was entitled "Is the Critical Care Unit Necessary in Treating the Elderly?"

9. An article entitled "Critical Care—Is It Worth the Cost?" It appeared in *Focus on Health,* a monthly magazine. The article, by Linda Hoover, appeared on pages 112 to 121 in issue 9 of the magazine, published in September 1986.

IMPROVING YOUR PUNCTUATION AND EXPRESSION

PART SIX
Punctuation

By now you realize that there's much more to good writing than just getting all the commas and apostrophes in the right places, but those commas and apostrophes are also important. This part of the book begins with a brief chapter on grammar—but only what you need to know in order to learn the relatively few important rules of punctuation. The other chapters then teach punctuation.

We don't attempt to teach you all the rules of punctuation because, for example, you already know how to use question marks and exclamation points. This part, then, teaches you only those common rules of punctuation we think you need to learn.

23
Definitions

Why begin studying punctuation with a review of grammar? If you understand the terms in this chapter, learning to punctuate a sentence will be easy, for punctuation is not really very mysterious. In fact, once you understand these terms, you will probably be surprised just how easy punctuation can be. The catch (and, of course, there is a catch) is that you must work hard to understand them. Skimming this chapter once, or even reading it once through carefully, will not suffice. You have to (gasp!) memorize a few terms. So learn this material well, because all of it is essential in later chapters.

1. Clause   *A clause is a group of words containing a subject (S) and a verb (V).*

<pre>
              S   V
</pre>
Clause: Sharon ran the New York marathon.

Sometimes people are fooled into believing a group of words is a clause simply because it contains something that looks like a verb:

Not a clause: Running a marathon.

The above group of words cannot be a clause for two reasons: (1) it has no subject; (2) it has no verb. Words that end in *-ing* and seem like verbs are really *verbals*. Just remember that an *-ing* word can never function by itself as a verb, and you will stay out of trouble. To be a verb, the *-ing* word must have a helper:

<pre>
        S   V
</pre>
Rosemary is running along the beach. (The word *is* is a helping verb.)

Because we have added a subject and a helping verb to the *-ing* word, we now
have a clause.

Clauses are either *independent* or *dependent*.

2. **Independent clause (IC)** *An independent clause is a clause that makes
a complete statement and therefore may stand alone as a sentence.*

                S   V

Independent clauses: The monkey is brown.

                S   V

The automobile runs smoothly.

              S   V

Marilyn knows her.

              S   V

(You) Close the door.

3. **Dependent clause (DC)** *A dependent clause is a clause that makes an
incomplete statement and therefore may not stand alone as a sentence.*

                S   V

Dependent clauses: *Although* the monkey is brown . . .

                S   V

If the automobile runs smoothly . . .

                S   V

. . . *whom* Marilyn knows.

             S   V

After you close the door . . .

Notice that a dependent clause is not a sentence by itself. That is why it is
dependent—it depends on an independent clause in order to make a complete, or even an intelligible, statement. By itself, a dependent clause does
not make any sense.

This definition and the one above on independent clauses—though fairly
standard, of course—may not satisfy you. Fortunately, we can offer another
definition that works almost all the time (and the exceptions you don't need
to worry about). A *dependent clause* almost always contains a subordinating

conjunction or a relative pronoun (both covered later in this chapter; we've italicized them in the examples of dependent clauses above so you can see where they are). The subordinating conjunctions and relative pronouns are like red flags signaling dependent clauses. You can recognize an *independent clause,* then, because it's a clause not containing a subordinating conjunction or a relative pronoun.

4. Sentence *A sentence is a group of words containing at least one independent clause.*
Sentences (independent clauses are underlined once):

Marilyn knows her.

Although Marilyn knows her, she does not know Marilyn.

After you close the door, Susan will turn on the record player, and Sally will get the potato chips.

5. Phrase (P) *A phrase is a group of two or more related words not containing both a subject and a verb.*

Phrases: in the submarine

running along the beach (remember, *-ing* words are not verbs)

6. Subordinating conjunction (SC) *A subordinating conjunction is a kind of word that begins a* dependent *clause.* You should memorize the italicized words (which are quite common) in the list of subordinating conjunctions below.

after	how	though
although	*if*	unless
as	in order that	until
as if	inasmuch as	*when*
as long as	provided	whenever
as much as	provided that	where
as though	*since*	wherever
because	so that	whether
before	than	while

Here are some examples of subordinating conjunctions beginning dependent clauses (the dependent clauses are underlined twice):

SC

Because your horse is properly registered, it may run in the race.

SC

The race will be canceled if the rain falls.

SC

Sign up for the trip to Memphis while vacancies still exist.

7. Relative pronoun (RP) *A relative pronoun is a kind of word that marks a* dependent *clause*. However, unlike a subordinating conjunction, it does not always come at the beginning of the dependent clause, although it usually does. You should memorize these five common relative pronouns:

who, whose, whom, which, that

Here are some examples of relative pronouns used in dependent clauses (the dependent clauses are underlined twice):

RP

The woman who runs the bank is registering her horse.

RP

The man whose car lights are on is in the grocery store.

RP

The woman whom I met is in the broker's office.

RP

The schedule with which I was familiar is now obsolete.

RP

The schedule that I knew is now obsolete.

Sometimes, unfortunately, these same five words can function as words other than relative pronouns, in which case they *do not* mark dependent clauses:

Not relative pronouns: *Who* is that masked man?

                                      Whose golf club is this?

                                      Whom do you wish to see?

                                      Which car is yours?

                                      That car is mine.

As a general rule, unless they are part of a question, the four words in our list that begin with *w* (*who, whose, whom,* and *which*) are relative pronouns. The other word, *that,* is trickier, but we can generally say that unless it is pointing out something, it is a relative pronoun. In the sentence "That car is mine," *that* points out a car, so it is not a relative pronoun.

    8. Conjunctive adverb (CA)   *A conjunctive adverb is a kind of word that marks an* independent *clause.* Many students make punctuation errors because they confuse subordinating conjunctions (which mark dependent clauses) with conjunctive adverbs (which mark independent clauses). You should memorize the italicized words (which are quite common) in the list of conjunctive adverbs below:

accordingly	hence	*nevertheless*
as a result	*however*	next
consequently	indeed	otherwise
first	in fact	second
for example	instead	still
for instance	likewise	*therefore*
furthermore	meanwhile	thus
	moreover	unfortunately

    You may remember seeing some of these words in Chapter 5, "Coherence." A conjunctive adverb serves as a *transition,* showing the relationship between the independent clause it is in and the independent clause that preceded it.

    A conjunctive adverb may not seem to mark an independent clause, but it does. The following examples are perfectly correct as sentences because they are independent clauses:

    CA
Therefore, I am the winner.

CA

However, the car is red.

Often a conjunctive adverb begins the second independent clause in a sentence because that clause is closely related in meaning to the first independent clause:

CA

I finished in first place; therefore, I am the winner.

CA

You thought your new car would be blue; however, the car is metallic brown.

Sometimes a conjunctive adverb will appear in the middle or even at the end of a clause (that clause, of course, is still independent):

CA

I finished in first place; I am, therefore, the winner.

CA

I finished in first place; I am the winner, therefore.

9. Coordinating conjunction (CC)   *A coordinating conjunction is a word that joins two or more units that are grammatically alike.* You should learn these seven coordinating conjunctions:

and, but, or, nor, for, so, yet

A helpful learning aid is that the coordinating conjunctions are all two or three letters long.
A coordinating conjunction can do the following:

CC

Join two or more words: Billy and Mary

CC

Join two or more phrases: in the car and beside the horse

CC

Join two or more dependent clauses: after the dance was over but before the party began

Join two or more independent clauses: He won the Philadelphia marathon,

CC
for he had been practicing several months.

Remember: Unlike subordinating conjunctions, relative pronouns, and conjunctive adverbs, the coordinating conjunction is not a marker for either an independent clause or a dependent clause. It simply joins two or more like items.

EXERCISES

A. Define these terms:

1. *Clause* _____

_____

_____

2. *Independent clause* _____

_____

_____

3. *Dependent clause* _____

_____

_____

4. *Sentence* _____

_____

_____

5. *Phrase* _____

_____

B. After reading this chapter, you should know seven subordinating conjunctions, five relative pronouns, seven conjunctive adverbs, and seven coordinating conjunctions. Without referring to the lists in the chapter, see how well you can do in the following.

1. Write seven subordinating conjunctions. _____

_____

2. Write five relative pronouns. _____

_____

3. Write seven conjunctive adverbs. _____

_____

4. Write seven coordinating conjunctions. _____

_____

C. 1. What two kinds of words mark dependent clauses? _____

_____

2. What kind of word may mark an independent clause (an independent clause, of course, does not necessarily have a marker)? _____

_____

3. What kind of word joins two or more units that are grammatically alike? ___

_____

D. 1. Write two closely related independent clauses, the second of which contains a conjunctive adverb, and label the conjunctive adverb (CA). _____

_____

_____

2. Write an independent clause not containing a conjunctive adverb. _____

_____

_____

3. Write a dependent clause containing a subordinating conjunction and label the subordinating conjunction (SC). _____

_____

4. Write a dependent clause containing a relative pronoun and label the relative pronoun (RP). _____

_____

5. Write two words joined by a coordinating conjunction and label the coordinating conjunction (CC). _____

_____

6. Write two phrases joined by a coordinating conjunction and label the coordinating conjunction (CC). _____

_____

7. Write two dependent clauses joined by a coordinating conjunction and label the coordinating conjunction (CC). _____

_____

8. Write two independent clauses joined by a coordinating conjunction you have not used earlier in this exercise and label the coordinating conjunction (CC). _____

_____

E. In the sentences below, underline the independent clauses once and the dependent clauses twice. Then label all subordinating conjunctions (SC), relative pronouns (RP), conjunctive adverbs (CA), and coordinating conjunctions (CC).
   1. Humphrey Bogart was Lauren Bacall's first husband.
   2. Which Shakespeare play is your favorite?
   3. When you go out, mail the rent check.
   4. Although it has no nutritional value, fiber still affects nutrition, so high-fiber diets are worth considering.
   5. Insoluble fibers reduce constipation, and soluble fibers help to produce a sense of fullness.
   6. Because they provoke a sense of fullness or satisfaction and because they function as natural laxatives, fiber-rich foods are encouraged in weight reduction plans.
   7. Sunshine is dangerous for unprotected skin; this does not mean that exposure to the sun is unacceptable, however.
   8. Sir Walter Raleigh discovered and named Virginia.
   9. Jackie Gleason and Art Carney made famous the characters Ralph Kramden and Ed Norton; Kramden was a bus driver, while Norton was a sewer worker.
   10. Brisk walking may be all that is needed for a sound exercise program; this should be, however, a period dedicated to walking as an exercise.
   11. In tiddlywinks the piece that you flip into the cup is the wink.
   12. What are your plans for the summer?
   13. Many people believe that they should continue playing sports even though they hurt; nevertheless, pain is a natural warning that they should heed.
   14. Mammals have self-regulating body temperature, hair, and, in the females, glands to produce milk.
   15. Herman kept the stereo very loud until his father threatened to cut off the power plug.
   16. Emotions do affect health, and hard-driving, aggressive people appear to be prone to heart attacks.
   17. Excitable, hurried people have an increased risk of heart problems; they can, however, reduce the risk by modifying their approach to life.
   18. The dandelion's name comes from the French for "tooth of the lion."
   19. In *The Mouse That Roared* the country of Grand Fenwick declares war on the United States so that the country can receive aid after losing the war.

20. "Low impact" aerobics involves reduced stress; nevertheless, it still includes impact.

21. Because he brought liberal reforms to the Soviet Union, Mikhail Gorbachev upset many old party bosses.
22. Remember to send the application before Monday.
23. William Styron's *The Confessions of Nat Turner* is about a black preacher who leads a slave revolt.
24. The Treaty of Versailles ended World War I.
25. James Michener won the 1948 Pulitzer Prize for *Tales of the South Pacific,* which is a collection of related short stories.

24

Sentence Fragment

A sentence fragment is an error involving punctuation.

Sentence fragment (Frag) *A sentence fragment is a group of words punctuated like a sentence but not containing an independent clause.* Because it lacks an independent clause, a sentence fragment is just a piece of a sentence. Here are some examples:

Sentence fragments: Running along the beach.

Even though the movie won an Oscar.

See? These so-called sentences are really frauds: they begin with a capital letter and end with a period, but they don't contain an independent clause.

Usually a sentence fragment is very closely related to the sentence that preceded it. The two examples above might have appeared in the following contexts:

Sentence fragments: I finally found that stray mutt. Running along the beach.

Marie absolutely refused to go to the theater. Even though the movie had won an Oscar.

To correct a sentence fragment, either connect it to an independent clause or add a subject and a verb to convert it to an independent clause.

Fragments connected to independent clauses:

I finally found that stray mutt running along the beach.

Marie absolutely refused to go to the theater even though the movie had won an Oscar.

Fragments converted to independent clauses:

I finally found that stray mutt. He was running along the beach.

Marie absolutely refused to go to the theater. The movie had won an Oscar.

Of the two types of changes above, most readers would prefer the connection of the fragment to an independent clause. That solution provides smoother writing, avoiding the choppiness resulting from converting each fragment to its own independent clause. More important, however, the first solution increases coherence: connecting the fragment to an independent clause links the thought of the fragment to the thought of the independent clause.

Are fragments always wrong? No, of course not. Fragments are common in speech and appear frequently in informal types of writing, such as advertisements. You'll even find a few examples in this book because the writing was designed to communicate to you directly, as if the authors were speaking to you. Because fragments break the conventional pattern of writing, they can create a useful effect. For example, the second "sentence" of this paragraph—really a fragment—communicates the desired thought more directly and simply than would this sentence combination: "Are fragments always wrong? No, of course fragments are not always wrong." And because the fragment answers the question in the first sentence, there is no loss of coherence. However, keep these cautions in mind:

- Fragments are never acceptable if they destroy coherence.
- Be aware of your probable readers. Some may never find fragments acceptable.
- Use fragments sparingly for good effect.

If breaking the writing convention of complete sentences becomes your normal style, the only effect you'll achieve is choppy prose that is difficult to comprehend. All right?

EXERCISES

A. Define *sentence fragment.* _____

_____

B. Correct the fragments in each of the following sentence-fragment combinations in two ways:

   1. The Canary Islands appear in legends. Seen as the highest peaks of the lost continent of Atlantis.

2. Milk is heavier than cream. Although many people guess the opposite.

3. Commonplace reading material in American barbershops once was the *National Police Gazette*. Printed on pink paper.

C. For each "sentence" below, indicate whether it is a complete sentence or only a fragment:

1. Turning white in winter.

2. Vichyssoise, sounding like an old European dish, having been invented for an American restaurant opening in 1910.

3. Seeds separated from the cotton in a cotton gin.

4. A fragment providing an incomplete thought.

5. Siberia's Lake Baikal is the deepest lake in the world.

6. A man with his hands covering his ears in Munch's famous painting *The Scream*.

7. In 1950 a "giant" television screen of 12 inches was introduced.

8. Are any peanuts left?

9. Because Harry Truman had bowling lanes installed in the White House.

10. We're almost there.

11. The mummified body of Francisco Pizarro residing in Lima, Peru.

12. So that astronaut John Glenn could see them, residents of Perth, Australia, turned on their lights.

13. After becoming popular on American college campuses in 1937, benzedrine, also known as pep pills.

14. You'll do.

15. Men being more prone than women to color blindness.

16. Amelia Earhart, called "Lady Lindy."

17. Named such because it sleeps at night.

18. A symbol used in calculating the area of a circle.

19. Most of the state's population residing on Oahu.

20. Turkey, named for what was thought to be its country of origin, although that wasn't true.

D. Correct the following sentence fragments:

1. In Naples, Italy, foreigners joke that traffic signals are only "recommendations." Because local drivers so often ignore traffic lights.

2. A manhole cover from the ancient Roman sewer system today is a tourist attraction. The reason being that the drainage hole is the mouth of a man's face and is supposed to bite the hand of anyone who tells a lie.

3. The manhole cover is named *Bocca della Verità*, or "Mouth of Truth." Because of the story about biting the hands of liars.

4. Rome's famous and emblematic "She Wolf" statue being actually from the Etruscans, with the figures of Romulus and Remus added in a later time.

5. The archaeological sites of Pompeii and Herculaneum never fail to fascinate visitors. Although the best of the artifacts are in a museum in downtown Naples rather than at the sites.

6. In Italian cities it is not unusual to see stray cats eating spaghetti. That being an inexpensive leftover that is readily available as a cat food.

25
Comma Splice and Fused Sentence

Comma splices and fused sentences are sentences that are punctuated incorrectly.

1. Comma splice (CS) *A comma splice occurs when two independent clauses are joined by only a comma.* In other words, it is two independent clauses "spliced" together with only a comma. Using the abbreviation IC for independent clause, we can express the comma splice as follows:

Comma splice: IC,IC.

Here are some comma splice errors:

Wrong: We hiked for three days, we were very tired.

Wrong: The television is too loud, the picture is fuzzy.

There are five ways to correct a comma splice:

a. Change the comma to a period and capitalize the next word. (IC. IC.)

Correct: We hiked for three days. We were very tired.

b. Change the comma to a semicolon. (IC;IC.)

Correct: We hiked for three days; we were very tired.

c. Change the comma to a semicolon and add a conjunctive adverb. (IC;CA,IC.)

Correct: We hiked for three days; hence, we were very tired.

245

d. Add a coordinating conjunction before the second independent clause. (IC,CC IC.)

Correct: We hiked for three days, so we were very tired.

e. Change one independent clause to a dependent clause. (DC,IC.)

Correct: Because we hiked for three days, we were very tired.

A very common form of comma splice occurs when only a comma precedes a conjunctive adverb at the beginning of the second independent clause in a sentence.

Wrong: Mount Rainier is beautiful, however, it is also forbidding.

The best way to correct this kind of comma splice is to change the first comma to a semicolon. (IC;CA,IC.)

Correct: Mount Rainier is beautiful; however, it is also forbidding.

Another form of comma splice occurs when two independent clauses are separated by a dependent clause but the strongest mark of punctuation is still only a comma.

Wrong: The artist is selling the portrait, because he does not have enough money, he has run out of paint.

How would you correct the above sentence? Does the writer mean that the artist is selling the portrait because he does not have enough money? Or does the writer mean the artist has run out of paint because he does not have enough money? Here is one instance in which correct punctuation is important to meaning. One of several ways to correct the sentence is to place a period on the appropriate side of the dependent clause, depending on the meaning you wish to express. (IC DC.IC.) or (IC.DC,IC.)

Correct: The artist is selling the portrait because he does not have enough money. He has run out of paint.

Correct: The artist is selling the portrait. Because he does not have enough money, he has run out of paint.

2. **Fused sentence (FS)** *A fused sentence occurs when two independent clauses are joined without punctuation or a coordinating conjunction.* In other words, a fused sentence is a comma splice without the comma.

Fused sentence: IC IC.

Here are some fused sentence errors:

Wrong: We hiked for three days we were very tired.

Wrong: The television is too loud the picture is fuzzy.

Correct a fused sentence with essentially the same methods you used to correct a comma splice:

a. Add a period after the first independent clause and capitalize the next word. (IC. IC.)

Correct: The television is too loud. The picture is fuzzy.

b. Add a semicolon after the first independent clause. (IC;IC.)

Correct: The television is too loud; the picture is fuzzy.

c. Add a semicolon and a conjunctive adverb after the first independent clause. (IC;CA,IC.)

Correct: The television is too loud; furthermore, the picture is fuzzy.

d. Add a comma and a coordinating conjunction after the first independent clause. (IC,CC IC.)

Correct: The television is too loud, and the picture is fuzzy.

e. Change one independent clause to a dependent clause. (DC,IC.)

Correct: Whenever the television is too loud, the picture is fuzzy.

EXERCISES

A. Define these terms:

1. *Comma splice* _____

_____

2. *Fused sentence* _____

_____

B. Correct the following comma splice in five different ways: *Lonesome Dove* won the Pulitzer Prize for fiction in 1986, the judges recognized that Larry McMurtry wrote much more than a cowboy tale.

C. Correct the following fused sentence in five different ways: McMurtry received critical attention for *The Last Picture Show* and *Terms of Endearment* both of these were made into very successful movies.

D. For each sentence below, write *CS* if the sentence has a comma splice *FS* if it is a fused sentence, or *Correct* if it is correct.

1. _____ Larry McMurtry also wrote *Horseman, Pass By* it was filmed as *Hud*.

2. _____ McMurtry has written that he thought *Horseman, Pass By* would be a memorable title, but he found that even his friends had trouble getting the title right.

3. _____ Because *Horseman, Pass By* seemed to be too literary Paramount Studios wanted to change the title *Hud* was the final compromise.

4. _____ For the movie Paul Newman played Hud, a middle-aged cowboy who could not follow the honorable model of his aged father.

5. _____ In the movie *Terms of Endearment,* Shirley MacLaine played mother Aurora Greenway, Debra Winger played her daughter Emma.

6. _____ In the novel *Terms of Endearment,* Aurora Greenway has many suitors, however, chief among them is a retired army general named Hector Scott.

7. _____ The movie of *Terms of Endearment* introduces an entirely new suitor, he is an aging astronaut named Garrett Breedlove.

8. _____ For the movie Jack Nicholson portrayed Garrett Breedlove; his character is a hard-drinking playboy, quite unlike the gruff but well-mannered General Hector Scott.

9. _____ Astronaut Breedlove appears in incidents and uses some dialogue that belongs to General Scott in the book, therefore, it is clear that Breedlove was created to replace Scott.

10. _____ *Lonesome Dove* begins in the Texas setting that is typical of Larry McMurtry's novels however a cattle drive places much of the story outside Texas.

11. _____ My favorite character in *Lonesome Dove* is Augustus McCrae although he prefers talking to acting he proves capable of decisive action when required.

12. _____ A second main character is Woodrow Call, he and Augustus McCrae rode together in earlier years as Texas Rangers.

13. _____ Even though they are retired from Ranger life Gus and Call feel compelled to uphold law much as they did in their Texas Ranger days.

14. _____ Gus and Call delay the start of their cattle drive until they can be joined by Jake Spoon, although he also had been a Ranger, Jake's difficulty with ethics proves his undoing.

15. _____ Larry McMurtry's novels often feature a boy who must learn the ways of the world in *Lonesome Dove* that character is a boy named Newt.

16. _____ Because it could not be an epic of the American West without a good-hearted barmaid of loose virtue, *Lonesome Dove* includes Lorena, she actually has little interest in pursuing her trade.

17. _____ Lorena's chief interest is getting to San Francisco, where she believes life will be better, because men offer passage west, much of Lorena's life is spent accompanying them.

18. _____ Most of the cowboys Gus and Call hire for their cattle drive are boys from neighboring ranches; however, the most unlikely cowboys on the drive are Allen and Sean O'Brien, two Irish tenderfeet they pick up lost in Mexico.

19. _____ Two interesting minor characters in *Lonesome Dove* are a pair of blue pigs that apparently will eat almost anything they are devouring a rattlesnake when the story opens.

20. _____ *The Last Picture Show* features two boys entering manhood in a small Texas town in the 1950s, in *Texasville,* however, the same characters and town reappear in the 1980s.

21. _____ Although *Texasville* repeats primary characters from *The Last Picture Show,* critics have complained that the *Texasville* characters have little in common with their counterparts from the earlier novel.

22. _____ The passing of thirty years between the time settings of the two novels causes significant differences in the situations of the main characters, nevertheless, both *Texasville* and *The Last Picture Show* deal with similar themes.

23. _____ In *The Last Picture Show* Sonny Crawford and Duane Moore are coming of age, while they are struggling with middle age in *Texasville.*

24. _____ In a series of essays published as *In a Narrow Grave: Essays on Texas,* Larry McMurtry discusses the passing away of the ideals of the Old West, clearly many of his novels deal with the same theme.

25. _____ Although *Horseman, Pass By, The Last Picture Show,* and *Texasville* focus on the loss of the Old West, *Lonesome Dove*—which shows the passing—celebrates the older ways, perhaps that celebration explains the appeal of *Lonesome Dove.*

26
Comma

This chapter presents the nine most important uses of the comma (,).

1. *Use a comma after every item in a series except the last item.*

Example: The ethics of contemporary surgery are often a problem for the patient, the doctor, and the patient's family.

You probably already knew to put a comma after the first item (*patient* in this case), but why do you need one after the next-to-last item *(doctor)*? Consider this example:

Example: The ethics of contemporary surgery are often a problem for the patient, the doctor and the hospital board, and the patient's family.

Commas tell your readers that you are moving to the next item in a series. When you omit a comma, you're telling them you're still in that same item—a compound item—so they won't have to reread your sentence.

2. *Use a comma before a coordinating conjunction that joins two independent clauses.* (IC,CC IC.)

Examples: I never liked parsnips, but my mother made me eat them.

She thought they were great, and she thought they would make me grow taller.

Note: Do not confuse a coordinating conjunction that joins two verbs with a coordinating conjunction that joins two independent clauses:

S   V   CC   V

The parsnips tasted awful and looked like paste.

The coordinating conjunction above is not preceded by a comma because it connects only the two verbs *tasted* and *looked.*

3. *Use a comma after a dependent clause that begins a sentence.* (DC,IC.)

Examples:
DC   IC

Although Harriet tried as hard as she could, she could not

win even a fun-run.

DC   IC

Because she couldn't run fast enough, she couldn't have

the free T-shirt we awarded to the first 200 runners to cross

the finish line.

4. *Use a comma after a long phrase that begins a sentence.* (Long phrase, IC.) The word *long* is rather vague, of course, but usually you will wish to place a comma after an introductory phrase of three or more words.

Long phrase

Examples: Even after a grueling night of writing, I didn't get the paper entirely finished.

Long phrase

Running to my next class, I tried to think of an excuse to give my professor.

5. *Use commas to set off any word, phrase, or clause that interrupts the flow of the sentence.* In other words, if you could set off a word or group of words with parentheses but do not wish to, then set off that word or group of words with commas.

Examples: My excuse, wild as it was, didn't sound convincing.
The class, together with the professor, turned their heads as I plowed into the classroom.
John, who has the seat next to mine, laughed at me as I sat down.
The professor ignored me as he finished the course, "Freshman English for Nonconformists."

Notice that interrupters in the middle of sentences have commas on *both* sides.

6. *Use commas to set off nonrestrictive clauses.* This rule is actually an expansion of rule 5, because all nonrestrictive clauses are interrupters. You may wonder, though, just what restrictive and nonrestrictive clauses are.

A *restrictive clause* is essential to defining whatever it modifies. In the following example, let's assume you have several brothers:

My brother *who is wearing a red motorcycle helmet* is meaner than I am.

The restrictive clause ("who is wearing a red motorcycle helmet") is essential because it tells us which of your several brothers is meaner than you are. It *restricts* the word *brother* from any one of your brothers to the one wearing the helmet. If you left out the restrictive clause, we would not know which brother you meant. You probably noticed that these restrictive clauses are not interrupters and, therefore, are not set off with commas.

A *nonrestrictive clause* is not essential in defining whatever it modifies. Since it is not essential, you could omit it and everybody would still know who (or what) you are talking about. Now let's assume that you have only one brother:

My brother, *who is wearing a red motorcycle helmet,* is meaner than I am.

Because you have only one brother, you could omit the nonrestrictive clause and still make sense. The word modified—*brother*—is not *limited* in any way by the clause; it is only described in more detail. In other words, without the clause we still know which brother you're talking about. Set off these nonrestrictive clauses with commas.

7. *Use a comma after a conjunctive adverb unless it is the last word in the sentence.* (CA,IC.) or (IC;CA,IC.) This rule applies no matter where the conjunctive adverb appears within the sentence.

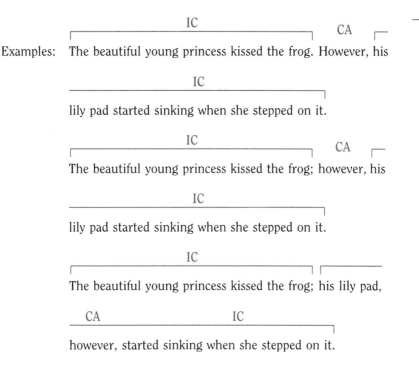

Examples: The beautiful young princess kissed the frog. However, his lily pad started sinking when she stepped on it.

The beautiful young princess kissed the frog; however, his lily pad started sinking when she stepped on it.

The beautiful young princess kissed the frog; his lily pad, however, started sinking when she stepped on it.

Note: If, as in the last example, the conjunctive adverb is in the middle of the independent clause, it will have commas on *both* sides of it.

8. *Use a comma between coordinate adjectives unless they are joined by "and."* Coordinate adjectives are sets of adjectives that independently modify a noun.

Example: The bulldog is noted for its wrinkled, flattened face.

Both *wrinkled* and *flattened* modify *face* independently. That is not the case with cumulative adjectives. When an adjective's modification is cumulative, it modifies not only the noun but also the whole adjective-noun phrase it precedes.

Example: Alicia wore a red felt hat.

Here *red* modifies not just *hat* but the phrase *felt hat.* Notice that no comma is used with cumulative adjectives.

Distinguishing between coordinate and cumulative adjectives isn't always simple. However, because of the independence of coordinate adjectives, you can check for two characteristics that help identify them.

- Coordinate adjectives are reversible, whereas cumulative adjectives aren't. That is, *flattened, wrinkled face* works as well as *wrinkled, flattened face.* On the other hand, *felt red hat* just sounds foolish.
- *And* fits naturally between coordinate adjectives, but not between cumulative adjectives. Thus, you could write *wrinkled and flattened face* but not *red and felt hat.*

Of course, modifier chains can include both coordinate and cumulative adjectives.

Example: The stands were full for the homecoming game even though it was a cold, rainy autumn day.

Cold and *rainy* are coordinate and are separated by a comma. However, both modify *autumn day* rather than just *day,* so there is no comma after *rainy.*

9. *Use a comma to set off words in direct address.* Words in direct address normally are names but can be phrases used in place of names.

Examples: Kristina, have you washed the dishes?
Where are you going now, little sister?
You look charming, Alicia, wearing that red felt hat.

Notice that the word in direct address in the last example has commas on *both* sides because it occurs in the middle of the sentence.

EXERCISES

A. Write the nine important rules for using a comma.

1. _____

_____

2. _____

_____

3. _____

_____

4. _____

_____

5. _____

_____

6. _____

_____

7. _____

_____

8. _____

_____

9. _____

_____

B. Write a sentence illustrating each of the above rules.

1. _____

_____

2. _____

_____

3. _____

_____

4. _____

_____

5. _____

_____

6. _____

_____

7. _____

_____

8. _____

_____

9. _____

_____

C. For each pair of sentences below, answer the accompanying questions.
   1. Which of the following implies that there were more topics but the Secretary of State covered only the three high-interest ones?
      a. The Secretary of State briefed the President on the three topics which were of extremely high interest.

    b. The Secretary of State briefed the President on the three topics, which were of extremely high interest.

2. Which sentence indicates that there will be no questions at all (because the Research Department has prepared well)? Which sentence implies that the board members are likely to attack some of the Research Department's initiatives?

    a. The board members are not likely to question the Research Department's initiatives, which are generally well prepared.

    b. The board members are not likely to question the Research Department's initiatives which are generally well prepared.

3. Which sentence implies that there was at least one version of the competency test before the one mandated in 1986?

    a. The high school competency test, which was mandated in 1986, has changed the way teachers do their jobs.

    b. The high school competency test which was mandated in 1986 has changed the way teachers do their jobs.

D. In the following sentences, add commas where necessary.

1. Juan do you know which part Peter Lorre played in *Casablanca*?

2. Alligators have broad short snouts but crocodiles have longer more pointed snouts.

3. My little brother brought home two large hairy stray dogs and asked if he could keep them.

4. As a result Sir Walter Raleigh was buried with a pipe and tobacco.

5. Authorities say that truckers who drive unsafe rigs cause most of the accidents on the Beltway. (Punctuate to imply that all truckers drive unsafe equipment.)

6. Authorities say that truckers who drive unsafe rigs cause most of the accidents on the Beltway. (Punctuate to imply that some truckers have safe rigs.)

7. *Pâté de foie gras* hard as it is to say sounds more appetizing than goose liver.

8. No matter how rushed don't miss the *David* in Florence.

9. Although they aren't the best known and certainly aren't designed for quick reference the Blue Guide tour books offer the best in-depth coverage of European cities.

10. The six possible murder weapons in *Clue* are a candlestick a knife a lead pipe a revolver a rope and a wrench.

11. Enrico thought he had impressed the charming elegant woman but that was before he tripped and spilled red wine on her gown.

12. The board has requested therefore that all tenants wait until morning before putting their garbage bags outside.

13. Lee Harvey Oswald who was accused of shooting John F. Kennedy was himself shot only two days after the assassination.

14. Even though he ruled Bavaria for only twenty-two years Ludwig II was responsible for constructing three magnificent castles today among the most visited spots in southern Germany.

15. Ludwig II of Bavaria built the castles of Neuschwanstein Linderhof and Herrenchiemsee.
16. Was Goya Spanish or Italian Rosalie?
17. Tourists who show proper respect are welcome in the churches of Italy. (Punctuate to imply that not all tourists show proper respect.)
18. Tourists who show proper respect are welcome in the churches of Italy. (Punctuate to imply that all tourists show proper respect.)
19. Although he made his name in music with *Cats Evita* and *Starlight Express* Andrew Lloyd Webber changed style dramatically in 1984 with *Requiem* a work in very traditional style.
20. Rated at 550 times the sweetness of sugar saccharin was the basis of the diet food industry for years.
21. Simone was dressed for success in a dark gray wool suit; however she hadn't noticed the ink splotch on her blouse.
22. Named for a Cuban city a daiquiri is composed of rum lime and sugar.
23. I visited Rome four times over a three-year period yet I was never able to see Trajan's Column because it was covered by scaffolding and drapes; however I was able to see a copy of it in London's Victoria and Albert Museum.
24. When you look for the airport in Rome Harry you'll have to remember that some highway signs say "Leonardo da Vinci" but others say "Fulmacino."
25. The most widely used seasoning in the world salt is not always the safest seasoning.
26. If you visit Rome don't miss the Trevi Fountain only a few blocks from the Spanish Steps.
27. A number of U.S. presidents have been shot in office; however Ronald Reagan was the first incumbent to survive being shot.
28. Because they didn't understand what being "chief" meant in many Indian tribal organizations Americans often didn't deal with leaders who actually had the type of control the whites believed they had.
29. Of the ruins recovered from the A.D. 79 eruption of Vesuvius Pompeii best shows the religious social and political aspects of Roman life and Herculaneum provides the best sense of living structures.
30. Herculaneum shows well the range of building styles for homes and even has remnants of wood and fabric from A.D. 79.

27
Semicolon

The semicolon (;) is stronger than a comma but weaker than a period. This chapter presents the three most important uses of the semicolon.

1. *Use a semicolon between two independent clauses closely related in meaning but not joined by a coordinating conjunction.* (IC;IC.)

IC   IC

Examples: Lee won some battles; Grant won the war.

IC   IC

The pale sun rose over the frozen land; the arctic fox gazed

quietly at the sky.

2. *Use a semicolon between two independent clauses when the second independent clause is joined to the first with a conjunctive adverb.* (IC;CA,IC.)

IC   CA

Examples: Auto theft is a major national crime; however, people

IC

keep leaving their cars unlocked.

IC   CA

Most stolen cars are recovered; unfortunately, many have

IC

been vandalized.

Note: If a conjunctive adverb is moved from the beginning of the second independent clause into the middle of it, the conjunctive adverb is then preceded by a comma instead of a semicolon; the semicolon, however, remains between the independent clauses.

$$\overset{\text{IC}}{\overbrace{\hspace{4cm}}} \quad \overset{\text{CA}}{\overbrace{\hspace{2cm}}}$$

Example: Most stolen cars are recovered; many, unfortunately, have

$$\overset{\text{IC}}{\overbrace{\hspace{2.5cm}}}$$

been vandalized.

3. *When commas occur within one or more of the items in a series, use semicolons rather than commas to separate the items in the series.* Commas normally separate the items, with the commas clearly indicating where each portion of the series begins and ends. When any portion needs its own commas, however, readers may become confused if commas separate the portions of the series.

Confusing: Maria turned first to the doctor, then to her father, mother, and sister, and finally to the priest.

The second item of the major series in this sentence is itself a smaller series—"father, mother, and sister"—requiring its own commas. From the context, readers probably would understand this sample, especially since each of the major items begins with a time indicator (*first, then,* and *finally*). However, you can make the readers' job easier by using semicolons to separate the major items in the series.

Better: Maria turned first to the doctor; then to her father, mother, and sister; and finally to the priest.

This way readers won't have to reread to understand the structure of the series.

EXERCISES

A. Write the three most important rules for using the semicolon.

1. _____

_____

2. _____

_____

3. _____

_____

B. Write a sentence illustrating each of the above rules.

1. _____

_____

2. _____

_____

3. _____

_____

C. In the following sentences, add semicolons and commas where necessary.

1. Rosencrantz and Guildenstern have very minor roles in Shakespeare's *Hamlet* in Tom Stoppard's *Rosencrantz and Guildenstern Are Dead* however they become the chief characters.

2. Some software companies devise complicated programming schemes to prevent copying of their programs nevertheless other companies market software packages to permit users to copy those protected programs.

3. Leon's cousins live in Indianapolis Indiana Omaha Nebraska and Colorado Springs Colorado.

4. General George Patton slapped a private one Paul Bennett because of the outcry that resulted General Patton was forced to apologize publicly.

5. Garrison Keillor has written humorously but also precisely about small towns in America several times as I read about Lake Wobegon I caught myself reaching for an atlas to see where the town is in Minnesota.

6. Ancient Romans liked their dining rooms to open onto a pleasant garden people too poor to afford a real garden sometimes had one painted on the walls of the dining room instead.

7. Romans built walls with a rubble core and they found that adding mortar to the rubble strengthened the wall over time this practice brought about the development of concrete.

8. To deal with housing shortages Roman engineers developed an inexpensive rapid-construction building style for which square wooden frames were filled with rough stones and mortar although the Romans didn't consider this type of building permanent one such house at Herculaneum has survived over 1,900 years.

9. As he strode into the village Luis saw old women most dressed all in black old men all wearing the clothes of farm laborers and a few small children.

10. Live television can create embarrassing moments for example many fans of *The Tonight Show* even ones who didn't actually see the show remember Ed Ames for throwing a badly aimed tomahawk.

11. Dolby technology advanced the state of art of tape players by reducing significant levels of background noise compact disc players however went a step further by eliminating almost all background noise.

12. For several years I thought compact disc players were just another electronic toy but I've changed my mind since I heard the clarity of the music they produce.

13. Because playing a compact disc causes no wear on the disc many people believe that compact discs are indestructible in fact manufacturers warn that the disc itself is subject to damage from improper handling.

14. For high school graduation my parents bought me a passport a round-trip airplane ticket to Europe and a Eurorail Pass I spent two months traveling in France Germany and Italy.

15. Humphrey Bogart had important roles in the 1950s including his Oscar-winning part in *The African Queen* but he's admired most for his films of the 1940s: *The Maltese Falcon Casablanca To Have and Have Not* and *The Big Sleep.*

16. Bogart and Lauren Bacall worked together well in *The Big Sleep* however the attraction between the two in *To Have and Have Not* clearly demonstrates why their partnership was so effective.

17. When Kerry prayed at night she was careful to include her three aunts in Hawaii her only uncle a relative stranger she had met only once and who also lived in Hawaii and her grandparents though all four were dead.

18. Michelangelo's *Pietà* is still on display in St. Peter's but it is less visible than it was prior to 1972 today the art treasure sits behind a bulletproof glass wall that was erected after an individual attacked the statue with a hammer.

19. For hundreds of years residents of Rome believed that Peter's tomb lay directly beneath St. Peter's Basilica excavations beneath St. Peter's have provided considerable evidence that this popular belief was true.

20. Because of the media attention they receive, few U.S. presidents today can avoid being criticized for some simple act or comment that meant little at the time Lyndon Johnson learned this when the media saw him pick up a pet beagle by the ears.

28
Colon

There are many rules for the colon, several of them relatively obscure. But there is one important rule you should know:

Use a colon after the last independent clause in a sentence to point to some more useful information about what you just said.

Virtually any grammatical unit can then follow the colon:

- a word or phrase
- a series of words or phrases
- a dependent clause
- an independent clause (or sentence)
- even a series of independent clauses or sentences

Examples:

The used car had one large defect: no engine.

The used car had three large defects: no tires, no brakes, no engine.

She sold the car for good reason: because it had no engine.

She sold the car for good reason: it had no engine.

She sold the car for three good reasons: It had no tires. It had no brakes. It had no engine.

When you have one entire sentence after the colon, should you capitalize the first letter of that sentence? There's no real standard: some people do and some people don't. (*Or* There's no real standard: *Some* people do and some people don't.) When you have a *series of sentences* after the colon, though, you should begin each with a capital letter.

The rule in this chapter says to put a colon after an independent clause. There are ways to put colons after only words, phrases, and dependent clauses. However, we suggest you learn and apply the one simple rule we give you: it can do wonderful things for your writing.

You should avoid unnecessary colons, however. If your sentence would read fine with no punctuation at all where you have a colon, simply leave the colon out. Here are some examples of unnecessary colons:

He bought: two bicycle tires, a bicycle pump, and a tire repair kit.

The weather radar showed the blizzard was: crossing the Rocky Mountains, heading for Kansas, and building up strength.

EXERCISES

A. Write five sentences using a colon correctly. Follow the colon with these grammatical units (using a different grammatical unit for each of the five sentences you write):

- a word or phrase
- a series of words or phrases
- a dependent clause
- an independent clause (or sentence)
- a series of independent clauses or sentences

B. What different effects do these two sentences have?

She worked all weekend for one reason: money.

She worked all weekend for money.

C. In the following sentences, add colons where appropriate.

1. The leaves fell slowly from the trees the people were even slower raking the leaves.
2. Most places don't let people burn leaves for two good reasons the danger of fire and the pollution to the air.
3. Most places don't let people burn leaves because of the danger of fire and the pollution to the air.
4. The tie was tight around the boxer's neck he preferred being in the gym.
5. The two boxers glared ferociously at one another showing one primal emotion hatred.
6. The two boxers glared ferociously at one another showing the primal emotions of hatred and fear.
7. The rugby shirt had many colors burgundy, green, white, and blue.
8. The rugby shirt had one dominant color blue.
9. The rugby shirts were popular because they were colorful, rugged, and cheap.
10. The rugby shirts were popular for three reasons because they were colorful, because they were rugged, and because they were cheap.

29
Dash

Years ago, people considered the dash too informal for most writing other than letters home. Today, though, the dash has come into its own—it's an extremely handy mark if you want to give a slightly more personal feeling to your writing. If you want to close the gap between you and the readers, use dashes. If you want to widen the gap, don't.

We'll discuss two common rules for the dash. Notice that the first rule we discuss is identical to the one we gave you for the colon (but—yes—the dash gives a more personal feeling).

1. *Use a dash after the last independent clause in a sentence to point to some more useful information about what you just said.*

Virtually any grammatical unit can then follow the dash (though not normally a series of independent clauses):

- a word or phrase
- a series of words or phrases
- a dependent clause
- an independent clause (or sentence)

Examples:

The used car had one large defect—no engine.

The used car had three large defects—no tires, no brakes, no engine.

She sold the car for good reason—because it had no engine.

She sold the car for good reason—it had no engine.

2. Use a dash the same place you could use parentheses to set off some useful information in the middle of a sentence.

In the following sentences notice these points:

- The dashes add emphasis to the words they set off.
- The parentheses take emphasis away, making the words set off like a whispered aside.
- The commas provide standard emphasis.

With dashes: The store—the one around the corner—was robbed again.

With parentheses: The store (the one around the corner) was robbed again.

With commas: The store, the one around the corner, was robbed again.

Note: A dash is a line that's a little longer than a hyphen. So . . . how should you make a dash on a typewriter? A typewriter has only a hyphen (-) but not a dash (--). There are two ways:

- You can make a dash - which isn't on a typewriter - by using a hyphen with spaces on each side, as in this sentence.
- Or you can make a dash--this way--with two hyphens in a row (and no space at all on either side).

Your choice.

EXERCISES

A. Write four sentences using a dash correctly. Follow the dash with these grammatical units (using a different grammatical unit for each of the four sentences you write):

- a word or phrase
- a series of words or phrases
- a dependent clause
- an independent clause (or sentence)

B. Write four sentences, with dashes, that have useful information in the middle of the sentence. The topic? Four different places you'd like to visit on a vacation.

C. What different effects do these two sentences have?

She worked all weekend for one reason—money.

She worked all weekend for one reason: money.

D. What different effects do these two sentences have?

The August breeze—surprisingly chilly—made spring seem far away.

The August breeze (surprisingly chilly) made spring seem far away.

E. In the following sentences, add dashes or colons where appropriate.
1. The mirror the one with small cracks running through it said the queen was the fairest in the land.
2. The queen was beautiful on the outside, but that beauty concealed an inner and ugly spirit.
3. The tree had a reminder of summer a single leaf.
4. The leaf looking like a brown scrap was clinging despite a terrific snowstorm.
5. Leaves normally fall during autumn not during winter.
6. The brick house the one with white, peeling paint was the oldest one on the block.
7. The house was really old it was built in 1723.
8. The house preceded one of our nation's key events the Revolutionary War.
9. The slipper tossed around the den by a new puppy was no longer useful.
10. The puppy was no longer very popular, either it had eaten a Gucci slipper.

30
Apostrophe

The apostrophe (') is, for very good reason, one of the most neglected marks of punctuation. Unlike the other punctuation marks, the apostrophe can usually be omitted without any loss of meaning. Because it is still an accepted convention of our language, however, we should know its two important uses.

1. *Use an apostrophe to show possession.*

Examples: Sara's silver Honda
            the dog's fleas

Note A: To form the possessive, follow these general rules:

(1) If the word does not end in an *s,* add an apostrophe and an *s:*

Base word: carpet
Possessive: carpet's design

(2) If the word ends in an *s,* add only an apostrophe:

Base word: dolls
Possessive: three dolls' dresses

Notice that if the word is singular, you simply apply these rules. If the word is to be plural, however, you make the word plural first, and then apply the rules.

Examples: dog (singular)
a dog's fleas (singular possessive)
two dogs (plural)
two dogs' fleas (plural possessive)

Note B: Some words—particularly those expressing units of time—may not seem possessive but still require an apostrophe:

Examples: a day's work
seven minutes' delay
a month's pay

Note C: Do not use an apostrophe to show possession for personal pronouns *(yours, his, hers, its, ours, theirs).*

Wrong: It's shell is broken.
Correct: Its shell is broken.

2. Use an apostrophe to show that letters have been left out of a word.

Examples: *cannot* becomes *can't*
do not becomes *don't*
does not becomes *doesn't*
I will becomes *I'll*
let us becomes *let's*
it is becomes *it's*

Note: The word *it's,* by the way, has only two meanings: "it is" or "it has."

EXERCISES

A. Write the two important rules for using an apostrophe.

1. _____

_____

2. _____

_____

B. Write an example that illustrates each of the above rules.

1. _____

_____

2. _____

_____

C. What class of words does not use an apostrophe to show possession?

_____

D. Form the singular and plural possessives of these words:

	singular possessive	plural possessive
second	_____	_____
piano	_____	_____
chairman	_____	_____
elephant	_____	_____
train	_____	_____
week	_____	_____
terra-cotta	_____	_____
potato	_____	_____
scissors	_____	_____
engine	_____	_____

E. Add the necessary apostrophes to these sentences:
1. Shelley said its been too long since weve visited my family or hers.
2. Zelda Fitzgeralds life is described in Nancy Mitfords *Zelda*.
3. Lisa didnt know that Mount McKinley is the United States highest mountain.
4. The squirrel collected its seeds into a small pile on the sheds roof.
5. The sound wasnt clear because one of the speakers wires was loose.
6. I dont know whether its true, but Janet claims that her neighbors dog has been howling for three nights.
7. As we slowly climbed the monasterys steps, we looked forward to seeing the chapels mosaic floor.
8. Germanys invasion of Poland in 1939 proved the might of the modern worlds weapons.
9. Lets discuss your companys offer over tomorrows lunch.
10. Its been too long since we visited that hunting cabin of yours.
11. After two days sightseeing in Florence wed seen the Baptistrys famous doors, the Uffizis paintings, and Michelangelos *David* in the Academy Gallery.
12. Enid indicated he wouldnt tolerate a seconds delay in making the stock his.
13. When you check the car to see if its finish was damaged by last nights hail, move the car back to its proper parking place.
14. Jacob stopped at the jewelers shop to see if both girls bracelets were engraved.
15. If that scarf is yours, see that its put away immediately.

31
Quotation Marks

This chapter presents the two important uses of quotation marks (" ") and three rules for using other punctuation with quotation marks.

1. *Use quotation marks to enclose the exact words written or spoken by someone else.*

> Example: Irving Knoke stated, "If someone is looking for an easy way to commit suicide, all he needs to do is stick his thumb out on any road."

2. *Use quotation marks to enclose the title of a poem, short story, magazine article, or newspaper article.* In other words, use quotation marks to enclose the title of a work that is published as part of another work. Poems and short stories are rarely published separately; rather, they are usually part of a book that includes other poems or stories. Similarly, magazine articles appear as part of a magazine, and newspaper articles appear as part of a newspaper.

Note: The book, magazine, or newspaper title—that is, the title of the larger work containing the poem, short story, or article—should be underlined (or italicized).

> Examples: "The Lottery," *Learning Fiction* (a short story in a collection of fiction)
>
> "The Love Song of J. Alfred Prufrock," *Poetry for First Graders* (a poem in a collection of poetry)
>
> "The Problems of Bigamy," *Gentlemen's Weekly Journal* (an article in a magazine)
>
> "Mayor Silvers wins again!" *Cripple Creek News* (an article in a newspaper)

The following rules explain how to use other punctuation with quotation marks:

1. *Always place periods and commas inside quotation marks.*

Examples: I enjoyed reading "The Lottery."
I just read "The Lottery," a strange story by Shirley Jackson.

2. *Always place semicolons and colons outside quotation marks.*

Examples: I just read "The Lottery"; it is weird.
There are three really interesting characters in "The Lottery": Mrs. Hutchinson, Old Man Warner, and Mr. Summers.

3. A. *Place question marks and exclamation points inside quotation marks if the quotation is a question or an exclamation.*

Examples: Tessie Hutchinson yelled, "That's not fair!"
The crowd answered, "Why do you say that, Tessie?"

Note: This rule applies even if the sentence is also a question or an exclamation.

Example: Was the crowd afraid of something when it asked Tessie, "Why do you say that, Tessie?"

B. *Place question marks and exclamation points outside quotation marks if the sentence is a question or an exclamation but the quotation is not.*

Examples: Who just said, "Steak fries are good"?
I can't believe you said, "Steak fries are better than noodles"!

EXERCISES

A. 1. What two marks of punctuation should you always place outside quotation marks? _____

_____

2. When are question marks and exclamation points placed inside quotation marks? _____

_____

3. What two marks of punctuation should you always place inside quotation marks? _____

   _____

4. When are question marks and exclamation points placed outside quotation marks? _____

   _____

B. What are the two important uses of quotation marks?

   1. _____

      _____

   2. _____

      _____

C. Add the necessary quotation marks in these sentences. Be careful to place quotation marks clearly inside or outside any other punctuation.

   1. I'm particularly fond of three short stories by H. H. Munro, who wrote under the name Saki: Sredni Vashtar, about a boy and his pet ferret; Tobermory, about a cat who talks; and Mrs. Packeltide's Tiger, about a wealthy woman and her tiger skin.

   2. In the story Sredni Vashtar, the title character is a polecat-ferret that is being kept by a boy named Conradin.

   3. When Conradin's cousin and keeper, Mrs. de Ropp, notices the time Conradin spends at the toolshed, she asks, What are you keeping in that locked hutch?

   4. After Mrs. de Ropp looks in the toolshed to find out Conradin's secret, only the ferret leaves the shed; Munro describes the exiting ferret this way: out through that doorway came a long, low, yellow-and-brown beast, with eyes a-blink at the waning daylight, and dark wet stains around the fur of jaws and throat.

   5. Do you know why Mrs. de Ropp's maid says, Whoever will break it to the poor child?

   6. The maid also exclaims, I couldn't for the life of me!

   7. In H. H. Munro's Tobermory, the main character is the house cat of Sir Wilfrid and Lady Blemley; a guest at their house party has taught the cat to talk.

   8. After looking for Tobermory to give a demonstration, Sir Wilfrid returns to his guests saying this about Tobermory: by Gad! he drawled out in a most horribly natural voice, that he'd come when he dashed well pleased! I nearly jumped out of my skin!

   9. Mavis Pellington makes the mistake of asking Tobermory this: What do you think of human intelligence?

   10. Tobermory counters, Of whose intelligence in particular?

11. When Mavis makes clear she is asking about her own intelligence, Tobermory replies, Sir Wilfrid protested that you were the most brainless woman of his acquaintance, and that there was a wide distinction between hospitality and the care of the feeble-minded.

12. Why does Major Barfield try to change the subject by asking, How about your carryings-on with the tortoise-shell puss up at the stables, eh?

13. Tobermory causes general panic at the house party when he answers, From a slight observation of your ways since you've been in the house I should imagine you'd find it inconvenient if I were to shift the conversation on to your own little affairs.

14. Can you blame Sir Wilfrid when he announces, We can put some strychnine in the scraps he always gets at dinner-time?

15. Like the story Tobermory, Mrs. Packeltide's Tiger is also a satire about life among the English gentry.

PART SEVEN
Expression

You can learn everything in Parts One through Six, but unless you express yourself skillfully, you'll still have trouble writing. This section offers some "dos" and "don'ts" that can help you improve your expression. Again, as in Part Six, we don't try to cover expression completely; we just talk about the problems most college students need to correct to improve their writing style.

32
Subordination

You probably know what *in*subordination is, but subordination is something else altogether.

When you first learned to read and write, almost every sentence was an independent clause: "Jane, see Spot." Every idea—small as it was—had exactly the same emphasis as every other idea. Of course, nobody in college writes like that, but too often college students have not progressed far enough from that grade-school style.

Your challenge is to combine related ideas into one sentence, giving them just the right emphasis. To succeed, you must learn subordination. We all know that a subordinate is someone who ranks lower than someone else. English has a rank structure, too:

Independent Clause	more important
Dependent Clause	↑
Phrase	↓
Word	less important

Ideas expressed in an independent clause naturally seem more important than ideas expressed by only a word. Subordination, then, reduces the emphasis of an idea by lowering its position on the rank structure. We might subordinate an idea originally in an independent clause by placing it in a dependent clause, a phrase, or—sometimes—even a word. For example:

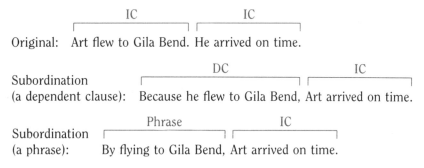

Original: Art flew to Gila Bend. He arrived on time.

Subordination
(a dependent clause):   Because he flew to Gila Bend, Art arrived on time.

Subordination
(a phrase):   By flying to Gila Bend, Art arrived on time.

Notice that subordination here has two effects. First, it shows that Art's arriving on time (expressed above in the independent clause) is the important idea to the writer. Second, it shows the relationship between the two ideas: the words *because* in the first revision and *by* in the second revision act as road signs, telling readers to be ready for a cause-effect relationship ("Because something happened, something else resulted." "Because he flew to Gila Bend, Art arrived on time."). These road signs make the readers' task much easier.

Now let's return to the example. We could have subordinated the second independent clause, instead, if we had decided that Art's flying to Gila Bend was more important than the idea that he arrived on time:

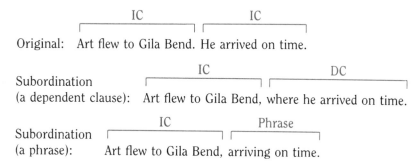

When you write, therefore, you have to decide which ideas you wish to emphasize and which you wish to subordinate.

"But," you might protest, "I use subordination all the time." Sure you do—though probably not enough. Let's express some ideas in grade-school style, early college style, and a more sophisticated style:

Grade-school style: The girl is playing tennis.
                        Her name is Sally.
                        She is a beginner.
                        She is taking lessons.
                        Karen is teaching her.
                        Karen is a professional.
                        Karen teaches at the Andromeda Club.
                        Karen teaches every Tuesday morning.

Early college style: Sally is playing tennis.
                        She is taking beginning lessons from Karen.
                        Karen is a professional, and she teaches at the Andromeda Club every Tuesday morning.

Improved style: Sally is taking beginning tennis lessons from Karen, a professional who teaches at the Andromeda Club every Tuesday morning.

This last revision certainly is easier to read than either of the other versions. Why? Subordination pushes the unimportant ideas to the side of the stage so the viewers can easily see the star, the independent clause.

Here's a final tip to help you with subordination. On a first draft, you're naturally too busy thinking of ideas to worry about the best way to piece them together. After you finish that draft, though, take another trip through your paper—beginning to end—just working on the best way to combine your ideas into better sentences.

Remember, your work while you write makes your readers' work much easier. Subordination lets readers see which ideas you consider important. And, after you finish school, that's the main reason you will write.

EXERCISES

A. Combine these simple sentences in two different ways, emphasizing a different idea each time.

1. The *Hindenburg* was the world's largest airship. It crashed at Lakehurst, New Jersey, in 1937.

   a. _____

   b. _____

2. Chung Wi-Suk is from Seoul, Korea. His father is a doctor who was educated at Stanford.

   a. _____

   b. _____

3. Tom Eliot was a drummer. He played in a group called The Wasteland.

   a. _____

   b. _____

4. Geraniums are the most common houseplant. They have red, white, or pink flowers.

   a. _____

   b. _____

5. My grandmother lived on a farm for forty-one years. Now she lives in a condo in Florida.

   a. _____

   b. _____

B. For each sentence below, combine all the ideas in the simple sentences into one good sentence:

1. Gloria Steinem founded *Ms.* magazine.
   She is a heroine to many people.
   She writes short stories and essays.
   She advocates feminist ideas.

   _____

   _____

   _____

2. The man was a con man.
   He looked like a real doctor.
   He wore a white coat.
   He wore a stethoscope.
   He spoke to the committee.
   He spoke convincingly.
   He spoke about the advantages of Thanatopsis Snake Oil.

   _____

   _____

   _____

3. Marla finally got home.
   She had been to track practice.
   She had run three miles of wind sprints.
   She had a flat tire.
   She had to stop for gasoline.
   She is tired.
   She is hungry.

   _____

   _____

   _____

4. Ellen Watkins wrote the "Student Manifesto."
   She is a political science major.
   Her home is in Fairfield, Washington.
   She is a junior.
   The manifesto demands more open hours for the library and better food at
     the cafeteria.
   The manifesto was approved by 94 percent of the students.

   _____

   _____

   _____

5. The state lottery drawing was held last week.
   A man named Oodles Goldsby won the jackpot.
   The jackpot amounted to $725,000.
   Goldsby collects cactus plants and raises rabbits.
   His name comes from his size.
   He weighs 320 pounds and is 5'9" tall.

   _____

   _____

   _____

33
Sentence Variety

After reading the preceding chapter, you may suspect that "good" writing consists of one complicated sentence after another. Not so; you'd lose the readers after a couple of pages. On the other hand, how would you like to read sentence after sentence in grade-school or early college style? You may think the solution is to write all medium-length sentences, but really good writing consists of a mixture, of both *sentence lengths* and *sentence structures.*

Now, variety just for the sake of variety is really not the goal. But good sentence variety is often an indication of good coherence—of the smooth flow of ideas from one to another. So if you find yourself writing many short sentences in a row, or beginning many sentences with the subject of the independent clause, ask yourself, "Do my sentence patterns help my ideas flow smoothly? Or do they make my ideas seem fragmented, choppy?"

This chapter will give you some tips on how to vary your sentences to achieve better coherence.

SENTENCE LENGTH

Actually, not very many people have poor sentence variety from writing only long sentences. The problem is usually a series of short sentences:

The new governor was sworn in today. He is a Democrat. Ten thousand people attended the ceremony. The governor gave a brief inaugural address. The governor promised to end unemployment. He said he would reduce inflation. He also promised to improve the environment. The audience gave him a standing ovation.

Pretty dismal, right? The average sentence length is only six and a quarter words, and all the sentences except the second are either six or seven words long—not overwhelming variety. Let's use the technique of subordination we learned in the last chapter to come up with something better:

> The new Democratic governor was sworn in today. At a ceremony attended by ten thousand people, he gave a brief inaugural address, promising to end unemployment, reduce inflation, and improve the environment. The audience gave him a standing ovation.

This version is certainly much easier to read, mainly because we've eliminated choppiness and subordinated some unimportant ideas. The average sentence is now thirteen words long, within the desirable goal of twelve to twenty words per sentence.

SENTENCE STRUCTURE

Let's look again at our bad example. Notice how many sentences begin with the subject (and its modifiers) of an independent clause:

> The new governor was sworn in today. He is a Democrat. Ten thousand people attended the ceremony. The governor gave a brief inaugural address. The governor promised to end unemployment. He said he would reduce inflation. He also promised to improve the environment. The audience gave him a standing ovation.

Every sentence begins with the subject of an independent clause. Surely there is a better way to move from sentence to sentence than to begin every one with the subject. Some should begin with dependent clauses, others with phrases, and still others with transitional words. For example, look again at the revision:

> The new Democratic governor was sworn in today. *At a ceremony attended by ten thousand people,* he gave a brief inaugural address, promising to end unemployment, reduce inflation, and improve the environment. The audience gave him a standing ovation.

The introductory phrases in the second sentence provide nice relief.

You may think *you* would never begin a lot of sentences the same way. Perhaps. However, during the first draft many writers think of an idea and then write it down: "Subject—verb"; they think of another idea and write it down: "Subject—verb"; and so on. Then, because they never revise that draft for sentence variety, their sentences all begin the same way. Check your last few papers to see if you have fallen into this bad habit.

Many sentences, of course, should begin with the subject of an independent clause; however, they should still not all look alike. They could end with a dependent clause, they could contain a couple of independent clauses, or they could contain a series of parallel phrases or clauses (see Chapter 34). The sentences in the paragraph you are now reading, for example, all begin with the subject of an independent clause, but after that beginning, their structures vary considerably.

SOME ADVICE

Good writing is not an automatic process, a flow of uninterrupted inspiration pouring forth from a pen. It is the result of a painstaking and *very conscious* process. If you want to write with good sentence variety, you have to check your draft to see if the variety is there. Don't just hope it will happen to you. After writing that draft, ask yourself these questions:

1. Are my sentences different lengths?
2. Do my sentences begin in a variety of ways?
3. Do those sentences that do begin with the subject of an independent clause have a variety of structures?

If your answers are "no," then edit your paper for sentence variety. Be careful, though, so you don't sacrifice clearness just for the sake of variety. And don't create grotesque, unnatural sentences. Variety is a means to achieve the goal of good writing—it is not the goal itself.

EXERCISES

Revise these paragraphs for better sentence variety. In both the original and your revision, circle the subject of the first independent clause in every sentence. Then compute the average number of words in each sentence (count all the words in the paragraph and divide by the number of sentences).

A. Original: I had never thought much about carpets before. They were always just there. Sometimes they were soft and dark like the ones in movie houses. Other times they were shaggy and yellow. That's the kind my aunt has in her house in Philadelphia. Then I got a job in a carpet store. I had to learn a whole lot more about carpets. I had to learn about the backing, the pile, and the density. The backing is the material on the bottom of the rug. It can be made of jute, or rubber mixture, or a kind of plastic. The pile describes the height of the carpet. The density tells you how many threads per square inch. I also learned about the materials. There is wool, but it is very expensive. It costs about $48 per square yard. Sometimes wool is blended with artificial fibers. Those carpets are not quite so expensive and are easier to clean. The lowest-cost carpets are made of plastic and look like artificial grass. They cost about $2 per yard. For most people, a carpet that is made of an artificial fiber is best. A good-quality one will cost about $12 per square yard. It will last for ten or fifteen years. But the color is another problem. I can now help customers with carpet quality. They have to choose the color.

Average number of words per sentence _____

Your revision:

_____

_____

_____

_____

_____

_____

_____

_____

_____

_____

_____

Average number of words per sentence _____

B. Original:

Many people today associate Mickey Spillane only with television commercials for low-calorie beer. Paperback book racks reveal the real Spillane legacy. Mickey Spillane popularized a type of tough detective. For this detective ends justify means. Mike Hammer is the "hero" in Spillane's *I, the Jury*. Hammer seeks revenge for the brutal killing of a close friend. Hammer declares himself judge, jury, and executioner. Then Hammer breaks most ethical and social laws while he pursues his private brand of justice. Hammer's actions in other books are equally immoral. However, the ugliness always occurs as Hammer rights some wrong. For years the marketplace success of Spillane's books has been tremendous. *I, the Jury* was first published in 1947. Authors still routinely reproduce Mike Hammer and his ethic. The questionable honor of spawning modern paperback series belongs to Mickey Spillane. These series include the Avenger, the Revenger, and the Executioner. You are sure to find some of these wherever cheap literature is sold.

Average number of words per sentence _____

Your revision: _____

_____

_____

_____

_____

_____

_____

_____

_____

_____

_____

_____

Average number of words per sentence _____

34
Parallelism

Now that you've studied sentence variety, you may be afraid of writing sentences that repeat simple patterns. Don't be. Some ideas work best in sentences that clearly show a pattern. When you analyze an idea, you take pains to discover similarities and differences among its parts. Whether you intend to compare or contrast those elements, you want readers to see how the parts are alike or different. Parallelism is the key.

The principle of parallel construction is simple: *be sure ideas that are similar in content and function look the same.* Parallelism works in a sentence because the similarity of the appearance of the items shows clearly the pattern of the thought. The principle of parallelism applies most often to two or more items in a series with a coordinating conjunction and to pairs of items with correlative conjunctions (explained below).

ITEMS IN A SERIES WITH A COORDINATING CONJUNCTION

The principle of parallelism requires that all items in a series must be grammatically alike. That is, all words in a series must be the same type of word, all phrases the same type of phrase, and all clauses the same type of clause. Two or more items in a series normally use a coordinating conjunction (CC): *and, but, or, nor, for, so,* or *yet.* Thus, the series looks like this:

item CC item

or this

item, item, CC item.

286

Here are sentences with parallel constructions:

Words in series:

item CC item

I saw John and Mary.

item item CC item

I saw John, Bill, and Mary.

Phrases in series:

item CC item

I see him going to work and coming home.

item CC item

I plan to eat in a restaurant and to see a movie.

Dependent clauses in series:

item CC

The phone rang when I reached the motel but

item

before I unpacked my suitcases.

Independent clauses in series:

item CC item

I liked the parrot, so I bought it for my mother.

Notice that each item—word, phrase, or clause—in a series has the same form as the other items in the same series.

Although words in a series seldom present special problems, if the words are preceded by the articles *a, an,* or *the,* be sure the articles fall in one of these two patterns:

article word, word, CC word

article word, *article* word, CC *article* word

Notice the placement of the articles in these sample sentences:

Wrong: I bought food for *the* dog, cat, and *the* horse.

Correct: I bought food for *the* dog, cat, and horse.

Correct: I bought food for *the* dog, *the* cat, and *the* horse.

The correct sentences have either an article before the entire series or an article before every item in the series.

Unlike words in a series, phrases often cause problems. Many times students mix types of phrases. Be sure that *-ing* phrases fit with other *-ing* phrases, *to* phrases with *to* phrases, and so forth.

Wrong: I like *swimming in the pond, cycling down the lane,* and *to ride horses in the pasture.*

Correct: I like *swimming in the pond, cycling down the lane,* and *riding horses in the pasture.*

Correct: I like *to swim in the pond, to cycle down the lane,* and *to ride horses in the pasture.*

Wrong: I plan *to study hard, doing well on my exams,* and *to graduate with honors.*

Correct: I plan *to study hard, to do well on my exams,* and *to graduate with honors.*

Correct: I plan on *studying hard, doing well on my exams,* and *graduating with honors.*

Clauses in a series seldom cause major problems. However, if the series contains dependent clauses, you can help your readers by signaling the beginning of each dependent clause. Consider this sentence:

I expect to be entertained if I'm going to pay $5 to get in a theater and I'm going to sit there for two hours.

What does the *and* join? Does it join the two independent clauses?

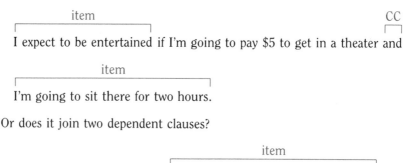

Or does it join two dependent clauses?

The intended meaning is probably the second one: the *and* joins two dependent clauses. Readers will more easily see the separation of items if the writer repeats the word that signals the beginning of the clauses:

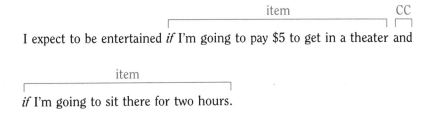

I expect to be entertained *if* I'm going to pay $5 to get in a theater and

if I'm going to sit there for two hours.

Now the meaning is clear. Here's another sample:

"I can see that you don't like the meal and that you'd rather not be here," she pouted.

Notice that the repetition of *that* (which signals the beginning of dependent clauses) makes the parallel construction clear.

In addition to having like words, like phrases, and like clauses in a series, be sure that the items in a series are the same type of grammatical unit. Do not, for instance, mix phrases and clauses in a series, as in this sentence:

item CC item

Wrong: My roommate likes to sleep in bed and when he's in class.

The sentence is awkward because the writer has joined a phrase *(in bed)* with a clause *(when he's in class)*. Here's what the writer should have written:

Correct: My roommate likes to sleep when he's in bed and when he's in class.

Now a clause fits with a clause. (Notice also that the sentence repeats *when,* the word that signals the beginning of each dependent clause.)

PAIRS OF ITEMS WITH CORRELATIVE CONJUNCTIONS

Correlative conjunctions mate pairs of related items. Common correlative conjunctions are these: *either . . . or; neither . . . nor; not (only) . . . but (also);* and *whether . . . or.* The rule for parallelism with correlative conjunctions is simple: the grammatical units following each of the correlative conjunctions must be alike. Items mated by correlative conjunctions (CorC) will look like this:

CorC item CorC item.

Here are sentences with such pairs:

CorC   item   CorC   item

I don't like either his appearance or his manners.

CorC   item CorC   item

Neither my aunt nor my cousin will speak to me.

Can you find the problem in this sentence?

Wrong: *Either* I go to bed early *or* get up late.

This sentence demonstrates the most common failure to maintain parallelism with correlative conjunctions: *either* precedes the subject of the sentence *(I)*, but *or* precedes the second verb *(get)*. There are two methods to deal with the problem:

Correct: I *either* go to bed early *or* get up late.

Correct: *Either* I go to bed early *or* I get up late.

The first solution moves *either* so that both correlative conjunctions precede verbs *(go* and *get)*. The second solution places *either* and *or* before subjects of clauses *(I* and *I)*. In both corrections, the grammatical units following each correlative conjunction are alike.

All of this may seem complicated, but it's not. You wouldn't try to compare apples and automobiles, because they're not alike. Similarly, you can't expect your readers to accept a comparison of items that don't appear to be alike. The principle of parallelism requires only that you make like items *look* alike so readers can see the similarity.

EXERCISES

A. 1. Name the seven coordinating conjunctions. _____

_____

2. Explain the principle of parallelism as it applies to a series with a coordinating conjunction. _____

_____

3. Name the four common pairs of correlative conjunctions.

_____

_____

4. Explain the principle of parallelism as it applies to a pair of items with correlative conjunctions. _____

_____

B. Improve the parallelism in each of the following sentences:
1. I had to write a physics paper, the phone company, and to my mother.
2. Stackley brought the compact disc player, discs, and the speakers.
3. After I wrote my physics paper, I went out to run, swim, and lifting weights.
4. Carlos came to the party for the food, music, and to see old friends.
5. Pat has always liked to cook and baking.
6. Elroy finally told his mother he wanted to go skiing, soak in the hot tub, and always avoiding work.
7. I'll decide to go to Stackley's party if it neither is on Saturday nor it happens to conflict with my brother's visit.
8. Overheated by the sun and with dehydration, I stopped running at mile seven in the July 4th road race.
9. Both the gardeners and workers who painted the garage were paid the same.
10. After running and I rewrote my physics paper, I ordered a pizza from Arny's.
11. We can go see a war film or to get something to eat.
12. As the buzzard rose into the air and stretching its wings, I thought it was ungainly and ugly.
13. Stackley had trouble getting the compact disc player to work, making the ice cream, and to move all the furniture.
14. The pizza delivery boy both wanted a new car and to quit his job.
15. Lifting weights, to swim, and run are all good exercises after hours of sitting in a computer lab.
16. After the party, Elroy picked up a purple bandana, stale tortilla, and Myra's cello bow.
17. Elroy, thinking the cello bow belonged to Myra and wanted to return it, borrowed Lafferty's bike.
18. Peg never liked running, football players, or to drive a stick-shift car.
19. The film director sought locations in the streets of New York and where people were scarce in Nevada.

20. Chung talked to an immigration officer, a bishop, and to his senator about ·helping.

21. Having borrowed Lafferty's bike and with Myra's bow held under his arm, Elroy rode off looking like a medieval knight.

22. But to travel, reading, and going to the opera were always important.

23. Carlos left the party early because he didn't have the time, the interest, and he lacked the energy to dance.

24. The delivery boy picked up the empty pizza box, five-cent tip, and red cap he wore.

25. Finishing my run and as I crossed Fourth Street, I was hit by a fellow on a bicycle and the cello bow he was carrying.

35
Misused Modifiers

Dangling participle! Nothing—not even "split infinitive"—can strike such terror in the heart of an English student. But don't be afraid. Behind the fancy name is a simple concept you'll understand after studying this chapter. You won't learn the differences between dangling participles, dangling gerunds, and dangling infinitives because the differences aren't really important: we'll treat them all more simply as *dangling modifiers*. In addition to the special type of modifier problem, you'll also study *misplaced modifiers*. But first, you may wonder what a modifier is.

Modifiers are words, phrases, or clauses that limit or describe other words. For example, in "I never saw a purple cow," the modifier *purple* limits the discussion from "all cows" to only "purple cows."

As you've seen in earlier chapters, modifiers allow you to combine several ideas into one sentence. You might write this:

Jonathan ate the doughnut. It was the only doughnut.

However, you save time and space by reducing the second sentence to a modifier:

Jonathan ate the *only* doughnut.

Still, there is a catch: word order in an English sentence often determines meaning; therefore, different word arrangements may yield different meanings. Let's see what happens if we place *only* in every possible position in "Jonathan ate the doughnut."

Only Jonathan ate the doughnut.   (No one else ate it.)

Jonathan *only* ate the doughnut.   (He didn't do anything else to it.)

Jonathan ate *only* the doughnut.   (He ate nothing else.)

Jonathan ate the *only* doughnut.   (There were no other doughnuts.)

Jonathan ate the doughnut *only*.   (He ate nothing else.)

Five combinations yield four distinctly different meanings. Play this game with other sentences and with words such as *only, almost, most, just, every, merely,* and *nearly.*

The game's implication is obvious: unless you carefully place the modifiers in your sentences, you may not write what you really mean. If modifiers do not clearly modify what they are supposed to, they may obscure your meaning, or they may make you look ridiculous.

MISPLACED MODIFIERS

Placing a modifier in a sentence requires good judgment and careful editing. No particular place in a sentence is always right for a modifier, but this much is true: a modifier tends to modify what it is close to. "Close to" may be before or after the thing modified, so long as the sentence makes sense. These sentences don't make much sense:

A jeep ran over the soldier *that had muddy tires.*

People stared in amazement *on the sidewalk.*

The accident left *neatly pressed* tire marks on the soldier's shirt.

In these sentences something comes between the modifiers and the things modified. As a result, the modifiers appear to refer to the things they are closest to: *that had muddy tires* seems to modify *soldier; on the sidewalk* seems to refer to *amazement;* and *neatly pressed* appears to modify *tire marks.*

Let's move the modifiers so that they modify what they should.

A jeep *that had muddy tires* ran over the soldier.

On the sidewalk, people stared in amazement.

or

People *on the sidewalk* stared in amazement.

The accident left tire marks on the soldier's *neatly pressed* shirt.

Notice that *on the sidewalk* works before or after *people,* whereas *that had muddy tires* works only after *jeep* and *neatly pressed* works only before *shirt.* What matters, then, is that the modifier must be close enough to the thing it modifies to complete the thought logically.

A second type of placement problem occurs when you write strings of modifiers. Consider this example:

A man *with red hair in a green suit* crossed the street.

Both *with red hair* and *in a green suit* should modify *man,* but instead *in a green suit* seems to refer to *hair.* One solution is to put one modifier before and another after the thing modified:

A *red-haired* man *in a green suit* crossed the street.

or

Wearing a green suit, a man *with red hair* crossed the street.

A second solution is to combine the modifiers with a coordinating conjunction:

A man *with red hair and a green suit* crossed the street.

Again, the exact position of the modifier doesn't matter if the result makes sense.

DANGLING MODIFIERS

Dangling modifiers can occur anywhere in a sentence, but the most common problem is at the beginning. A modifier that *begins* a sentence must refer to something that follows. Because of convention, readers expect an introductory word or phrase modifier to refer to the subject of the sentence.

Walking along the beach, Mary found a sand dollar.

Since we expect the opening phrase *(walking along the beach)* to modify the subject of the sentence *(Mary),* we know that Mary, not the sand dollar, was walking along the beach. But what if the sentence reads as follows?

Walking along the beach, a sand dollar was found by Mary.

Again we expect the introductory phrase to modify the subject of the sentence, but sand dollars don't walk. Since the modifier cannot logically modify the subject of the sentence, we say that the modifier "dangles."

The following sentences contain dangling modifiers:

Enthusiastic, the hour seemed to pass quickly.

Finishing the game, the crowd loudly booed the home team.

After examining the data, the steam engine appeared to be the best choice.

To enjoy surfing, the waves must be high.

When only nine, John's mother took him to a circus.

Was the hour enthusiastic? Did the crowd actually finish the game? Did the steam engine examine the data? Can waves enjoy surfing? Do you really believe that John had a mother who was only nine years old? Because the modifiers above have no logical connection to the subjects of the sentences, the modifiers dangle.

You have two options to correct dangling modifiers. The most obvious method is to rewrite the sentence so that the subject matches the modifier.

Enthusiastic, we thought the hour passed quickly.

Finishing the game, the home team heard loud booing from the crowd.

After examining the data, we concluded that the steam engine was the best choice.

To enjoy surfing, you need high waves.

When only nine, John went to a circus with his mother.

These corrections leave the modifier unchanged.

The second method is to change the phrase or word modifier into a clause.

Because we were enthusiastic, the hour seemed to pass quickly.

As the game ended, the crowd loudly booed the home team.

After we examined the data, the steam engine appeared to be the best choice.

If you want to enjoy surfing, the waves must be high.

When John was only nine, his mother took him to a circus.

You can avoid problem modifiers—misplaced as well as dangling—if you keep in mind the essential relationship between modifiers and the things they refer to: a modifier tends to modify what it is close to, and a modifier should be close to what it must modify.

EXERCISES

A. 1. When is a modifier misplaced? _____

_____

2. How can you correct a misplaced modifier? _____

_____

3. When does a modifier dangle? _____

_____

4. How can you correct a dangling modifier? Name two ways.

a. _____

_____

b. _____

_____

B. 1. Write one sentence with a misplaced modifier and one with a dangling modifier.

a. _____

_____

b. _____

_____

2. Now correct your sentences.

a. _____

_____

b. _____

_____

C. Rewrite the following sentences to eliminate the modifier problems.
1. Walking on the sidewalk, the Volkswagen ran into me.
2. Professor Snidely returned the exams to the students covered with blotches of red ink.

3. He was only a child a mother could love.
4. Running the word processing program, the printer jammed.
5. Professor Snidely sipped the decaffeinated tea with an expression of arrogance.
6. He almost seemed disappointed.
7. I quit at Wendy's after two years' employment on Monday.
8. The president wishes you to notify her if you will attend on the enclosed card.
9. My mother borrowed an egg from Mr. Eldritch that was rotten.
10. His trainer told him frequently to do back stretches.
11. Being made of plastic, I did not expect the coffee filter to last very long.
12. He put the cowboy hat on his head which he had bought in Phoenix.
13. Driving through Yellowstone, five bears were seen by my family.
14. Grades will only be released after all final examinations are turned in.
15. Who is the man who gave you directions to the gym in the business suit?
16. She bought the Irish setter from a neighbor with a sore front paw.
17. The furnace exploded shortly after the dancers left rehearsal with a roar.
18. When completely exhausted, the researcher should refill the experimental atmospheric beaker.
19. Having finished the third act, the audience applauded long and loud in response to the actress's performance.
20. Professor Snidely only has class meetings on Fridays at 4:00 P.M.
21. Bleating piteously, Mary allowed the lamb to follow her to school.
22. The mortician figured that he had very nearly embalmed twelve hundred bodies.
23. Opening the door, the mountain peak in the distance became visible.
24. Being nervous, the interview might get off on the wrong note for the journalism student.
25. Having been precise and honest all her life, the dice game Helen's aunt runs in Corona shows the results of her experience as dean of women.

36
Subject-Verb Agreement

You've learned in school that there are many rules in grammar, and you've probably learned from experience that the ways to make mistakes in grammar are more numerous than the rules. But you can apply most of the rules correctly already. This chapter deals with only one grammar problem—agreement between subjects and verbs. The rule itself is quite simple: *a verb must agree in number with its subject.* If the subject is singular, the verb must be singular; if the subject is plural, the verb must be plural.

Usually the verb itself doesn't cause trouble. In fact, the forms for many singular and plural verbs are identical, so you can't make a mistake in agreement. Yet English verbs retain one peculiarity that some students find troublesome. You know that an *-s* or *-es* ending on a noun makes the noun plural. The same would seem to be true for verbs, but it isn't. An *-s* or *-es* ending on a verb makes the verb singular:

Plural	*Singular*
They run.	He run*s*.
They go.	She go*es*.
They jump.	It jump*s*.

Other than this simple difference between verbs and nouns, the verb doesn't cause much difficulty. Most errors in agreement, then, occur because of some difficulty related to the subject. Some problems arise from trouble with *identifying the subject;* others result from uncertainty in *recognizing the subject's number.*

IDENTIFYING THE SUBJECT

We can usually find the subject if it comes in its ordinary place—just before the verb—but we may have trouble if it follows the verb. Watch for

299

sentences opening with *there* or *here*. These words delay the subject so that it appears after the verb. You'll have to think through such a sentence because you won't know whether the verb should be singular or plural until you get beyond it to the subject.

          V   S

There *are* three *sailboats* at the dock.

          V   S

There *is* the *sailboat* with the sail on upside down.

          V   S

Here *are* the *supplies* you ordered.

          V   S

Here *is* the *box* you wanted first.

Sometimes even when the subject comes before the verb, it is still hard to identify, especially if we have written a phrase between the subject and the verb. Then we might think a word in that phrase is the subject or (just as bad) that the phrase is part of the subject and therefore makes it plural. Let's look first at an example in which a word in the phrase might seem to be the subject:

                      S   V

Wrong: One of the Coyne *boys have climbed* the water tower.

Here the word *boys* is so close to the verb that the writer thought it was the subject. He was wrong. *Boys* is simply part of a phrase that comes between the subject and the verb. The real subject is *one:*

              S   V

Correct: *One* of the Coyne boys *has climbed* the water tower.

Now let's look at a phrase that might seem to be part of the subject:

                      S   V

Wrong: *Martha, as well as her sisters, work* in the fields regularly.

As well as her sisters seems to be part of the subject. It seems to be equivalent to *and her sisters.* But it isn't. *As well as* and these other words below

are merely prepositions and therefore have nothing to do with determining
the agreement between a subject and its verb.

as well as	including
accompanied by	like
along with	together with
in addition to	with

How can we find the subject in our example above? Mentally eliminate the
entire phrase:

     S   V

Correct: *Martha* (~~as well as her sisters~~) *works* in the fields regularly.

The subject is now clear.

RECOGNIZING THE SUBJECT'S NUMBER

The problems we just looked at occur because the subject isn't where we
expect it to be. Sometimes, though, we can find the subject and still not
know whether it is singular or plural. These rules will help you:

1. Two or more subjects joined by *and* are almost always plural. The *and*
    joins the items—singular, plural, or mixed—into one plural unit.

   S   S   V

Charlotte and her *mother drive* the metallic brown dune buggy.

     S   S   V

That *woman* and her *husband look* a lot alike.

There is an exception: if the two subjects joined by *and* refer to a single
person or act as a single unit, then use a singular verb.

     S   S   V

A *scholar* and *gentleman is* what we need for a leader.

2. If *or* or *nor* joins subjects, the verb agrees with whichever subject is
    closer to the verb.

     S   S   V

Either *Beverly* or my other *aunts have* my thanks.

Here *aunts* is closer to the verb than is *Beverly,* so the verb is plural. What if we reverse the subjects?

S   S   V

Either my other *aunts* or *Beverly has* my thanks.

Now *Beverly* is closer, so the verb is singular.

This rule still applies if both items are singular or if both items are plural. If both are singular, naturally a singular subject will be next to the verb, so the verb is singular. Likewise, if both subjects are plural, a plural subject will be next to the verb, so the verb is plural.

3. *Some, all, none, part, half* (and other fractions) may be either singular or plural, depending on the phrase that follows them. You probably think we're crazy because we told you in the first part of the chapter not to let a phrase between the subject and the verb influence subject-verb agreement. Well, here is an exception to that rule.

   Many times the words in the list above are followed by a phrase beginning with *of* ("All *of* the jurors . . . ," "Some *of* the tea . . ."). If the main word in the *of*-phrase is plural, then the verb should be plural. However, if the main word is singular or just can't be counted (we wouldn't say "one *milk*" or "thirteen *tea,*" for example), then the verb should be singular.

S   V

Some of the grapes *are* still on the table. (*Grapes* is plural, so the verb is plural.)

S   V

Some of the milk *is dripping* on the floor. (*Milk* cannot be counted, so the verb is singular.)

4. Relative pronouns (*who, whose, whom, which,* and *that*) may be singular or plural, depending on the word they refer to. Usually the relative pronoun refers to the word just before it:

S   V

Jeannette is one of the children *who love* to read. (*Who* is a pronoun replacing *children.* Not just one child but all the children love to read.)

Again, here comes an exception. What if Jeannette is the only one in the group who loves to read? Then the pronoun *who* refers to the word *one,* not the word *children:*

$$\overset{\text{S} \quad \text{V}}{}$$

Jeannette is the only one of the children *who loves* to read.

The exception, then, is that in the phrase *the only one . . . who/that*, the relative pronoun refers to the word *one*, so the verb must be singular (after all, what can be more singular than *one*?).

EXERCISES

A. Use one of the following verbs when completing this exercise:
Singular verbs: *throws, goes, misses, takes*
Plural verbs: *throw, go, miss, take*
Do not use other forms of these verbs (such as *threw, had thrown*, or the like).

1. a. Write a sentence that has the subject following the verb. Use a singular verb.

   _____

   b. Now use a plural verb.

   _____

2. Write a sentence with a singular subject and the phrase *as well as (fill in a word)* between the subject and the verb.

   _____

3. Write a sentence that has two subjects joined by *and*.

   _____

4. a. Write a sentence with two plural subjects joined by *or*.

   _____

   b. Write a sentence with two singular subjects joined by *or*.

   _____

   c. Write a sentence with a singular and a plural subject joined by *or*.

   _____

   d. Rewrite sentence *c* but reverse the order of the subjects.

   _____

5. Write a sentence with *all* as the subject and a phrase beginning with *of* between it and the verb.

   _____

6. Write a sentence that contains a relative pronoun as a subject and draw an arrow to the word it refers to.

_____

B. Circle the correct verb.

1. Hester is the only one of the divers who (has, have) a chance for a letter.
2. Either Mike or his brother (have, has) the mumps.
3. There (is, are) only a chair and desk left to sell.
4. One of the kids or the dog (is, are) banging into the fence.
5. Each of the secretaries (complain, complains) about the smoke in the office hallway.
6. There (is, are) fewer burglaries since the "Gentleman Bandit" was arrested last month.
7. The type of bread dough that bakers use in some recipes (is, are) very difficult to knead.
8. Angie is one of the women who (is, are) driving in the race.
9. Mike is the only one of the brothers who (like, likes) diet soft drinks.
10. Consequently, there (is, are) bloodshed, revolution, and chaos.
11. The coach, as well as the fans, (was, were) elated about the last-second goal.
12. The first three chapters of the physics book (was, were) uninspiring.
13. The rest of the book, however, along with the illustrations, (was, were) fascinating.
14. The committee on the selection of the new dean (do, does) not approve of Professor Snidely.
15. Ignorance is one of the major failures that (cause, causes) crime.
16. Two suggestions to solve the traffic problem have been submitted but so far neither (has, have) been tried.
17. Lackley's earnestness and his logical mind (make, makes) him a favorite with the freshman girls.
18. Not one of his many relatives (was, were) at his funeral.
19. Neither the bird nor the bee (has, have) to be told about people.
20. There (was, were), according to Congressman Gasjet's ideas, at least one objection to a frank discussion of his record.
21. Each of the oysters (is, are) to be stewed in its own juice.
22. A chorus of hoots and jeers (was, were) heard throughout the stadium.
23. Stanley Williams believed that one of the greatest crimes (was, were) poverty.
24. Hester may be the only one of the girls who (win, wins) her letter.
25. Economics (is, are) a difficult course to finish because there (is, are) so many things to consider.

37
Pronoun Agreement

This chapter deals with another agreement problem—agreement between pronouns and the things they refer to.

Because pronouns replace nouns or other pronouns in sentences, a pronoun must have something to refer to (called the *antecedent* of the pronoun). Look for the antecedent for *his* in this sentence:

The boy found his dog.

Clearly, *his* refers to *boy,* so *boy* is the antecedent for *his.*

The grammar rule that students often find troublesome is this: *A pronoun must agree in number with its antecedent.* If the antecedent is singular, the pronoun must be singular; if the antecedent is plural, the pronoun must be plural.

Because the pronoun's number depends on the antecedent, our attention should be on problem antecedents. When the antecedent is simple, making the pronoun agree is a simple task. You wouldn't write this:

The *boys* looked for *his* books. (Assume all the boys are missing books.)

Boys is a plural antecedent, so you'd write this:

The *boys* looked for *their* books.

Yet, special problems do arise with two types of antecedents: *indefinite pronoun antecedents* and *compound antecedents.*

INDEFINITE PRONOUN ANTECEDENTS

The biggest headache connected with pronoun agreement occurs when the antecedent is an indefinite pronoun like *everyone* or *nobody.* We needn't be concerned here with all indefinite pronouns, but we must look at one problem group.

The following indefinite pronouns are singular and always require singular pronoun references:

each	everyone	everybody
either	someone	somebody
neither	anyone	anybody
another	no one	nobody
one		

The words formed from *-one* (like *everyone*) and from *-body* (like *everybody*) often seem to be plural, but they're not. Try thinking of them as if they had the word *single* in the middle, like this: *every-single-one* or *every-single-body*. Now they seem to be singular, as they really are.

An unusual mental block is associated with these indefinite pronouns. Few people would write this:

Everyone *have* a coat.

Have just doesn't sound right following *everyone*. And for good reason. *Have* is plural, but *everyone* is singular. Yet, often the same people who recognize *everyone* as a singular subject have trouble recognizing *everyone* as a singular antecedent. Far too often they write this:

Everyone *has their* coat.

Has, of course, is correct: the singular verb agrees with the singular subject. But plural *their* cannot refer to singular *everyone*. As illogical as this problem seems, it is still common.

Study these samples:

Wrong: Everyone wore *their* coat.

Correct: Everyone wore *his* coat.

Wrong: Nobody looked at *their* books.

Correct: Nobody looked at *his* books.

You may be uneasy with these correct answers because often the *everyone* you are talking about refers to a mixed group of men and women, in which case the word *his* may seem inappropriate. You're right, of course. Usage is changing, though in formal English the conventional use of *his* to refer to both sexes is still common. But considerate writers will avoid the kind of sexist tone that comes from using only the masculine form when writing about people in general. Using words like *his* or *mankind* omits more than half the population.

We know of at least three ways to solve the problem. First, you might use "his or her," as in these sentences:

No one read his or her assignment.

Everybody brought her or his book instead.

But you certainly won't want to use several of this kind of sentence close together because the repetition grows awkward and tiresome, attracting attention to itself.

A second way simply omits the pronoun.

Instead of this: Everyone wore his coat.

Better: Everyone wore a coat.

Instead of this: Each of the voters cast his ballot.

Better: Each of the voters cast a ballot.

The third (and best) method avoids the problem by changing both antecedent and pronoun reference to plural forms.

Instead of this: Everyone wore his coat.

Better: All wore their coats.

Instead of this: Each of the voters cast his ballot.

Better: All of the voters cast their ballots.

Similar problems occur with words like *each, either, neither, another,* and *one.* Usually, however, these pronouns are followed by a phrase beginning with *of* and ending with a plural noun, like these:

Each of the girls . . .

Either of the students . . .

Don't be fooled. The singular indefinite pronoun, not the word in the *of*-phrase, is the antecedent for a pronoun in the rest of the sentence.

> Wrong: Each of the girls gave me *their* money.

> Correct: Each of the girls gave me *her* money.

The pronoun refers to *each,* not to *girls.*

> Wrong: Either of the students may bring *their* books.

> Correct: Either of the students may bring *his or her* books.

His or her refers to *either,* not to *students.*

> Better: Either of the students may bring the books.

COMPOUND ANTECEDENTS

Compound antecedents may be joined with *and, or,* or *nor.* And the antecedents themselves may be all singular, all plural, or a mixture of singular and plural. The rules for agreement depend on the various combinations of these factors.

1. Two or more antecedents joined by *and* require a plural pronoun. It makes no difference whether the antecedents are singular, plural, or mixed: the *and* makes the compound antecedent plural.

   John and the other boy found *their* seats.

   John and the other boys found *their* seats.

2. Plural antecedents joined by *or* or *nor* require a plural pronoun.

   Either the boys or the girls will clean *their* rooms first.

   Neither the boys nor the girls want to clean *their* rooms.

3. Singular pronouns joined by *or* or *nor* require a singular pronoun.

   Either the dog or the cat will get *its* food first.

   Neither the dog nor the cat will eat *its* food.

4. When *or* or *nor* joins a singular antecedent and a plural antecedent, the pronoun agrees with whichever antecedent it is closer to.

Neither Freddy nor the other boys like *their* jobs. (The pronoun *their* agrees with *boys.*)

Neither the other boys nor Freddy likes *his* job. (*His* agrees with *Freddy.*)

You may not like the second sample sentence here, even though it is technically correct. Many readers feel uncomfortable when the singular antecedent of a singular-plural set determines the number of the pronoun reference. It's a good idea, then, to place the plural antecedent closer to the pronoun reference so that the pronoun may be plural.

EXERCISES

A. Circle the correct pronoun in each set of choices below.
  1. Another of the men applied to change (his, their) job today.
  2. One of the women used (her, their) credit card to pay the highway toll.
  3. Neither Tom nor Steve can get (his, their) truck started in this weather.
  4. Anyone else from the student council would gladly have acknowledged (their, his, his or her) contributions.
  5. Every Canadian may enter the United States without showing (her, their, his or her) passport.
  6. Each car that needs a new license must have (their, its) exhaust inspected.
  7. The family is traveling together to New Orleans for (their, its) vacation.
  8. Political action groups differ from political parties in (its, their) funding and purpose.
  9. The Chamber of Commerce tries to earn support for (its, their) fair-practices program.
  10. Members of the Chamber of Commerce try to earn support for (its, their) businesses.
  11. Even the national food chains have pushed hard for (their, its) goal of lower wages for teenagers.
  12. Either the waiter or waitress will seat you in (his, her, his or her) section.
  13. Elroy and Myra found (his, her, their) seats in the theater.
  14. Neither Mr. Anderson nor the programmers finished (his, their) work early.
  15. Everybody may help (himself or herself, themselves, himself) to the ice cream on the table.
B. Correct errors in pronoun agreement in the sentences below.
  1. Sheila and Edna both said she had been chased by a gorilla.
  2. Drought and revolution ravaged the land, and nothing could be done to stop it.

3. Not only the girls but Mrs. Alatorre had on their best clothes.

4. The Cancer Society seeks members for their fund drive.

5. Another of the owls escaped from their cage last night.

6. I hope everyone knows what to do before their number is called.

7. Each car in the parade has their sponsor's banner taped to the driver's door.

8. Eleanor and Nina each knew her part but neither of the women knew their stand-in.

9. Before Lori and Myra practiced the cello together, each practiced their parts alone.

10. Neither of the tenors sang their best.

C. Change the following sentences to eliminate gender-specific language. We have underlined the problem words in the first ten sentences.

1. A man's best friend is his dog.

2. Some of America's greatest businessmen come from the South.

3. No doctor can read much outside his specialty.

4. Everyone hopes he will win the lottery.

5. The common man always surprises the pollsters.

6. The lady lawyer was hired to be an assistant district prosecutor.

7. The earth belongs to all mankind.

8. Man is a social animal.

9. Each soldier must get his field equipment by Thursday.

10. Every nurse will find an invitation to join in her pay envelope.

11. When a city person runs into a farmer, he may think the farmer is old-fashioned.

12. That seven-year-old just ate a man-sized sandwich.

13. Each pilot is responsible for making sure his flaps are in the right position before beginning a landing.

14. A successful business owner knows he has to work long hours.

15. Will everyone be able to find his way back home?

16. One of the nurses tried to use her influence to get the hospital charges lowered.

17. Each vice president of this company must pick up his personal mail in the mail room.

18. Each of the workers put his tools away for the day.

19. Every musician knows how to care for his instrument.

20. Everybody in the cast knew his lines.

38
Passive Voice

Ever wonder why you have trouble reading something even though you know all the words? Perhaps you're struggling through sentence after sentence of passive voice. Like most readers you've come to expect sentences in the active voice, although you may not know what active and passive mean.

The natural order for an English sentence—actor-action-acted upon—requires *active voice,* as in the following:

Jonathan   ate   the doughnut.
(actor)   (action)   (acted upon)

Notice that the subject of the sentence is the actor (the one doing the eating).

You risk distracting or annoying your readers with passive voice because it reverses this normal, expected order. Instead, the subject changes: it is no longer the actor. The new subject is acted upon, as in this *passive voice* sentence:

The *doughnut   was eaten   by Jonathan.*
(acted upon)   (action)   (actor)

Notice that the actor now appears in a phrase after the verb. However, the passive sentence may not even name the actor, as in this version:

The *doughnut   was eaten.*
(acted upon)   (action)

A simple comparison of the active and passive sentences above allows us to see the disadvantages of the passive voice: (1) passive constructions are more wordy than active constructions; (2) because passive voice reverses the normal sentence order, passive constructions are indirect; (3) as the name "passive" implies, passive constructions lack the vigor inherent in active verbs; and (4) if the writer forgets to tell us who the actor is, the passive construction is vague. For these reasons, active voice is better than passive, suggesting a simple rule for you to follow: write with the active voice unless you have an excellent reason for using the passive.

RECOGNIZING PASSIVE VOICE

Students often complain that they cannot tell whether a verb is active or passive, but identification is really quite simple. Only a passive sentence will receive "yes" answers in all of the following tests:

1. Is the subject of the sentence *acted upon?* In our sample passive sentence, *doughnut,* the subject of the sentence, is acted upon (eaten) by Jonathan.
2. Does the sentence use a form of the verb *to be* followed by the kind of main verb that almost always ends in *-ed* or *-en?* The simple forms of *to be* are these: *is, am, are, was,* and *were.* Compound forms of *to be* use *be, being,* or *been* (for example, *will be, is being, has been*). Thus, passive verbs look like these: *is divided, was beaten,* and *will have been destroyed.* In our sample passive sentence, *was eaten* is the passive verb form.
3. If the actor appears in the sentence, is the actor in the prepositional phrase "by someone or something"? If the actor is not given, does the sense of the sentence imply "by someone or something"? "The doughnut was eaten by Jonathan" ends with "by Jonathan," whereas "The doughnut was eaten" implies "by someone."

USING PASSIVE VOICE

You may have decided by now that the passive voice was created (by someone) merely to entrap you. Not so. In fact, passive constructions do have legitimate uses:

1. Passive voice is useful when the object of the action is more important than the actor.

Residents of Sandstone, Nevada, are afraid that a lethal gas manufactured in nearby Cactus Flower may someday poison them. They fear, for example, that the *lethal gas may be released* by a defective valve or a worn gasket.

The emphasis in the last sentence is clearly on the lethal gas. That is, the context of the passage makes the gas more important than the parts that might allow a leak. Only passive voice will allow the object of the action (lethal gas) to gain emphasis by appearing first in the sentence.

2. Because passive voice can hide the actor, it is useful when the actor is obvious, unimportant, or uncertain. For example, if we did not know who dropped a canister of gas, we might write this:

When a canister *was dropped,* a lethal gas enveloped the laboratory workers.

However, a strong warning is necessary here: the worst misuse of passive voice occurs when the readers want or need to know who the actor is and the writer doesn't bother to say. Imagine being told this:

Leave your application in the box. If you *are found* acceptable, you *will be notified.*

Because you want to know who will judge you, or at least who will notify you, the omission of the actors is very irritating.

Deciding when the rules apply requires good judgment. If you try hard enough to convince yourself, you can stretch these justifications for passive voice to cover most sentences. Therefore, keep in mind the general rule: use the passive voice only when you have a strong reason.

ACTIVATING THE PASSIVE

Far too often students use passive voice because they can't think how to write the sentence in the active voice; in such cases the passive is more accidental than intentional. You can prevent this lack of control in your own writing by learning the following three methods to convert passive voice into active:

1. Reverse the object and the subject.
   Passive: An example *is shown* in Figure 3.
   Active: Figure 3 *shows* an example.
2. Delete the main verb, leaving the sentence with a form of *to be* as the only verb.
   Passive: Your cousin *is seen* as the best candidate.
   Active: Your cousin *is* the best candidate.
3. Change the verb.
   Passive: Jonathan *was given* a new book.
   Active: Jonathan *received* a new book.

If you learn to recognize the passive voice and determine to avoid the passive whenever you can, these three methods will provide you the tools you need to write simple, direct, and vigorous active sentences.

EXERCISES

A. Explain the three tests that identify passive voice.

1. _____

_____

2. _____

_____

3. _____

_____

B. Name the two justifications for using passive voice.

1. _____

_____

2. _____

_____

C. Write the three methods for changing passive voice to active voice.

1. _____

_____

2. _____

_____

3. _____

_____

D. Rewrite the following sentences to eliminate all passive voice. When necessary, supply the actors.
1. Cracks in the foundation were not considered serious before the building collapsed.
2. Self-reliance was gained by me when I was allowed to set up my own experiment.
3. Hundreds of balloons were released by the children at the festival.
4. The *Titanic* was found and explored by a French and American team seventy-three years after its sinking.
5. Equipment for underwater sonar exploration was used by the team.
6. It was discovered by the team that the stern of the *Titanic* was missing.
7. Reclaimed by the explorers were sets of dishes and bottles of wine.
8. The sinking was survived by Molly Brown, a Denver heiress, who later was nicknamed "Unsinkable."

9. A musical was produced about Molly Brown's life; it was later turned into a film.

10. Although his shape was peculiar, the UFO pilot was ignored by the customers at the doughnut shop.

11. Later, for lunch, enchiladas with green chilies were ordered by the bewildered pilot.

12. The Special Olympics for handicapped children were canceled when funds were not raised by the sponsors.

13. We regret to inform you that your medical records have been lost.

14. The gunman and his accomplice were chased down by six irate citizens from Arny's Pizza Place.

15. The news that a congressman's aide has been indicted by a federal grand jury no longer surprises us.

16. Opposition to the new sales tax was voiced by the 150 angry residents.

17. It can be seen by any observer that most people over thirty-five have not been exposed to computer training.

18. Four serious accidents at the corner of Grant and Lee have been caused in the past week.

19. Emergency teams have been dispatched by the 911 operator six times in the last week; each time it was a false alarm.

20. The little Italian sports car was run into by the yellow pickup truck with chrome exhaust stacks; the truck cannot be found by police.

21. Tanya's typewriter was fixed by the incompetent repairman for the third time this week.

22. Before the speech was delivered, the President rehearsed it with his advisers.

23. The grass was planted slowly by the reluctant gardener.

24. The incompetent repairman has already been fired by four bosses in the last eighteen months.

25. The end of the semester was welcomed by every student and professor.

39
Word Choice

The French have a phrase that could be the title of this chapter. The phrase is *le mot juste,* and it means—roughly—"the right word." *Le mot juste* is often the difference between an A paper and a merely ordinary C paper—not just one good word, of course, but a lot of them. This chapter covers some basic and advanced techniques for finding those good words.

BASIC TECHNIQUES

What is a good word? Is it something really impressive, a big word that proves how educated we are? No. Usually it's a word we all know. Unfortunately—even though it's a common word—we don't use it very often because another more general word is even more common. *See* is one of those more general words we might slap down on a rough draft, but think of all the synonyms that might work better: *glimpse, gaze, stare, peer, spot,* or *witness.*

Let's take a longer example. Suppose you are reading a paragraph and run across these words:

The man walked into the room.

The words are so general they could fit into a number of strikingly different contexts:

The policeman, hidden behind a parked car, watched as *the man walked into the room.*

or

The Capitol guard smiled as *the man walked into the room.*

or

The class quieted somewhat as *the man walked into the room.*

or

The patients gasped as *the man walked into the room.*

"What a great clause!" you say. "I can use it anywhere." It's a lousy clause—you can use it anywhere. All the words are general, the kind of words that pop into your mind in a second. Let's think a second longer and try to make the words more exact. Here are some possibilities:

man: thief, senator, English teacher, Dr. Rodney

walked: sneaked, hurried, sauntered, reeled

room: motel room, antechamber, classroom, office

Now let's rewrite that all-purpose clause using more specific words:

The policeman, hidden behind a parked car, watched as *the thief sneaked into my motel room.*

or

The Capitol guard smiled as the *senator hurried into the antechamber.*

or

The class quieted somewhat as *the English teacher sauntered into the classroom.*

or

The patients gasped as *Dr. Rodney reeled into his office.*

Each clause is better—and certainly more interesting—because the writer took the time to come up with just the right words. Try it yourself. Look for those dull, general words in your own writing and make them more specific. This technique is one of the best ways to improve your writing dramatically.

Let's take a moment for a warning, though. Don't become so obsessed with the idea of seeking different words that you choose unusual ones. *Perambulate,* for example, means "to walk through," so we could write this sentence:

The senator perambulated the antechamber.

The readers probably will notice the peculiarity of *perambulated* rather than its preciseness. Your goal is getting the right word, not the unusual word.

The second basic technique, in addition to using the right word, is to use modifiers. Sometimes the nouns and verbs don't tell the whole story. To be really precise, you need to add some adjectives and adverbs. Let's work with one of the sentences we improved in the last section:

> The policeman, hidden behind a parked car, watched as the thief sneaked into my motel room.

From the clause we revised ("the thief sneaked into my motel room"), we can modify *thief, sneaked,* and *motel room.* Here are just a few possibilities:

We don't want to overload the sentence with modifiers, so let's just modify *thief* and *sneaked:*

> The policeman, hidden behind a parked car, watched as the furtive thief sneaked noiselessly into my motel room.

We've come a long way from "The man walked into the room," haven't we?

Again, a warning: don't get so carried away that you pile up modifier after modifier. Only the writer and the writer's mother could love this sentence:

> The diminutive, chunky, azure-eyed, eighteen-month-old boy toddled to his rocking horse.

ADVANCED TECHNIQUES

If you really want to get your readers' attention, use a comparison. It may be the most memorable part of your theme. Remember when we said transitions are like road signs? And when we said the blueprint for your paper is like the architect's design for the structure he plans to build? These and other comparisons really help your readers understand an idea.

Only one problem with comparisons: they're hard to think of, particularly good comparisons. We can all think of bad ones. The familiar phrases that come to mind almost automatically are clichés, and they are as bad as original comparisons are good. Consider this sentence:

> Although he was *blind as a bat,* Herman remained *cool as a cucumber* when he entered the arena.

See how clichés attract the wrong kind of attention to themselves? Hearing a cliché is like hearing a comedian go through the same routine time after time. After a while, nobody listens.

A good rule is that if you have heard a comparison before, don't use it. But do use original comparisons. Be daring. Try one in your next theme.

Here's something else to try in your next theme: when you want to use a general word that stands for an entire class of items—like *toys* or *vehicles* or *books*—use just one item from that class instead. Let the specific stand for the general. Take this sentence:

> Inflation means that most Americans can hardly afford to eat, but some congressmen don't seem to care how much *food* costs.

Let's make the sentence a little more interesting by replacing the word *food* (an entire class of items) with *a loaf of bread* (one item from that class):

> Inflation means that most Americans can hardly afford to eat, but some congressmen don't seem to care how much *a loaf of bread* costs.

Here's another example:

> As a photographer she is limited. She may be able to take pictures of *nature,* but she can't take good pictures of people.

We can make the second sentence more interesting by changing the word *nature* to something more specific:

> As a photographer she is limited. She may be able to take pictures of *trees,* but she can't take good pictures of people.

See how the detail instead of the generality makes the sentence livelier? Most college students don't use either of the advanced techniques in this section. Most of them don't get A's either. If you want to learn how to write an A paper, you might start by occasionally using a comparison or a specific word instead of a general one.

EXERCISES

A. Rewrite the following sentences two different ways, replacing the underlined general words with more precise words.

Example: The official talked to the man.
   a. The district attorney grilled the arsonist.
   b. The manager congratulated the pitcher.
1. The teacher demonstrated the experiment.

   a. _____

   b. _____

2. The employee greeted the public.

   a. _____

   b. _____

3. The people liked the plant.

   a. _____

   b. _____

4. The worker dropped the tool.

   a. _____

   b. _____

5. The scientist talked about her invention.

   a. _____

   b. _____

B. In each sentence below write a modifier in the blank. Make the modifier as colorful and specific as you can. Try to fit it to the context.

Example: The _____ policeman arrested the mayor.

Words like *short* and *young* may not help much. On the other hand, try these choices:

The *rookie* policeman arrested the mayor.

                    or

The *bitter* policeman arrested the mayor.

1. The _____ pitcher beaned the batter.

2. The _____ driver winced when her car backed over the glass.

3. The _____ survivor had nightmares about the avalanche.

4. The gardener was very surprised to find such a/an _____ bug on the end of his shovel.

5. The _____ editor was really angry about the mistake in the news column.

6. My first year in college is a/an _____ experience.

7. As the _____ safecracker gently touched the dial, the telephone suddenly rang.

8. I don't see how anybody can read this _____ map!

9. Seventeen of us piled into the _____ school van.

10. The _____ criminal fled to the Everglades.

C. We use comparisons every day, but too many of them are clichés, like "nervous as a cat on a hot tin roof" or "scared as a rabbit." For this exercise write one original comparison on any topic. (If you have trouble thinking of a topic, consider blind dates, a hobby, a famous person.)

_____

_____

_____

_____

D. List three clichés other than the ones we've used as examples. (Remember, clichés are bad. Avoid them like the plague.)

1. _____

2. _____

3. _____

E. Improve the sentences below by changing each italicized generalization to something more specific.

Example: Small movie houses that show film classics are going out of business. After all, who wants to pay *good money* to see *an old movie*?

Revision: Small movie houses that show film classics are going out of business. After all, who wants to pay *five dollars* to see *Humphrey Bogart*?

1. You have nearly finished *your work,* but you still need to do the *final cleanup.*

your work: _____

final cleanup: _____

2. Social critics claim that many *women's magazines* even today still depict women in *demeaning ways.*

   women's magazines: _____

   demeaning ways: _____

3. We learned, *some years ago,* that *kids in junior high school* had trouble with *basic arithmetic.*

   some years ago: _____

   kids in junior high school: _____

   basic arithmetic: _____

4. *Moving* through the crowd, we constantly bumped into a *variety of people.*

   Moving: _____

   variety of people: _____

5. If you listen to radio today, all you hear is *music* and *people talking.*

   music: _____

   people talking: _____

Appendix
Theme Format

Incredible as it may seem, English instructors are just like you and me (well—maybe a little more like me). Like you, they're human and have their little eccentricities. For example, they think that if students have done a good job writing their themes, they'll also want to make them as neat as possible. Silly idea—or is it?

That idea also has its corollary: the student who writes a theme at the last minute probably doesn't take—doesn't even *have*—the time to make it neat.

The moral is clear: be neat so that your instructors think they're looking at A papers before they've read even the first word. Here are some guidelines, although your instructors may wish to make some changes to suit individual preferences.

Handwriting or typing? Look at the two sample papers that follow. Which one would you rather read? If you can type at all, then do so. The early papers are short enough that typing them shouldn't take very long. If you don't type, use either black or blue ink. Other colors are hard to read.

Typing or word processing? Should you use a typewriter or a computer with a word processing program? The answer is easy: If you have a word processor, by all means use it. It has several overwhelming advantages over the typewriter:

- You can make corrections easily. That means you're far more likely to engage seriously in the revising process.
- With many programs, you can use a spelling checker. That means you'll not only correct words you've misspelled but correct typos, too. By helping with the technicalities, the word processor frees you to think about the larger, more important matters of writing. Be careful, though, because spelling checkers can't catch all errors—especially when your typo results in a legitimate word.

• Most important from our point of view, the word processor helps you get words on paper easily in the first place—especially if you can compose at the keyboard. People who have become comfortable with this method know that it is one of the primary benefits of the word processor, and often they refuse to write any other way.

Proofreading   Do it—*always,* but especially if you type, and even if you use a spelling checker with a word processor. Otherwise, you might be surprised by what your magic fingers did the night before.

Paper   If you type, use standard-sized (8½- × 11-inch) typing paper. For a typewriter, the erasable kind is especially good because you can make corrections easily. For a word processor, erasing is not required, so stick to a reasonably heavy bond paper. The thin "onionskin" typing paper is hard for your instructor to write on because it absorbs ink. Don't use it.

If you don't type or use a word processor, find a standard-sized tablet or pad of high-quality, lined theme paper. Don't use ordinary notebook paper (or paper torn from a spiral notebook) unless your instructor approves.

Corrections   On a short assignment (like the one-paragraph essay), avoid handing in a paper with obvious corrections. If, however, you're torn between making a correction at the last minute or handing in a neat paper, of course make the correction. What good is a neat error?

Spacing   If you're typing, double-space except where format requirements call for different spacing. If you're writing by hand, write on every other line.

Margins   Allow an inch on the top (except page one), left, right, and bottom. On page one, center your title two inches from the top; then quadruple-space to start your theme.

Page numbers   Don't number the first page, but do count it as page one. For other pages, use Arabic numerals (2, 3, 4, etc.) and put the number in the upper right-hand corner, ½ inch from the top of the page and in line with the right margin. Chapter 17 shows MLA format which uses a different pagination style for the research paper. Use that style for your own research paper if your instructor requests you use MLA format.

Identification   Put your name, course number, instructor's name, and date in the upper right-hand corner of page one. If you are using MLA format, follow the style used in the sample research paper shown in Chapter 17 and the pages shown here.

Fastening the paper   Use a stapler. Paper clips are fine in theory, but in a stack of themes they tend to clip themselves onto other themes.

Marilou Edwards

Professor Elser

English 111 H   2 inches

October 31, 1988

The Boundary Waters

Quadruple
space   _____

       The Boundary Waters Canoe Area, a wilderness park in
northern Minnesota, is a refreshing change from the city. Away
from the din of civilization, I have canoed silently across its
Double-
space   waters for an entire afternoon and not heard a single noise
except an occasional birdcall and the sound of waves beating
against the shore. Also, my partner and I were able to navigate
our way through a string of five lakes merely by following a
single campfire's scent drifting through the pure air. Most   ⊢—1 inch—⊣
refreshing, the park is so magnificently beautiful that even the
—1 inch—⊣ voyageurs of old were willing to endure its hardships in order
to settle there. The Boundary Waters Canoe Area is thus an
ideal place to clear your head of the congestion of urban life.

1 inch

Marilou Edwards
English III H
Professor Elser
October 31, 1988

The Boundary Waters

The Boundary Waters Canoe Area, a wilderness park in northern Minnesota, is a refreshing change from the city. Away from the din of civilization, I have canoed silently across its waters for an entire afternoon and not heard a single noise except an occasional bird call and the sound of the waves beating against the shore. Also, my partner and I were able to navigate our way through a string of five lakes merely by following a single campfire's scent drifting through the pure air. Most refreshing, the park is so magnificently beautiful that even the voyageurs of old were willing to endure its hardships in order to settle there. The Boundary Waters Canoe Area is thus an ideal place to clear your head of the congestion of urban life.

Index